GOD OF THE POOR

GOD OF THE POOR

Dewi Hughes
with
Matthew Bennett

**OM
publishing**

Copyright © 1998 Tearfund

First published in 1998 by OM Publishing

Reprinted 2000

06 05 04 03 02 01 00   7 6 5 4 3 2

OM Publishing is an imprint of Paternoster Publishing,
P.O. Box 300, Carlisle, Cumbria, CA3 0QS, U.K.
and P.O. Box 1047, Waynesboro, GA 30830-2047, USA
paternoster-publishing.com

Tearfund have asserted their right under the Copyright, Designs and
Patents Act 1988 to be identified as Author of this work

British Library Cataloguing in Publication Data

A catalogue record for this book is available from the British Library.

ISBN 1-85078-297-0

Typeset by WestKey Ltd., Falmouth, Cornwall
Printed in Great Britain by
Caledonian International Book Manufacturing, Glasgow

Contents

Preface

The heart of this volume has been born during ten years of preaching, teaching and thinking as an employee of Tearfund. When I set out to put some shape to the material accumulating for this project I was privileged to have Matthew Bennett, a then recent graduate in Theology and Philosophy at Oxford, to join me as a Research Assistant. Matthew worked unstintingly to provide material for me to work with, and as time went on, through his comments and writing, made a very substantial contribution to the final product. I have to take responsibility for the volume as a whole and all its blemishes, but in the last three chapters in particular Matthew was practically a co-author. This is primarily why his name appears on the cover; also because I feel that Research Assistants are seldom given the recognition which is their due. I treasure the memory of the happy eighteen months we had working together and the lasting friendship that has resulted from it.

A number of other Tearfund staff members also played a significant part. David Cohen almost forced my hand to get on with it. Stephen Rand, my director at the time, encouraged me to the task and approved Matthew's appointment. The many discussions with Stephen, going back to long before I even thought about joining Tearfund, have played an important part in shaping my thinking. Tim Chester became my Team Leader midstream and made an important contribution to turning a very big pile of material into a more coherent book. Many other colleagues have provided encouragement with their prayers and kind words. My colleagues in the Communications Department and the Research and Policy Team deserve special mention in this context. Many from the various Overseas Teams helped Matthew to find useful material; others made helpful comments. I must also thank the many workers and partners who gave of their time to talk to Matthew. Their insights have proved invaluable. Then there are those partners that I have had the privilege of visiting in their own countries so that I could see with my own eyes what is being done among the poor in Jesus' name. Finally, I must thank the publishers for owning a project they did not initiate and for their graciousness throughout the process of turning a manuscript into a book.

Some time ago I had the great pleasure of spending a week taking Rene Padilla to a number of theological colleges in England to promote holistic mission. It was my great admiration for his contribution to evangelical thinking that led me to invite him to speak in the colleges. Listening to his teaching and sharing the burden of our heart together during his visit was a great blessing. It was a great joy when he agreed to become a Tearfund President, and an even greater joy to me when he agreed to write the Foreword.

This book is really a product of Tearfund. I just hope that it is worthy of the great work God is doing through them in our generation. I therefore dedicate it to all Tearfund staff and partners.

It was Stephen Rand who suggested the title 'God of the poor', from the song which Graham Kendrick wrote for the twenty-fifth anniversary of Tearfund. My prayer for myself and for all those who read this book is beautifully expressed in the first verse and chorus of that lovely song:

Beauty for brokenness, hope for despair,
Lord, in your suff'ring world, this is our prayer.
Bread for the children, justice, joy, peace,
Sunrise to sunset your kingdom increase.

God of the poor, friend of the weak,
Give us compassion we pray,
Melt our cold hearts, let tears fall like rain,
Come change our love from a spark to a flame.

Dewi Hughes
Theological Advisor, Tearfund

Foreword

The last quarter of the twentieth century has witnessed a new awakening of social concern among evangelical Christians around the world. To be sure, there is still a long way to go on the journey toward a church that has learnt what it means to live out the gospel of God's Kingdom in the midst of a needy world. There is, however, plenty of evidence to affirm that evangelical Christians have definitely entered a new era in their pilgrimage – the era of holistic mission.

In essence holistic mission is Kingdom mission. In other words, the church is involved with the world in terms of transforming action of which the starting point and goal is God's Kingdom revealed in Jesus Christ. It is mission shaped by, and for the sake of, the Kingdom. From the perspective of the New Testament the gospel of the Kingdom is by definition 'good news to the poor'. Accordingly, the acid test of commitment to the Kingdom is practical concern for the poor.

Experience shows, however, that far more than goodwill is necessary to change the situation of the poor. If poverty were simply an economic problem, money would be the way to solve it. But poverty is not only material. It is also cultural and social, political and structural.

This book is a very good demonstration of the extent to which a Kingdom perspective can help us avoid the dangers of oversimplification as we approach different aspects of the mission of the church, including development. People are not poor merely because they lack certain things; rather, they are poor because of a complex combination of factors that often cannot be separated from one another. This book goes a long way to show the impact that issues such as religion, economics, politics and ethnic identity, as well as attitudes towards women, birth control and ecology, have on poverty. A holistic understanding of poverty is a good starting point for a holistic approach to development. From this perspective development is not something done to the *poor*. Rather, development concerns ways to deal with the root *causes* of poverty, including the spiritual dimensions of human life.

Christians are in a unique position to help alleviate poverty around the world. They have been given a message that has to do with the transformation of the totality of life through God's dynamic power, active in history – the gospel of the Kingdom. They have been called to form churches that live out the whole of that gospel and, as such, to become agents of change in society, not only in the Third World but everywhere.

Dewi Hughes helps us to see this. Beyond doubt, he has succeeded in sharing with us a biblical vision of what it means to be faithful to the gospel of the Kingdom in the face of massive poverty at the end of the twentieth century. May God use this book to encourage many Christians to participate in what God wants to do around the world – so that his justice may fill the earth!

C. Rene Padilla
Director, Kairos Institute, Argentina
President, Tearfund

Introduction

The one central fact that conditions everything that follows is the fact of poverty. It may be difficult to get precise figures but there is a consensus among statisticians that there are at least one thousand million people in the world today who have nothing like adequate food supply, clothing, shelter, medical care or education. The overwhelming majority of these poor people live in the Third World.[1] The central conviction that conditions all that follows is that the God who has revealed himself in Jesus makes it very clear in his word to those who welcome his revelation, that our response to poverty is a crucial test of the reality of our faith. It is impossible to really know Jesus and be indifferent to the plight of the poor.

This central conviction is not a new discovery but a common conviction among Christians of every type and in all ages. Evangelical Christianity, with which the author of this volume and his assistant are happy to identify, is no exception. In fact, we believe that care of the poor is a fundamental aspect of Evangelicalism.

---

[1] After a lot of thought we decided to use 'Third World' to describe the countries where the majority of the poor live. It is used in contrast to 'the West', the rich industrialized countries that claim the lion's share of the world's wealth. Other contrasting terms considered were 'Two-thirds World/the West', 'developed/developing countries', 'North/South'. The final choice was between Third World and Two-thirds World. It would take too much footnote space to explain why we opted for Third World but we believe it to be the best descriptive term available which has no suggestion of inferiority in it. So, from those who strongly advocate Two-thirds World we ask for forbearance.

We also recognize that Christians are not alone in their concern for the poor. The humanistic perspective, that has dominated Western thinking throughout the twentieth century, sees poverty as an evil which must be eliminated. For the humanist, who rejects any idea of an afterlife, earthly existence is an absolute value. Therefore, it is imperative that as many people as possible should enjoy a good life on earth since that is the only life that they have. Humanists have put in a lot of effort and resources into trying to make sure that this happens. The term that they use to describe the process of change required in order to eliminate poverty is 'development'.

If as Christians we are to be concerned about the poor we will not be able to ignore the various theories of development, and the practices that flow from them, that are current in the world around us. When we set out to bless the poor we will find ourselves shoulder to shoulder with those who also care but who do not share our faith. We will also find that they have thought very deeply about what they are doing and that we can learn much from their wisdom. This is so even if we have to reject their overall theory of development as inadequate, because in the last analysis, no theory or practice that ignores our relationship with God can give us a true picture of what a meaningful human life is.

So, in approaching the problem of poverty as evangelical Christians, we have to look towards three horizons: 1) The Bible. Evangelicals believe that the Bible is the final authority for what we believe and do. It is in the Bible that we learn how to relate to our Creator, to each other and to the earth. It explains the disorder in the world, of which poverty is a part, and shows us the way out. The Bible is the fundamental horizon in the light of which what comes from the other two horizons is assessed. 2) General development theory and practice. Christians working among the poor have been, and are, influenced by what is happening in general development theory and practice. It is impossible to do justice to the issue of Christians and poverty without taking note of what is happening in this general world of development. 3) Christian experience. Christians, including evangelicals, have been involved in work among the poor for many years so that there is a wealth of Christian experience to draw on. This volume draws particularly on the experience of Tearfund with its many partners over a period of 30 years.

The idea of 'development' in the Bible

As noted above, 'development' is a term Western humanists devised to describe the process that a community needs to go through in order to bring about the elimination of poverty. On one hand some Evangelicals have come to the conclusion that the process recommended is so tied to the structures that perpetuate poverty in the Third World that it is better to drop the term altogether. On the other hand such a large number of evangelicals from the West and in the Third World are so involved in what they themselves call 'development' that it may be better to attempt to redeem the term. In the light of heavy Christian involvement it may be worth thinking what the term could mean in a biblical context.

Like the term 'Trinity' or 'mission', the term 'development' is not to be found in the Bible. The question is whether, as in the case of Trinity or mission, the idea of development is present. The idea of development is that there is something potentially present which if given the right conditions will gradually unfold. A baby girl growing up into a woman is a good example. Genetically all the characteristics of a woman are already present at conception. Given the correct nourishment the physical form of the embryo and infant will inevitably change in such a way that the end result will be a woman. The idea of growth is, therefore, very close to the idea of development and growth is, unquestionably, a biblical idea.

In Ezekiel 16 God compares the growth or development of the nation of Israel under his care to the growth of an abandoned baby girl which a man rescued, cared for and eventually married. Through God's care the infant nation of Israel, in the form of Jacob and his family, was rescued through Joseph and went to live in Egypt. There it developed numerically but was unable to express its nationhood because of Egyptian oppression. So God came to the rescue again, brought the Israelites out of bondage, gave them a just set of laws and gave them the land which he had promised their forefathers. In the days of David and Solomon the abandoned baby girl became the beautifully adorned bride of the one who had rescued her. Israel had developed into a numerous nation where justice prevailed and the people lived in peace and contentment.

In Ezekiel 16 we have a very graphic allegorical description of the growth of God's nation. In Luke we find a straightforward description of the growth of an individual – the individual being our Lord Jesus himself. In Luke 2:40 there is a simple statement that Jesus grew physically like any other healthy boy: 'And the child grew and became strong.' The verb used here is *auxanō* which means 'to grow physically'. In v. 52 of the same chapter Luke says that 'Jesus grew in wisdom and stature, and in favour with God and men'. This time the verb that is translated 'grew' in the NIV is *prokoptō* which literally means 'to cut a way forward' or 'to advance'. It is used here in its metaphorical sense of 'making progress' or 'increasing'. Jesus, the eternal Son of God incarnate, grew or increased in four areas: intellectual (wisdom), physical size (stature), spiritual (favour with God) and social (favour with men). As we would expect, his was a fully orbed, perfect and totally real human development.[2] Here at least we find a perfect pattern of human development which we can follow.

Revelation is another biblical idea which is close in meaning to development.[3] There is only one Hebrew term for revelation, *gala*, which means 'to make bare, uncover'. The idea is that something that is hidden is uncovered and thus made known. In the New Testament there are a number of terms that convey the same idea. *Apokaluptō* is used exclusively of divine disclosure, although in a number of instances it seems that human beings are not only recipients of revelation but partakers in it. In the final reckoning true believers will *be* a revelation. 'I consider that our present sufferings', says Paul, 'are not worth comparing with the glory that will be revealed in us.'[4] In the

---

[2] Cf. Marshall, I. Howard, *The Gospel of Luke* (Exeter, Paternoster 1978), p. 130.
[3] I am indebted to Maurice Sinclair for this idea. See Sinclair, Maurice, *Green Finger of God* (Exeter, Paternoster 1980), p. 18.
[4] Rom. 8:18. For a helpful comment on this passage see Murray, J., *The Epistle to the Romans* (London, Marshall, Morgan & Scott 1967), Part 1, p. 301.

next verse Paul goes on to say that the whole creation is looking forward in eager anticipation for this revelation of God's children.

Phaneroō, 'to make visible, clear, manifest or known', is another word that can be translated by 'to reveal' in English. This term is used on a number of occasions to convey the idea that the reality of God can be made known through human action. 'Whoever lives by the truth', says Jesus, 'comes into the light, so that *it may be seen plainly* that what he has done has been done through God.'[5] The idea is that the one who believes in Jesus is prepared to allow the light to expose the evil of the heart so that evil can be replaced by virtue. Seen by the world this virtue reveals the reality of the work of God in the believer's life. The same idea is beautifully expressed in Paul's second letter to the Corinthians: 'But thanks be to God, who always leads us in triumphal procession in Christ and through us *spreads [phanerounti]* everywhere the fragrance of the knowledge of him.'[6] Through lives of obedience in the service of our great King we spread the perfume of his presence wherever we go.[7]

The idea that Jesus' followers can and should reveal God through the way they live becomes even more significant when viewed in the context of the doctrine of the creation of human beings in the image of God. To say that human beings were created to image God is one helpful way of understanding what the 'image' means. The way humans behave in relation to each other and to the rest of the natural world should be a revelation of God's character. The great tragedy of humankind is that this development has been horribly hindered by sin.

Development may not be a biblical term but the idea is certainly present in terms that express the ideas of growth and revelation. God created human beings full of potential for growth. He created us to handle the resources of the earth in co-operation with others in a way that would reveal the wisdom and glory of our Maker. The Fall thwarted this development but through Israel first, and then through his Son, God is

---

[5] Jn. 3:21.
[6] 2 Cor. 2:14.
[7] Cf. 2 Cor. 3:3; 4:10–11.

working towards our restoration. God is determined to develop human beings that will realize their potential for displaying his glory.

Because it has its root in the world of the spirit it is not surprising that some evangelicals prefer the term 'transformation' to development. They believe that development is too wedded to a secular agenda to convey the radical change that is needed in order to bring blessing to a world of need. Transformation is reminiscent of the new birth that Jesus spoke about or the new creation that Paul wrote about. It points to that radical reorientation towards God and away from sin at the heart of our being which bears fruit in true wisdom and real social harmony. But while transformation points to the radical nature of the change that is required, development points to the fact that even in those that are reborn the working out of the implications of their new birth is a gradual process.

The aim of this volume is to open out what it means for transformed people to develop, with God's strength, in wisdom, in stature and in favour with God and men. The cold bondage of poverty melts away in the warmth of this type of development.

This biblical development is not something needed by just one class of people, or only by people living in certain parts of the world. General development theory and what is basically the same theory slightly modified by evangelicals have focused attention on the Third World.[8] We in the West have assumed that the answer to the problem is to be found where the problem is found. But we need to realize that the Third World does not have a monopoly of the problems and that we are as much a part of the problem as anyone. Jim Wallis was right when he said that the poor are not our problem in the West but that we are their problem.

Everyone has 'sinned and fall[s] short of the glory of God'.[9] So, this volume will be concerned with holistic development, not only in the sense of developing every aspect of our being but

---

[8] Cf. Elliott, Charles, *Comfortable Compassion* (London, Hodder & Stoughton 1987), p. 117.

[9] Rom. 3:23.

also in the sense of developing all peoples. We are living in a global community. All the peoples of the world are interdependent so that there can be no real development away from poverty that does not affect the West and the Third World alike.

General theories of development

In coming to theories of development it is helpful to distinguish between development that is done by international government agencies and international business enterprise on the one hand and work that is done by non-governmental organizations (NGOs) on the other. In broad terms the NGOs were seen initially as existing to help realize the aims and objectives of the government agencies who defined the meaning of development. The government agencies had the large resources so the NGOs were viewed as minor contributors to the action. As time went on it was realized that the NGOs often made much better use of their limited resources so more government funds were channelled through them. Government agencies also began taking note of what the NGOs were saying about development so that they have come to play an important part in formulating development theory in general.

This change in the role and perception of agencies reflects the change in development theory. It will be helpful to take a brief look at some of these changes.

Macro or large-scale theories of development

The Second World War left the European economies in a very sorry state. The Marshall Plan, underwritten by American investment, was put in place in order to get them back on their feet. In some cases the execution of the Marshall Plan meant that the economies of some countries were rapidly industrialized with the result that living standards were dramatically raised. This seemed to prove that economies could be modernized very quickly with the resultant benefit to all. So 'development' came to be seen in terms of rapid increase in production through investment in modern industrial technology. This development could be easily measured in terms of Gross National Product (GNP) and per capita income (PCI). This is what is meant by the modernization theory of development.

The assumption behind this theory is that industrialized countries are 'developed' while non-industrialized nations are 'un/underdeveloped'. To be fair the industrialized countries could point to some notable economic achievements. In the 1950s and 1960s, for example, they had a very low level of unemployment. Prime Minister Harold Macmillan in England could declare that people had 'never had it so good'. With plenty of job opportunities in industry and a mechanized agricultural sector producing food very efficiently, a good communications, power and services infrastructure could be put in place and maintained. Added to this a system of welfare benefits for those unfortunate enough to fall through the net was affordable and a state pension could be paid to the old. Massive resources could be ploughed into education and health care. In the UK a national health system was established. Though some people could be described as deprived, absolute poverty was practically eliminated. In view of this it is understandable that economists and politicians in these countries were very confident that they had found the key to the elimination of poverty and to human well-being. If other countries followed their example, their problems could also be solved.

By the time the Western states were becoming 'developed' in the sense described above the greater part of what has become known as the Third World was gaining its political independence. The newly independent countries of Africa and Asia, and the older independent countries of Latin America, were certainly un/underdeveloped. The leaders of these emerging nations had generally gone through the educational system established by the imperial power so that it is not surprising that they embraced the theory of Western economists that development meant modernization. So the focus was very much on attracting investment in order to rapidly expand the modern industrial sector of these countries' economies.

In 1969, though recognizing that there were many problems still to be solved, the report of the Commission on International Development set up by the World Bank was fairly optimistic about the future of what it described as developing countries.[10] This was before the devastating oil price rises of the early seventies and the world recession of the eighties that left the best plans for worldwide modernization in shreds. The mood is now very pessimistic as the aim of eliminating poverty seems to become more and more elusive.

It also became apparent by the 1960s that large-scale economic development could not be divorced from social and intellectual development. This is clear, for example, in Gunnar Myrdal's monumental study of South Asian countries published in 1968.[11] In his list of 12 aspects of the modernization ideal only a few items were strictly economic. Among the non-economic ones was rationality, which essentially meant accepting a Western scientific view of the world. If people allowed superstition, or the suppression of facts because of social and cultural values, to intervene, it would be impossible to create an economy on the modern Western model. Democratic government was another aspect. Myrdal believed that only a Western style democracy could establish a strong local government which is vital to economic development. Another aspect was 'social and economic equalization'. This meant accepting that every member of the state is of equal value and that traditional hierarchical structures are not permanent. Economists were very critical of Myrdal's thesis because they saw the introduction of religion, politics and morality into the debate as merely muddying the waters for economics. Since then it has become generally accepted that economics cannot be divorced from these other aspects of human life.[12]

Some were sceptical that modernization would work even before the oil crisis of 1974. The most vociferous sceptics hailed from Latin America where most of the countries had been independent for over a hundred years but had made very little

---

[10] Published report entitled *Partners in Development* (London, Pall Mall 1969).

[11] *Asian Drama: An Inquiry into the Poverty of Nations*, 3 vols. (Harmondsworth Penguin 1968).

[12] Cf. Todaro, Michael P., *Economic Development in the Third World* (New York, Longman 1985³), pp. 85, 580, for a recent definition of development that recognizes Myrdal's point.

progress towards becoming modern industrial states. They argued that although Third World countries had gained their political independence they had never gained economic independence. The powerful business interests of the Western nations had made sure that the Third World economies were kept dependent. One clear symptom of this is the fact that Third World nations still produce the raw materials that Western business converts into the finished products that net the lion's share of the profits to be made from them. The dependency theorists see modernization as part of the strategy of Western commercial interest to make sure that the Third World never succeeds in joining the élite club of wealthy countries. To them modernization is the antithesis of development. They advocate development that is independent of the Western-dominated world of international trade. Commercial development within individual countries that is outside the modern industrial sector and trade between Third World countries is consistent with this theory.

Dependency theory has made a significant contribution to our understanding of international economics in particular and some of its conclusions have been widely accepted by development theorists. Its most significant contribution could be that it forces Western countries to focus on the way their economic life impacts the life of the Third World. It moves the focus for the West from thinking that it must help the Third World to become like itself to thinking that its being as it is is a major contributor to the problems of the Third World. In this model, development is not something that needs to happen in the Third World alone.

Since the early 1970s macro development theory has oscillated between various emphases in the modernization and dependency theories. The move to establish a New International Economic Order (NIEO) initiated by the United Nations in 1974 was really only another variation on the modernization theme. Since modernization means creating societies all over the world in the image of Western societies, that it failed may be more of a cause for rejoicing than for sorrow.

In 1975 another UN group based in Stockholm produced the Dag Hammarskjöld Report as an alternative to the NIEO. The report entitled 'What Now? Another Development' reflects many themes that are consistent with dependency theory. The central principle of modernization that poverty will only be eradicated by increased production is rejected in favour of a more equitable distribution of what is produced. Some of the fundamental policies of much contemporary development practice flowed from the principles expressed in this report. In health care in the Third World, for example, the emphasis has moved from hospital-based high-tech medical care in the Western style to primary health care in the community.

Where production of goods is concerned the emphasis moved to self-reliance, which meant a dependence on technologies that are appropriate to a Third World context as opposed to Western technology. Self-reliance demands that power be redistributed right down to grass-roots level and achieving this is much more likely if the technological resources needed to produce wealth are within easy reach. Schumacher popularized this approach in his famous book entitled *Small is Beautiful*.[13] Another factor that looms large in this approach is the importance of the environment. It cannot be gainsaid that Third World countries have paid a very high price for what industrialization they have experienced in environmental degradation. The 'Another Development' approach claims that the emphasis on self-reliance and small-scale technologically appropriate methods of production is much more likely to be friendly to the environment.[14]

Micro or NGO theories of development

As in the case of the macro theories an attempt has to be made here to simplify an extremely complex issue. The standard story of NGO involvement with the poor now begins with relief. NGOs at first existed to raise funds to provide emergency help for people who had been affected by natural or man-made disasters. OXFAM, which was originally a shortening of Oxford

---

[13] Schumacher, E.F., *Small is Beautiful, A Study of Economics as if People Mattered* (London, Abacus 1974).

[14] This outline of various theories of development is indebted to a very helpful outline and critique by Wayne G. Bragg in a chapter entitled 'From Development to Transformation' in Samuel, Vinay and Sugden, Chris (eds.), *The Church in Response to Human Need* (Oxford, Regnum 1987), pp. 20ff.

Committee for Famine Relief, was established in 1942 to help Greeks who were suffering as a result of a military blockade. The American Co-operative Agency for Relief Everywhere, established in 1945, was also initially involved in bringing relief to those affected by war. In the 1950s and 1960s the number of NGOs multiplied rapidly and their focus moved to the Third World.[15]

Emergencies may have been the spark that brought many NGOs into being but they soon plugged into the modernization ideal. The ethos of this phase in their story is encapsulated in the saying, 'Give a man a fish and you feed him for one meal, but if you teach him how to fish, you feed him for life.' The implication is that the poor are ignorant – they don't know how to fish – so they need someone to come along and teach them how to do it. Fundamental to this approach is the conviction that the West knows best. Development means the transference of Western ways of doing things. The poor need to be trained to do things in the Western way so that they can escape from poverty.

There is no denying that this approach has brought relief from poverty to many people. It also helped the NGOs in their relationship with the public from whom they got their funds. This type of work is project based and successful projects are very useful for fund-raising. The deep sense that Western know-how is superior among the general public is fed by this approach. It fits in well with the perception that the West has it altogether and that what is needed is simply to transfer something of the West's knowledge and expertise and the problem will be solved. It is being realized, however, that this type of development is often nothing more than a sophisticated version of relief in that it is still done to the poor. NGOs find that despite their genuine desire to help the poor to get on their own feet they never seem to do so. On the contrary this strategy seems to create long-term dependency on the NGO.

So the focus moved from what the NGO could do to the poor to what the poor could do for themselves. The work of the South American educationalist Paulo Freire was crucial in causing this

---

[15]   See Clark, John, *Democratising Development: The Role of Voluntary organizations* (London, Earthscan 1991), pp. 34ff.

shift in emphasis. Freire argues that education is not simply a matter of transferring certain skills but a process that has social and political dimensions.[16] The rich in any country go to great pains to make sure that their children have access to the best education because education is power. To be effective, the education of the poor must, therefore, be a means of empowerment as well as a simple transference of skills. Self-reliance must be the goal from the beginning. What this means for development is that much more attention is given to what the poor want rather than to what they are perceived to need. This means that the development worker becomes a facilitator and encourager rather than a deliverer. Korten believes that this approach has already brought into being a large network of grass-roots movements from among the poor themselves and that some NGOs are already seeing their role simply in terms of servicing these movements.[17]

Reflections on general theories of development

A number of conclusions can be drawn from this very brief and inadequate outline of development theory. Firstly, there is no one theory of development which commands universal agreement. A number of theories have been described in chronological order. But the appearance of a new theory does not mean the universal jettisoning of previous theories. What it means is the addition of another option to choose from although the latest theory is often presented as the only real option. Development theory is as subject to fashion as anything else in Western culture. Christians should always be on their guard against latching on to the latest fashion in any area.

Secondly, what is in view here is very much the creature of the West. As such it is very big business. A host of academics, government officials and employees of NGOs make a very good living out of it. This may be too cynical a view of things but it is undeniable that a great many people in the West and Western-trained experts in the Third World are doing very well out of

---

[16] Freire, Paulo, *Pedagogy of the Oppressed* (New York, Herder & Herder 1970).
[17] Korten, David C., *Getting to the 21st Century* (West Hartford, CN, Kumarian 1990).

trying to find answers to the plight of the poor. There would be
a lot of unemployed people in the West if poverty was eliminated!

Thirdly, despite all the theorizing and the actions that have
flowed from it, we have to face up to the fact that the problem
of poverty is as great as it ever was. The truth of the situation is
that in the second half of the twentieth century the rich have got
richer and the poor have got poorer. Development may have
succeeded here and there, and any success must not be despised,
but in global terms all the talking and working in the last 50 years
has not solved the problem. The poor are still with us in greater
numbers than ever. One wonders whether the now-fashionable
theory of empowerment is going to be any more successful than
the theory of modernization.

Evangelical Christian experience

Evangelicalism is a movement that came to maturity in the first
half of the nineteenth century as a result of a widespread revival
among Protestants in the eighteenth century. By the beginning
of the nineteenth century this revival had permeated very
deeply into the life of many Protestant denominations leading
to very significant church growth. It was a movement that
touched Christians in many countries and denominations. In
London in 1846 representatives of 52 denominations from many
countries gathered together to form a worldwide Evangelical
Alliance. They were able to unite on some basic doctrines but
the attempt to form a worldwide alliance failed because the
Europeans could not form a fellowship with those from the USA
who claimed to be evangelical but condoned slavery.

Within an orthodox Trinitarian framework evangelicals are
Bible people. They believe that the Bible is the word of God
and the only source of authority for faith and practice. The
whole Bible is inspired by God 'and is useful for teaching,
rebuking, correcting and training in righteousness'.[18] The heart
of the Bible's message is the life, death and resurrection of Jesus

---

[18] 2 Tim. 3:16.

Christ. Evangelicals focus very strongly on the atoning death of Jesus. On the cross Jesus paid the debt for our sin as he suffered the wrath of God in our place. Our greatest need as human beings is to realize what Jesus has done for us. For this to happen we need to become convinced of our sin and condemnation. It is only when we see how lost we are that we are ready to turn to Jesus in faith and forsake our life of sin. This is the process of conversion which evangelicals believe is necessary for everyone if they are to be saved. This conviction drove evangelicals out to make as many disciples as possible for Jesus. It was the driving force behind the missionary movement that started with the Moravians, was consolidated by Carey and which has spread all over the earth. Recharged by Pentecostalism the movement is now the fastest growing Christian missionary movement.

Evangelical activism was not limited to making converts. From the beginning it was a movement that laid heavy emphasis on social responsibility which spawned a host of organizations devoted to caring for people in need. When evangelicals went as missionaries all over the world they did not leave their strong social conscience behind. Wherever they went they preached the gospel and did everything in their power to improve the lives of the people through the introduction of education, medical care and even in many cases small-scale industry. The missionaries and those who became Christians as a result of their work continued to be involved in these activities until independence and even beyond in those places where they were granted the freedom to carry on. As NGOs evangelical churches and para-church organizations have been active in development in Third World countries since the beginning of the expansion of the Protestant missionary movement in the late eighteenth century!

The idea that evangelical NGOs' involvement in development in Third World countries began with a focus on disaster relief has more to do with the way things were seen from the Western perspective than with the reality of the situation. Western evangelicals probably assumed that when colonies became independent then government would exercise a similar responsibility for the people as was exercised in their own country. By then they had also generally adopted a theology which was happy to hand over the state and all its doings to the 'world' which is 'passing away' and focus all their efforts on getting people into the ark of the church before it was too late. Then the media, television in particular, intervened.

In the UK, for example, the television had found its way into a majority of homes by the early 1960s. This was the time when news broadcasting was revoluntionized and news ceased to be simply a man in the studio telling people what was happening but also included visual reports from correspondents who were on the scene of the action. Pictures began appearing of starving refugees or the result of floods and earthquakes. Evangelical Christians and non-Christians alike wanted to do something to help those who were suffering as a result of such disasters and this led to the formation of NGOs to deliver the aid. As a result Tearfund, (The Evangelical Alliance Relief Fund), was established in 1968.

Though born out of the common media-driven perception of what was needed at the time, Tearfund was never simply a relief fund. When it began operating in earnest it immediately plugged into the worldwide network of evangelical activity which had always been involved in education, health care and much more. One of Tearfund's earliest partners was Iniciativa Cristiana which was an evangelical Anglican work aimed at the economic and social enhancement of the life of the Chaco Indians of Argentina.

Despite a long history of care for the poor on the part of evangelicals their agenda has tended to be driven by general development theory and practice in the second half of the twentieth century. Though never in a position to introduce modernization on a large scale, evangelical development, like any other in the 1960s and 1970s, was really a matter of transferring Western expertise into a Third World context. At present evangelicals are in the process of embracing the latest fashion of empowerment. Freire, the prophet of this movement, was a devout Roman Catholic who saw his theories as an outworking of his faith, so empowerment may have more of a Christian foundation than some other theories. If Freire's views are consistent with God's word it makes no difference where they come from, but there is a pressing need for evangelicals to examine the development of this idea, like any other idea, from a biblical perspective.

Outline of contents

The brief outline of general development theory and practice above proves that the topic is very wide ranging. It includes government policy in Western and Third World countries. It has to do with the policy of large international institutions like the World Bank, the IMF and various bodies affiliated to the UN. But it also has to do with the provision of a good water supply or health care in remote rural villages. It has to do with enabling the poor to earn some sort of living in urban and rural slums. So, if helping the poor is a Christian virtue, there are a whole host of different avenues for Christian input, ranging from lobbying and being actively involved in government or commercial agencies, to supporting the work of Christians in the slums.

For such a broad agenda there is need for a wide biblical vision of what it means to live as a Christian in the shadow of the massive problem of poverty at the end of the twentieth century. The first section seeks to provide such a vision.

The first chapter focuses on the kingdom of God. The kingdom is seen as fundamental to any biblical understanding of development. Many have written about the kingdom and it has an important place in contemporary social theology. In this volume there is space only for considering some fundamental principles. Since Jesus as King claims not to destroy but to fulfil the revelation of God's will in the Old Testament, attention is then given to some of the principles that should condition the way in which we move from the Old Testament text to addressing the problem of poverty in our complex modern world. This is the theme of the second chapter. That Jesus, as King, wills to bring to birth a visible community (church) which belongs to him and reflects his character, is considered in the third chapter. The fourth chapter looks at Jesus' teaching on how the resources of his community are to be used for God's glory and to bless the poor. However, the growth of the church, as a community of peace and freedom, does not occur in a vacuum but in the face of opposition which has its ultimate source in the spiritual realm that is opposed to God. The first section concludes, therefore, with a chapter on spiritual warfare.

Section two deals with seven key topics that have a direct bearing on the issue of poverty in the light of the principles laid down in the first section. The first chapter in this section, (Chapter 6), focuses on religion. The Bible is very clear that what people do flows from what they believe, so it is appropriate to start by exploring the place of religion in perpetuating poverty. In the secular context the answer to the problem of poverty is still sought to a great extent in the application of the right economic principles. Chapter 7 suggests some ways of applying kingdom principles to the world of economics. Chapter 8 goes through the same exercise for the world of politics. It is becoming more and more apparent that we are witnessing a powerful surge of interest in ethnic identity at present. In many cases this is leading to poverty resulting from conflict and dislocation. So, chapter 9 looks at the issue of ethnic identity. The statistics tells us that the majority of the world's poor are women. Chapter 10 examines the reasons for this and the appropriate Christian response. The final two chapters deal with two issues that Western experts believe to be the cause of some poverty at present but which could be the cause of poverty on a catastrophic scale in the future. The issues are population growth and degradation of the environment. Chapter 11 deals with population and Chapter 12 with the environment.

General approach

The ground that is covered by this volume is enormous so it may be helpful to explain some of the principles that have conditioned its composition. Firstly, it has been written by theologians, with Christian leaders in mind. We believe that those who are involved in development or are just interested in the broad implications of what it means to be a Christian will find encouragement in it. But our heart is for those who have the responsibility of teaching God's word in all the various ways that that is done in the context of the church. The overwhelming majority of footnotes in this volume are Bible references. All the themes dealt with are Bible themes. Sadly they are dealt with too rarely from the pulpits and platforms of the churches. If this unworthy effort will give confidence to leaders to preach and teach God's counsel that is contained within it we shall be more than happy.

Secondly, we have purposely set out to raise issues without trying to give all the answers. Neither have we tried to be exhaustive in linking the principles of Section 1 with the themes considered in Section 2. We have left plenty of scope for further study. To facilitate this a resources section is attached to each chapter.

Thirdly, we consider that the earthing of theory in practice is vitally important. Even Christian theory that does not work is useless. It is here that the experience of Tearfund's partners all over the world is invaluable.

Resources

All the resources sections at the end of each chapter will be organized in the same way. A limited number of Christian, mainly evangelical, books will be mentioned first. Normally, the first book mentioned will be a fairly accessible introduction to further study of the subject of the chapter. The last book mentioned in this first section will be the most academic. An attempt will be made to grade the books between these two poles. In many cases the list of Christian books will be followed by a list of books that are not explicitly Christian. Finally there will be a list of journal articles or single chapters from books. The overwhelming majority of these will be Christian. Where books are concerned an effort has been made to refer to books which have been published recently and are, therefore, more likely to be available, although we recognize that the shelf-life of books is now very short. Inevitably some older books are so good that they have to be included. We just hope that they will not be too difficult to find. In most cases what is recommended is only a small selection of what is available.

This particular resources section is divided into two sections:

1) *Resources relevant to the whole volume*

The following volumes are all good introductions to what Christian development means from different perspectives:

Sinclair, Maurice, *Green Finger of God* (Exeter, Paternoster 1980), is a theology of development based on Bishop Sinclair's experience of working among the Indians of the Argentinian Chaco. Sadly, out of print but still one of the best books on the subject.

Batchelor, Peter, *People in Rural Development* (Carlisle, Paternoster 1993[2]). A beautiful book full of wisdom, grace and practical advice flowing from 40 years' experience of working with the rural poor in Africa.

Perkins, John M., *Beyond Charity: The Call to Christian Community Development* (Grand Rapids, Baker 1993). A super book by one of the great elder statesman of Christian social action in our day.

Maggay, Melba, *Transforming Society* (Oxford, Regnum Lynx 1994). A powerful testimony from a Filipino on the relevance of the gospel in the political upheavals that her country has passed through in recent years.

Bradshaw, Bruce, *Bridging the Gap* (Monrovia, MARC 1993). A stimulating attempt to bridge the gap between evangelism and development.

A composite volume from the World Evangelical Fellowship can be added here:

Nicholls, Bruce (ed.), *In Word and Deed, Evangelism and Social Responsibility* (Exeter, Paternoster 1985).

The following two volumes are helpful in placing the issue of addressing poverty in a wider context:

Stott, John, *Issues Facing Christians Today* (London, Marshall Pickering 1990). A magisterial volume on the many aspects of Christian social responsibility.

Chester, Tim, *Awakening to a World of Need* (Leicester, IVP 1993). A history of the awakening of social responsibility among British evangelicals since 1950 by Tearfund's Research and Policy Director.

There are also many books that are not written from a Christian perspective that are very helpful. Just four of these will be mentioned:

George, Susan, *How the Other Half Dies: The Real Reasons for World Hunger* (Harmondsworth, Penguin 1976). Nothing has changed fundamentally since this powerful book was first published over 20 years ago. It gives the Christian conscience a powerful stir.

Jackson, Ben, *Poverty and the Planet* (Harmondsworth, Penguin 1990). A clear and readable introduction to the problem of world poverty.

Todaro, M.P., *Economic Development in the Third World* (New York, Longman 1985[3]). A massive work that throws tremendous light on the Western economist's view of the Third World.

Eade, D. and Williams, S., *Oxfam Handbook of Development and Relief*, 3 vols. (Oxford, Oxfam 1995). This is the 'bible' of many development workers.

Finally, there are a number of periodicals that are particularly helpful:

Transformation is the journal of the International Fellowship of Mission Theologians. Published quarterly by Paternoster Periodicals it is by far the most helpful journal on issues that cluster around the problem of poverty.

Footsteps, published by Tearfund, is a quarterly paper linking health and development workers worldwide. It is very practical, is available in English, French, Portuguese and Spanish, is free – but donations are welcome. An index for issues 1–17 is available.

New Internationalist. A humanist magazine which is often anti-Christian but which usually contains a lot of useful information.

2) Resources relevant to the Introduction

Books

Maurice Sinclair's book referred to above and Viv Grigg's *Companion to the Poor* (Sutherland, Albatross 1984), are helpful in defining what development could mean biblically.

For material on general development theory, Elliott, Charles, *Comfortable Compassion* (London, Hodder & Stoughton 1987) is very helpful. He is a former director of Christian Aid and writes from a non-evangelical perspective. For an evangelical account see Wayne Bragg's chapter 'From Development to Transformation' in Samuel, Vinay and Sugden, Chris (eds.), *The Church in Response to Human Need* (Grand Rapids, Eerdmans/Oxford, Regnum 1987). A critique of general development theory which is not specifically Christian but very Christian in tone can be found in Chambers, Robert, *Whose Reality Counts? Putting the First Last* (London, Intermediate Technology 1997).

For a deeper understanding of Evangelicalism see Tidball, Derek J., *Who Are the Evangelicals?* (London, Marshall Pickering 1994), and Bebbington, D.W., *Evangelicalism in Modern Britain* (London, Unwin Hyman 1989).

Articles

There are a number of useful articles in *Transformation*, vol. 13 no. 4 (1996) as well as Deryke Belshaw's 'Socio-economic theology and ethical choices in contemporary development policy: an outline of Biblical approaches to social justice and poverty alleviation' in *Transformation*, vol. 14, no. 1 (1997).

SECTION 1

BIBLICAL FOUNDATIONS OF ACTION ON BEHALF OF THE POOR

ONE

The King and His Kingdom

Introduction

A big problem needs a big vision to sustain those who are brave enough to tackle it. Poverty is a massive problem but the vision of the kingdom of God is equal to it. It provides an adequate end for all human effort because it is ultimately rooted in a heavenly future. It sustains effort now because the king has promised to be with his disciples in the heat of the conflict. Because the king is endowed with indestructible life we can be sure that even if we lose our own life in his service that our self-sacrificing service will not be in vain.

The kingdom of God and the poor

The kingdom of God has become a central theme in the biblical underpinning given to much Christian action against poverty. For many the fight against poverty is an integral part of the coming of God's kingdom on earth. According to this view, any blow struck for justice is a blow struck for the kingdom even where this breakthrough has occurred among people who do not confess God as king and Jesus as lord. According to this view, the establishment of God's kingdom does not begin only when individuals accept the lordship of Jesus but occurs whenever God's values are established in a particular situation. The emergence of social justice, for example, is seen as part of the coming kingdom of God. Since one of God's key values is the protection and strengthening of the poor and vulnerable, much development work is therefore kingdom work even where no one personally accepts Jesus as king. Within this approach even the term 'redemption', normally reserved for those who have been redeemed out of the kingdom of Satan into that of God, can be appropriate to describe God's activity outside the church, when we see it not simply as the experience of regeneration, forgiveness and new life, but in wider terms as God's work of fulfilling his intention for the world.

Other Christians are worried by this appropriation of kingdom language to describe success in the fight against poverty. Ronald Sider, for example, comments that 'There seems no warrant in the New Testament for talking about the coming of the kingdom of God via societal change apart from confession of Christ.'[1] The root of this argument is that 'absolutely none of the scores of New Testament texts on the kingdom of God speak of the presence of the kingdom apart from the conscious confession of Christ'.[2] Advocates of this position still maintain that God is very much at work among the people of the world who do not confess him as king. However, they describe this activity in terms of his role as Creator, Sustainer and Judge of all humanity. They reserve kingdom and redemption language for God's rule over the redeemed and his work of saving them from their sin.

Both sides of the debate see real dangers in the other side's position. Those who use kingdom language to describe the establishment of justice and peace in communities which still do not accept Jesus as Lord are worried that their opponents denigrate the importance of striving for justice and freedom from want in the world. They are afraid that the world outside the community of those who accept Christ as Lord will come to be seen simply as a hopelessly depraved sinking ship from which all effort should be made to rescue individuals into the kingdom of God. The world meanwhile can continue to sink until the return of Jesus. In so doing they forget that God's redemptive purposes encompass the whole of his created world.

---

[1]   Sider, R. with Parker, J., 'How Broad is Salvation in Scripture?' in Nicholls, B., *In Word and Deed* (Carlisle, Paternoster 1985), p. 104.

[2]   Ibid. p. 104.

Those who confine kingdom language to the conscious acceptance of Jesus' lordship predict that their opponents' position will encourage a movement away from making conscious disciples of Jesus Christ as king to merely seeking people's physical and social improvement. They are afraid that striving for the kingdom will be reduced to improving the material conditions of the poor and thereby forgetting that it is no profit to gain the whole world and lose one's soul.

Since there is evidence to support the fears of both sides it is important to examine the biblical evidence on the kingdom carefully. We shall focus on the scope, timing and qualities of the kingdom of God.

The scope of the kingdom of God

In the Old Testament

Though the Old Testament does not contain the phrase 'the kingdom of God', the kingship of God is one of its central themes.

The God of Israel is presented as the God who rules the whole world.[3] His sovereignty over all nations is seen in two contexts in particular. First, God uses other nations to punish and to teach his chosen people. Second, he judges and punishes the foreign nations themselves because of their idolatry which leads them to stray from his requirements of justice. Since God is the creator and sustainer of the earth and all its creatures his rule is universal and he has the right to demand obedience from all human beings. Everyone knows what his standards are to a certain extent and are responsible for living by them. Therefore, God's judgment, when it strikes, is just.

These themes emerge particularly strongly in the book of Daniel. For example, the rule of God even over the mighty Nebuchadnezzar, king of Babylon, is revealed to Nebuchadnezzar in a dream.[4] Daniel interprets the dream in terms of

---

[3] See for example 1 Chron. 16:31; 29:11–12; Ps. 9:7–8; 45:6; 47:7–9; 93:1–2; 103:19; 145:11–13; Isa. 37:16.

[4] Dan. 2:31–5.

God's sovereignty even over Nebuchadnezzar: 'The God of heaven has given you dominion and power and might and glory; in your hands he has placed mankind.'[5] This fact of divine delegation entails ethical requirements for Nebuchadnezzar. This emerges in his second dream.[6] Daniel tells Nebuchadnezzar how to avoid God's punishment revealed in the dream, 'Renounce your sins by doing what is right, and your wickedness by being kind to the oppressed.'[7] God's rule over all powers, therefore, involves a demand for standards of behaviour that reflect God's character.

Whilst God reigns universally, he is the ruler of his chosen people in a unique way. The exodus from Egypt was really the removal of the Israelites from the oppressive dominion of the Pharaoh to the just dominion of God. At Sinai, God gave the Israelites the law as an expression of his rule over them. When they eventually arrived in the promised land God apportioned it to them according to their tribes and families. Israelite government was theocratic and when there was need for a unifying figure to unite the tribes against an enemy, judges were equipped by God to act as his representatives. It is not surprising that Samuel, the last of the judges, saw the demand of the Israelites for a king as a crisis in their history, because, in his eyes, it was tantamount to rejecting God as king.[8]

When David became king the situation was restored because he was anointed by God and ruled very consciously as God's representative. God promised David that his throne would remain for ever. When Solomon proved unfaithful it started to become clear that this promise did not simply relate to David's physical descendants and to the occupation of a particular territory. This became very clear when Judah and its king were taken into exile in Babylon, and Jerusalem and its temple were reduced to ruins. It is at this point that it becomes clearer that God's rule is something God does rather than the geographical area in which he does it. Although it is impossible to divorce rule from its locus entirely, it became possible, after the exile, to think

---

[5] Dan. 2:37–8.
[6] Dan. 4:10–18.
[7] Dan. 4:27.
[8] 1 Sam. 8:6–8; 12:12.

of God ruling without that rule being confined to a defined territory. God continued to rule over his faithful remnant even though they were scattered among the nations. Meanwhile, God's prophets continued to hold out the hope of a full and glorious restoration of Israel when it would become the centre of a territorial kingdom subject to the benign rule of the heavenly king.

The promise to David was now attached to the idea of an ideal king, the Messiah, who was to come and restore the glory of Israel and to fulfil the promise to Abraham that all the nations of the world would be blessed through his descendants. It is this idea of kingdom as a dynamic power which will ultimately have a territorial locus that is developed in the New Testament.

Before turning to the New Testament it is important to note how the special sovereignty exercised by God over his chosen people has continuity with his universal sovereignty over all peoples. God creates and sustains all humanity, but his sustaining activity is particularly clearly seen in his intimate upholding of his chosen people. God rules and delegates authority to all nations, but he rules his chosen people in a special way, revealing his awesome authority to them. God expects certain standards of behaviour from all people, but he has revealed the nature of his righteousness in far greater depth to his chosen people. He has mercy on all nations, but his mercy is uniquely long-suffering in relation to his chosen people. All people can and are required to worship God, but his chosen people have a unique responsibility to worship given their privileged access to the wonder of God. Overall, therefore, God's redemptive dealings with Israel develop and extend his creative and sustaining dealings with the whole of humanity.

In the New Testament

As we would expect, the New Testament confirms the Old Testament teaching that God's rule over humanity is universal and ethical. God is sovereign over the destiny of all things from sparrows to nations.[9] God's reign over all humanity is merciful

---

[9] Mt. 10:29; Acts 17:26.

and just.[10] Consequently he expects justice and mercy from all
people. Furthermore, his continual creative upholding of the
universe testifies to his nature and his power, so that humanity
is 'without excuse'.[11] However, whilst his rule is absolute over
humanity, humans universally choose to rebel against his
authority.[12]

The major difference between the Old and New Testaments
is the revelation of the role of the pre-incarnate and eternal Son
of God, who became flesh in Jesus, in this universal rule. We
know now that God the Father made everything through the Son
and that it is through and for the Son that everything is sustained.[13] God's rule over the universe is now expressed through
the reign of his Messiah, the Son of Man, Jesus. The Old Testament had established a pattern of expectation that God would
set up a kingdom on earth which would be given to his anointed
one, the Son of Man, to rule over.[14] In fulfilment of these expectations God exalted Jesus 'when he raised him from the dead
and seated him at his right hand in the heavenly realms, far
above all rule and authority, power and dominion, and every
title that can be given not only in the present age, but in the one
to come'.[15] Jesus has been given universal dominion and God
assures us of his ultimate victory over all opposition. The time
will come when 'the kingdom of the world [will] become the
kingdom of our Lord and his Christ'.[16] Meanwhile we have to
live with one of the great mysteries of this present age, that many
humans prefer the rule of the Prince of this world to the benign
jurisdiction of the Prince of Peace.

Whilst in the New Testament God's rule is universal, the
'kingdom of God' or the 'kingdom of heaven' is the expression
used, particularly in the Synoptic Gospels, of the sphere in
which people, enabled by the Holy Spirit, confess Christ as their

---

[10] Mt. 5:45; Acts 17:31.
[11] Rom. 1:18–20.
[12] Rom. 3:23.
[13] Heb. 1:1–3; Col. 1:15–20; Jn. 1:1–18.
[14] Isa. 9:1–7; 11:1–9; Mic. 5:1–4; Jer. 23:5–6 and Ezek. 34:22–4. For Son of Man
expectation, see Dan. 7:13–14.
[15] Eph. 1:20–1.
[16] Rev. 11:15.

Lord and Saviour and worship God as their Father. A clear distinction is made between God's universal rule and his reign over those who accept his authority and forgiveness. Jesus says to Nicodemus that no one can see the kingdom of God unless they are born again.[17] The discontinuity between the kingdom of God and the kingdom of this world is so complete that new birth is necessary. This radical discontinuity is also expressed vividly in Jesus' teaching on how to deal with the cause of sin.[18] Such is the incompatibility of sin with the kingdom that Jesus teaches that it would be worth removing anything from oneself that causes sin, however painful that might be. Only then can one enter 'life' or the 'kingdom of God'.

The fact that 'life' and the 'kingdom of God' are seen to be synonymous in this section of Mark's gospel is particularly significant for our understanding of Jesus' teaching in John's gospel. In John the 'kingdom' is only mentioned twice, in the conversations with Nicodemus and with Pilate. John prefers to use 'life' (19 times), or 'everlasting life' (17 times), to express the same truth. One of the major weaknesses of contemporary Evangelicalism is that it tends to drive a wedge between the ideas of 'the kingdom of God' and 'everlasting life' while in the New Testament they are just different ways of representing the same reality. This reality exists in radical discontinuity with life outside Christ's lordship.

Yet, the kingdom, which is so different from the world which has not bowed before God, continually seeks to reach out to the world. Jesus consequently offends the Pharisees by breaking their rules of separation from sinners as he seeks to win more people for the kingdom. Jesus' 'parables of the kingdom', which focus on growth, emphasize that members of the kingdom are part of an organism which has begun to grow into something that will fill the whole world.[19] In the parable of 'The

---

[17] Jn. 3:3; cf. v. 5.
[18] Mk. 9:43–7.
[19] 'The Mustard Seed and the Leaven': Mk. 4:30–2; Mt. 13:31–2; Lk. 13:18–19; Mt. 13:33 and Lk. 13:20–1. 'The Seed Growing Secretly': Mk. 4:26–9. 'The Sower': Mk. 4:1–9; Mt. 13:1–9; Lk. 8:4–8. 'The Wheat and the Weeds': Mt. 13:24–30. 'The Dragnet': Mt. 13:47–50.

Wheat and the Weeds',[20] for example, the field, which is the 'world', and which contains in the present 'sons of the kingdom' and 'sons of the evil one', can also be described as God's 'kingdom'. Though it may not appear to be the case, those who belong to the kingdom represent the primary reality in the world. This world rightly belongs to God and his people so, in the end, the Usurper and his followers will be weeded out and 'the kingdom of the world' will 'become the kingdom of our Lord and his Christ'.[21]

While there is discontinuity between the kingdom of God and the kingdom of this world, there is also a sense in which God rules over all. This universal rule has continuity with God's rule over the redeemed. This is as true of the New Testament as it was of the Old. In his mercy God sustains and provides for all his creatures irrespective of their response to him, but he promises to provide in a particular way for those who seek his kingdom and righteousness first.[22] He reveals his power and nature to all through creation, but he reveals himself far more fully to those in the kingdom.[23] He rules over and will judge all nations and individuals, however evil their actions, but he rules in a unique way over those who confess him as Lord.[24] He delegates the care of creation and the protection of humanity to Christians and non-Christians, but he delegates a unique authority to those who have entered his kingdom.[25]

God fulfils his aims for the world through a humanity that retains something of the image of God, but he works particularly through those who are being 'transformed' into the 'likeness' of Jesus.[26] Overall, God intends that his providential concern for the whole of humanity should point humanity to the fuller experience of his care and authority that awaits them if they bow before him and enter his kingdom. Similarly, the realization of

---

[20] Mt. 13:24–30.

[21] Rev. 11:15.

[22] Mt. 5:45; Acts 14:17; Mt. 6:33.

[23] Rom. 1:19–20; Mk. 4:11–12.

[24] Acts 17:26,31; 2:23.

[25] Rom. 13:1ff.; Mt. 16:19.

[26] Jas. 3:9; 2 Cor. 3:18 – *eikōn*, 'likeness' here, is the word used in the Septuagint to render *ṣelem*, 'image', in Gen. 1:26.

God's redemptive provision reawakens individuals to the wonder of his provision for all in creation.

The timing of the kingdom of God

When Jesus began his ministry the heart of his message was 'The time has come. The kingdom of God is near. Repent and believe the good news'.[27] The translation begs the following question: Was Jesus saying 'Repent, for the kingdom of heaven is present with you in me', or 'Repent, for the kingdom from which every evil will be banished for ever is going to be established at some point in the future'. An examination of the broader teaching of Jesus on the kingdom, recorded particularly in the Synoptics, seems to suggest that Jesus would have replied affirmatively to both interpretations. The kingdom has come with Jesus, but it will only come in its fullness when Jesus comes to earth a second time as judge. This picture is confirmed if we agree with most biblical scholars that 'everlasting life' or just 'life' takes the place of 'kingdom' in John. In John's gospel 'everlasting life' is both something that comes with Jesus in the present and something that will occur in the future.[28] These two truths run through the New Testament.

The kingdom of God in the present

There can be no doubt that whilst the New Testament looks forward to a kingdom that is yet to come, the king of that coming kingdom has already come into our world. Because Jesus is the king established by God and ruling through the power of the Holy Spirit, his very existence among us was a judgment on sin. So he could claim that if he drove 'out demons by the Spirit of God, then the kingdom of God has come upon you'.[29] It is

---

[27] Mk. 1:15; Mt. 4:17, Lk. 4:43.

[28] Jn. 5:24; 6:40.

[29] Mt. 12:28; cf. Lk. 11:20 where Jesus says, 'if I drive out demons by the *finger* of God'. This saying has crucial importance in the debate between those who believe that the kingdom has come in Jesus and those who believe that Jesus taught that the kingdom is yet to come.

inevitable that where the king is those forces that are arraigned against him should be challenged and banished. The dynamic core of the kingdom is the presence and power of the king. So, where the king is exercising his rule the kingdom must already be present.[30]

This current reality of the kingdom is the key to understanding the much-debated statement of Jesus in Luke: 'Once, having been asked by the Pharisees when the kingdom of God would come, Jesus replied, "The kingdom of God does not come with your careful observation, nor will people say, 'Here it is', or 'There it is', because the kingdom of God is within you." '[31] The key phrase in this saying is 'the kingdom of God is within you'. Many commentators now argue that 'within you' should be translated 'among you' or 'in your midst'. These words of Jesus were spoken in response to a question by the Pharisees about when the kingdom would come. Their understanding of the kingdom was tied to the territory of Israel and the hope that a world empire ruled by a son of David would be established in Jerusalem. They were enquiring about the signs they should look for to know that this kingdom was about to be established. Jesus says that their question displays a fundamental misunderstanding of the nature of the kingdom of God. It is not essentially about the territorial rule of some future king but about inward submission to the king who was standing in the midst of them. It is our response to the king's rule now that is the crucial factor in considering our preparation for the future coming of the kingdom.

If the kingdom is essentially the king's rule then the encouragement in the Sermon on the Mount, to 'seek first [God's] kingdom and his righteousness/justice' must have a present as well as a future reference.[32] Commenting on these words Leon Morris says: 'The kingdom has both present and future significance, and we should seek to exclude neither from the . . . passage. Kingdom points to rule, and the expression is to be

---

[30] Various sayings of Jesus confirm this. The more obvious are Mk. 4:11 (similarly Mt. 13:16–17; Lk. 10:23–4); Mt. 11:11 (with parallel in Lk. 7:28); Mt. 11:12 (with parallel in Lk. 16:16); Mt. 12:28 (with parallel in Lk. 11:20).

[31] 17:20–1.

[32] Mt. 6:33.

understood in terms of doing the will of God now as well as looking for the coming of the final kingdom. The important thing for the disciple is to be constantly seeking to do the things that God wills, that is, to be submissive to the King.'[33]

The kingdom of God in the future

Many of Jesus' parables which emphasize the reality of the kingdom in the present experience of Jesus and his followers, simultaneously point to its future development. The parable which compares the kingdom of God to a seed which grows from humble beginnings to a world-embracing dominion is a good example.[34] A seed contains within itself, in the present, the reality of the future. The present and future activity of that seed are a unified whole. Similarly, in the present, the kingdom of God spreads gradually and in conjunction with the continued existence of evil. However, at the final harvest[35] all evil will be rooted out and the kingdom of God will be established as the only kingdom on earth. The current spread of the kingdom and the final judgment, when it will be fully established, are parts of one process. So, the kingdom was initiated with the first coming of Jesus, continues to come in the post-Pentecost power of the Holy Spirit and will come with the return in judgment of the Son of Man.

The present reality of the kingdom, through the Holy Spirit, should mould the behaviour of its members. However, there is an equally strong emphasis in the New Testament that the coming final consummation should influence behaviour to the same degree. Christians should be constantly looking for, and hoping for, the final stage of the kingdom's development. They should be warning others of the judgment to come. The 'near expectation [of the return of Jesus to rule] is endemic to hope itself'.[36] At the same time, Jesus recognizes the need to make

---

[33] Morris, L., *The Gospel According to Matthew* (Grand Rapids, Eerdmans/Leicester, IVP 1992), pp. 161–2.

[34] 'The Mustard Seed': Mk. 4:30–2; Mt. 13:31–2; Lk. 13:18–19 and 'The Seed Growing Secretly': Mk. 4:26–9. All the parables of growth mentioned earlier are also relevant to this theme.

[35] Mt. 25:31–46.

[36] Beasley-Murray, G.R., *Jesus and the Kingdom of God* (Grand Rapids, Eerdmans/Carlisle, Paternoster 1986), p. 343.

planned, long-term and sensible use of whatever time is left.
This balance of sleepless expectation and a sensible long-term
perspective is seen clearly in the juxtaposition of the parable of
the 'Ten Virgins', which advocates sleepless waiting for the
master's return, and that of 'The Talents', which encourages the
planned use of 'a long time'.[37]

The hope of the final consummation of the kingdom is a hope
for the whole of creation. As such, it is consistent with the hope
of the Old Testament for 'new heavens and a new earth'. The
picture Isaiah gives is of a renewed earth that will be a blessing
to its godly inhabitants. Sin and sorrow will be banished from
within it and its inhabitants will dwell in eternal felicity. Peace
between people and with, and among, the animals will be its
hallmark. The earth will yield its bounty for all to enjoy. Most of
all, righteousness will reign supreme at that time.[38] This theme
is picked up by Peter, in his second letter, and by John in
Revelation.[39] The kingdom, therefore, affirms and renews the
whole creation.[40]

Qualities of the kingdom of God

Having looked at when the kingdom comes we shall now look
at how it comes. What are those fundamental qualities that
indicate its presence? We shall focus on four qualities in particular.

1. New birth

Jesus states that we need to be born again if we are to enter the
kingdom of heaven. Paul underlines this need for total transformation when he states that those who are in Christ are a 'new
creation'.[41] The kingdom is essentially a work of God in people's
hearts. Its fundamental interface is not to be found in human

---

[37] Mt. 25:1–13; 25:14–28; 25:19.

[38] Isa. 65:17–25; 66:22.

[39] 2 Pet. 3:13 and Rev. 21.

[40] See Romans 8:18–25. The future of the creation is explored in ch. 12,
'Environment, Poverty and the Kingdom'.

[41] Jn. 3:3,5; 2 Cor. 5:17.

relations with each other but in human relations with a God who has graciously revealed himself in Jesus.

This can be seen in the way Jesus reverses the standard human way of defining what people are by means of what they do. People seeing those who are generous to the poor, who pray a lot and who obviously fast conclude that they must be very holy. Jesus rejects that conclusion and says that if we know how generous someone is and how much they pray and fast, then they may not be holy because they may be doing their good deeds in order to be seen and praised by other people.[42] For Jesus it is what people are inside that is crucial. That is what defines them. The flow is not from the outside in but from the inside out. His concern is with motivation and not action. In the case of alms the crucial issue for Jesus is that they are offered from a heart that is full of genuine love for God and the needy. Such inner transformation can only come in those whom God has 'rescued . . . from the dominion of darkness and brought . . . into the kingdom of the Son he loves'.[43]

The nature of the spiritual renewal illustrated by the metaphor of new birth is also seen in the fact that humility is one of its main attributes. Jesus' disciples found it very difficult to think of the kingdom in any way other than in terms of the exercise of earthly authority and power. On more than one occasion we find them arguing about who was to have the positions of authority in the kingdom. They accepted that Jesus was the king, but kings have chief ministers and advisers, and they were very curious to know which of them were to occupy these positions. That is what lies behind their question about who is the greatest in the kingdom of heaven. Jesus responds by calling a little child to him and, giving him a hug, says: 'I tell you the truth, unless you change and become like little children you will never enter the kingdom of heaven. Therefore, whoever humbles himself like this child is the greatest in the kingdom of heaven.'[44] Children lacked all authority or power in the society of Jesus' day. They were dependents in the fullest sense. So Jesus is saying that we

---

[42] Mt. 6:1–18.
[43] Col. 1:13.
[44] Mt. 18:1–4; cf. Mk. 9:33–7; Lk. 9:46–8. It is Mark who says that Jesus took the child into his arms.

must give up any idea of power and authority in their earthly sense and yield our wills to the determination of Jesus and others if we are to enter the kingdom of heaven. As we shall see when we come to look at this principle in the context of the church, this is the key to the sort of servanthood that should be a central characteristic of citizens of the kingdom of God. In fact it is one of the foundations of any real community.

2. Forgiveness

Because the kingdom is essentially a divine invasion from above no limits can be placed on who can be invaded. It is not a matter of human qualification but of divine forgiveness – and everyone and anyone needs forgiveness. So, it is not surprising that the ministry of Jesus was marked by close contact with those who were called 'sinners' by their more religious contemporaries. The 'sinners' were those who had fallen foul of God's law in some specific way such as adultery or who, because of their poverty, found it very difficult to fulfil the ritual demands of the law. Those who had collaborated with the Roman authorities in collecting taxes were singled out as a particularly bad case of 'sinner'. They broke ritual law and oppressed the poor, so they were reviled by all. Unlike his contemporaries Jesus ate and drank with 'sinners' and tax collectors.[45] He even allowed a prostitute to anoint him.[46] He kept such close contact with sinners because he had a message of forgiveness for them.

Accepting the forgiveness of Jesus is the way sinful human beings enter the kingdom of God. But in entering the kingdom of God we take our leave of another kingdom – the kingdom of darkness/Satan. Paul says that Jesus 'has rescued us from the dominion of darkness and brought us into the kingdom of the

---

[45] Beasley-Murray warns us that this close contact is 'so familiar a picture of the ministry of Jesus that we are in danger of overlooking how greatly he differed from what we know of his contemporaries in this respect: John the Baptist in the wilderness waiting for the penitent to come to him; the Essenes in Qumran, watching and waiting for the call to march to the Day of the Lord; the Pharisees keeping their skirts clear of the defiled; the Sadducees maintaining the cultus in the temple and trying to maintain good relations with the Romans; the Zealots raising the flag of God against his foes . . .' Beasley-Murray, *Jesus and the Kingdom*, p. 137.
[46] Lk. 7:36–50.

Son he loves, in whom we have redemption, the forgiveness of sins'.[47]

Those who have found forgiveness in Jesus have been transplanted from the kingdom of Satan to the kingdom of Jesus. Though Satan may still have access to the citizens of the kingdom of Jesus it is clear from what Paul says that transfer from one kingdom to the other is permanent, just as birth into the family of God cannot be undone. The struggle is not over being in the kingdom of God or not, but over behaving in a way that is consistent with its citizenship. So we can move to the third quality, obedience.

3. Obedience

Jesus says that 'not everyone who says to me, "Lord, Lord", will enter the kingdom of heaven, but only he who does the will of my Father who is in heaven'.[48] This close correlation between the kingdom and the Father's will emerges again in Paul's farewell address to the Ephesian elders at Miletus. Paul says 'that none of you among whom I have gone about preaching the kingdom, will ever see me again'. Then he adds, 'For I have not hesitated to declare to you the whole counsel/will of God'.[49]

In the Lord's Prayer we say, 'your kingdom come, your will be done on earth as it is in heaven'.[50] Some commentators understand the request that the kingdom come as exclusively a prayer for the final manifestation of the kingdom at the end of the world. But 'kingdom' is a dynamic concept referring more to the doing of what God wants than to the place where his wishes are performed. In this case, while it includes a petition for the final manifestation of the kingdom, it can also be seen as a parallel to the next petition that God's will should be done on earth as it is done in heaven.

To do God's will now is to practise righteousness or justice in all human relationships. His kingdom is not some privatized and marginalized religion that is concerned only with the rela-

---

[47] Col. 1:13–14.
[48] Mt. 7:21; cf. 12:50; 18:14.
[49] Acts 20:25,27.
[50] Mt. 6:10.

tionship between an individual and God. This is not to deny the fact that the relationship between people and God is pivotal. Many of us have power points in our homes into which we plug a panel of sockets from which we can run a number of appliances. Human beings are like those panels. We will have no power unless we are plugged into the mains, but the power that we have from the mains is useless unless we become channels of power into a whole range of human relationships. We were made not simply to enjoy God, but to be channels of his kingdom into the world – the world of economics, politics and so on.

This is made clear by John the Baptist whose message was endorsed by Jesus. The coming of the kingdom demands repentance. This will involve very practical steps towards justice in human relationships. The rich should share with the poor, tax collectors should only collect what they are required to and soldiers should stop extorting money from ordinary people.[51]

4. Power through suffering

During his ministry on earth Jesus provided external signs of his right to rule over human hearts and lives. So, when the rabbis questioned his right and ability to forgive the sins of a paralysed man he proved that he could by healing that man's paralysis.[52] When Jesus sent out his disciples into the villages of Galilee he said, 'as you go, preach the message, "The kingdom of heaven is near". Heal the sick, raise the dead, cleanse those who have leprosy, drive out demons.'[53] Where the king is, power is unleashed and broken lives and communities are put together again.

There is a tendency today to focus on the more dramatic manifestations of kingdom power. Yet miracles and victories over demonic powers, which are seen in many parts of the world today, must not distract from the fact that Jesus' awesome power was ultimately exercised through the suffering of the cross, on which he finally overcame the powers of evil.[54] This pattern of

---

[51] Lk. 3:11–14.
[52] Mk. 2:3–12.
[53] Mt. 10:7–8; cf. Mt. 11:5.
[54] Col. 2:15.

power through suffering remains the pattern for all members of the kingdom.[55] Even in the new heaven and new earth the Lamb will still be at the centre witnessing eternally that the way to the glorious kingdom was the way of the cross.[56]

Jesus' suffering came from the opposition of men held in sway by Satan. But because his kingdom is qualitatively different from the kingdom of this world he refused to fight back, choosing the path of suffering. His kingdom powerfully advances through the proclamation of the truth in word and self-sacrificial action.[57] When, therefore, Christians bear witness to the truth they must expect persecution.[58] In this situation they must not meet violence with violence. 'Anyone', Jesus says, 'who does not take his cross and follow me is not worthy of me. Whoever finds his life will lose it, and whoever loses his life for my sake will find it.'[59] Living under the yoke of Jesus and seeking to establish righteousness in this world is difficult and dangerous work. It has never progressed, and never will progress, without sacrifice and suffering until the kingdom is fully revealed. The kingdom can indeed come with power into this present world and affect all human relationships but it never comes without suffering.

The significance of the scope, timing and qualities of the kingdom for ministry among the poor

God's rule over the redeemed

While God rules universally, he reigns through his Son, Jesus and by the operation of the Holy Spirit in those who have accepted his mercy and authority. To experience this reign, in the language of John's Gospel, is to experience 'life'. To know Jesus is to know 'life' because *he* is 'life'. Jesus and the kingdom

---

[55] Phil. 3:10.

[56] Rev. 21:3–4; 22:22–3.

[57] Jn. 18:37–8, cf. Carson, D.A., *The Gospel According to John* (Leicester, IVP 1991), p. 595.

[58] Mt. 5:10; 10:22ff.

[59] Mt. 10:38–9.

are inseparable. Much modern theology is scandalized by what it sees as the limitations put on the kingdom by the intensely personal and particular emphasis of the New Testament. Strenuous efforts have been made to convert Jesus from a personal Lord and Saviour to an ideal pattern of attitudes and behaviour. The kingdom can then be reduced to a way of living that does not need to have anything to do with the person of Jesus. Jesus did not say 'this is the way' but 'I am the way' to life in all its fullness. The kingdom is and will be only where Jesus is worshipped, honoured and obeyed.

What this means for Christian work among the poor is that it must be focused on the person of Jesus Christ. After all, it is he who is able to transform our life so that we move from being self-centred to being God-centred; it is he who is able to forgive our failings and who makes possible a life of joyful obedience to him, and of service to our fellow human beings; it is he who can enable us to take up our cross, and embrace what this world sees as suffering, in order to release the power of Jesus into the world to transform people's lives for time and for eternity.

Christians working with the poor, therefore, need to keep their vision strongly on the ultimate goal for humanity which is the kingdom of God. It is good if individuals and communities are transformed from powerless victims of circumstance to purposeful controllers of their own destiny. However, this development must point people to a far deeper need for salvation from the tyranny of Satan and self. Similarly, while it is good that people are enabled, perhaps for the first time, to enjoy God's creative provision for them, it is ultimately inadequate if they do not experience the riches that are in Christ Jesus for those who accept his forgiveness and lordship. Christians must always keep a biblical perspective of God's ultimate vision for human beings, which is, that through redemption they come to know him in Jesus Christ. Anything less is short-changing the poor.

God's universal rule

God is Lord of the whole universe and the whole of humanity even though many do not acknowledge it. God's universal rule provides the basis for his redemptive rule over those who accept his authority over their lives. The way he rules over the whole universe has continuity with the way he rules over the redeemed. Everyone is created in God's image although the image, in every human being, has been severely marred by the fall. God's provision for all people has continued to be consistent and generous since the flood. In this sense he has been, and will continue to be, just. The problems lie with his rebellious subjects. But the rebels are never ultimately able to subvert his rule or to destroy absolutely the image of God in them.

An awareness of this reality of God's universal rule should encourage Christians working among the poor who do not believe in Jesus. They are co-operating with God's sovereign will which is that all should experience the fullness of his creative provision. In striving for justice in the economic and political spheres they are working within God's plan for the whole of his creation. In pursuing peace between different ethnic groups and different genders, they are co-operating with his universally applicable standards of inter-human relations. In seeking the sustainable use of the world's natural resources, they are reflecting God's concern and joy in his creation. Christians expect to find marks of the image of God among the poor with whom they work and these marks will enable improvements and development to take place. There are many testimonies to the transformations that have occurred within communities and individuals even where those communities and individuals have not yet accepted Jesus as their Saviour and Lord.

Christians working in these situations, often seeing good changes happen among the lives of the poor, realize that God's universal provision for all people is meant to point to his plan of redemption through Jesus Christ. The goal ultimately is that all people come to realize their need of a Lord and Saviour. Similarly, Christians who see truly admirable qualities among the non-Christian poor with whom they work, realize that those people, like themselves, are fallen and in need of being recreated in the image of Jesus Christ. God's universal sovereignty, therefore, must point onwards to the need for him to become sovereign over the lives of fallen people through faith in Jesus.

The power of hope in the coming kingdom

Whilst the kingdom of God is a present reality, nevertheless, its full revelation remains in the future. Jesus is indeed king now and has been given a name which is above every other name. Everyone will one day recognize that he is king and bow the knee to him. But that is far from being the case at present. The world in which we live is torn apart by pride, injustice and greed. As a result, the weight of suffering as a direct consequence of sin seems immeasurable. It makes us cry from the depth of our heart, 'Come, Lord Jesus, come. Come and right the wrongs; come and punish the wicked who have trampled the poor into the dust; come to establish justice in the earth.'

Our hope in the coming glorious rule of Jesus does not leave us paralysed face to face with the enormous problems of a fallen world. Rather it should inspire us to prepare for his coming. Our consuming passion should be to live in obedience to our glorious king and to see others also coming to recognize him and live under his authority. Because Jesus is a living Lord who has sent his Spirit into our hearts to empower us we labour in his kingdom now with hope in our hearts as we look forward to the day of his coming. Our hope is a living hope.

Amazingly, hope for a future kingdom also transforms present reality. As human beings we were created to find our true meaning and purpose in God. Much of the suffering and poverty in the world is a consequence of people seeking meaning and purpose somewhere else – in wealth, power or pleasure. For the poor, having no future hope is reflected in hopelessness about the present. Finding hope in Christ and the future establishment of his kingdom transforms everything. Those who once made wealth, power or pleasure their aim now seek justice and use their resources to bless their neighbour. The poor, whose life was drenched in blackness, see light at the end of the tunnel and even their present material circumstances begin to change for the better in its glow. Hope in the coming kingdom is a powerful force for development.

Resources

Books

Gnanakan, Ken, *Kingdom Concerns* (Bangalore, Theological Book Trust/Leicester, IVP 1990), is a good introduction to the kingdom from a Third World perspective and Padilla, Rene, *Mission Between the Times* (Grand Rapids, Eerdmans 1985), is an excellent collection of essays on the kingdom.

The most comprehensive examination of the New Testament teaching is Beasley-Murray, G.R., *Jesus and the Kingdom of God* (Grand Rapids, Eerdmans 1986), and the most substantial theological treatment is Ridderbos, H., *The Coming of the Kingdom* (Philadelphia, Presbyterian and Reformed 1962).

A little book by Louis Berkhof entitled *The Kingdom of God: The Development of the Idea of the Kingdom Especially since the Eighteenth Century* (Philadelphia, Presbyterian and Reformed 1951), may not be easy to find but it is a very helpful analysis of movements like 'The Social Gospel'.

Articles/Chapters

Caragounis, C.C., 'Kingdom of God/Heaven' in Green J.B. and McKnight, S., *Dictionary of Jesus and the Gospels* (Downers Grove/Leicester, IVP 1992).

McCloughry, Roy, 'The Signpost to the Kingdom' in *The Eye of the Needle* (Leicester, IVP 1990).

Johnstone, A.P., 'The Kingdom in relation to the church and the world' in Nicholls, Bruce (ed.), *In Word and Deed, Evangelism and Social Responsibility* (Exeter, Paternoster 1985), represents the branch of Evangelicalism that is suspicious of social action. Rene Padilla responds powerfully to this chapter.

Kuzmic, P., 'The church and the Kingdom of God' in Nicholls, Bruce (ed.), *The Church, God's Agent for Change* (Exeter, Paternoster 1985). This chapter is also relevant to the chapter on the church.

TWO

The Law of the King

Introduction

As the one appointed by God to bring in the kingdom, Jesus wants to control our lives in every detail. That leaves us with the question of how we can know what his will is in the many different situations that we have to face from day to day. We have the example and teaching of Jesus and his apostles to help. But Jesus also bequeathed us the Old Testament as an authoritative source of instruction. The Law found in the Pentateuch has much to say on how the Jews were to behave towards God and each other. The difficulty comes when, as Christians, we try to apply the Old Testament law to our lives today. However, Jesus leaves us with no option but to accept the Old Testament law as a word from God.

Christians have recognized from the beginning that there are different categories of law in the Old Testament. The clearest definition of the different categories before modern times was made by John Calvin who divided the laws into the three categories of moral, civil and ceremonial. The Ten Commandments is the fundamental expression of the moral law, according to Calvin. He argues that it contains law that is relevant to everyone, everywhere and at all times. The ceremonial law includes all the legislation that has to do with the tabernacle/temple cult and the matter of cleanness/uncleanness. All these laws have been fulfilled in Christ and need not be observed any more though they are still very instructive in helping us to understand the full meaning of the life and death of our Lord.

The civil laws are the laws that were given by God to Israel as a nation. Because God's people in Old Testament times lived within specified territorial boundaries they needed a legal code to regulate their life within those boundaries. The Jubilee is a good example of this type of law. While the details of these civil laws are no longer binding they may be instructive because they are founded on the principles of the moral law.

The paradigmatic approach

There has been a recent revival of interest in Old Testament law and its application to our lives today.[1] Christopher Wright is one of the key figures in the discussion. In dialogue with others, such as Walter Kaiser,[2] John Goldingay[3] and also Michael Schluter and Roy Clements[4] of the Jubilee Centre in Cambridge, England, he has developed a comprehensive method for interpreting Old Testament law in the light of the New Testament and our contemporary situation. He calls his approach paradigmatic. It is really a development of the older Calvinistic approach which takes into account the modern study of the Old Testament and the present state of society.

Wright's description of his approach is divided into two sections: assumptions and method. His first assumption is that the Old Testament continues to be authoritative and relevant for Christians. As Paul says to Timothy when reminding him of his Jewish upbringing in the law of God: 'All Scripture is God-breathed and is useful for teaching, rebuking, correcting and training in righteousness, so that the man of God may be thor-

---

[1] For a very useful introduction to the contemporary discussion among evangelicals about the precise nature of the continuing validity of the law, see, Wright, C.J.H., 'The Ethical Authority of the Old Testament: A Survey of Approaches. Part 2', *Tyndale Bulletin*, vol. 43, no. 2 (1992), pp. 203–31.

[2] Kaiser, W.C. (jr)., *Toward Old Testament Ethics* (Grand Rapids, Academie 1983).

[3] Goldingay, J., *Approaches to Old Testament Interpretation*, updated edition (Leicester, Apollos 1990).

[4] Schluter, M. and Clements, R.D., *Reactivating the Extended Family: From Biblical Norms to Public Policy in Britain* (Cambridge, Jubilee Centre 1986). See also Schluter, M. and Lee, D., *The R Factor* (London, Hodder & Stoughton 1993).

oughly equipped for every good work.'[5] Paul is a faithful fol-
lower of Jesus here. Both present us with the Old Testament as
authoritative Scripture. The question we face is not *whether* it is
relevant to our lives as Christians in the modern world, but *how*.

Wright's second assumption is the unity of Scripture. He
believes that despite its diversity the Bible tells one story of
revelation and redemption. It is a story that begins with the call
of Abraham and ends with the second coming of Jesus. If this is
the case then the story of Abraham or Moses or any other of the
great saints of the Old and New Testaments is my story as a
believer in the twentieth century. So, since we belong to the same
unchanging God, what God revealed to his people of old must
still be relevant and instructive.

The third assumption is the priority of grace. Here Wright is
among those who question the validity of the idea of a 'covenant
of works' that has been so important in Reformed thinking for
centuries. He argues, rightly, that the law of Moses was never,
even hypothetically, given as a means of salvation. It was rather
given as a gift to a people who had already been saved. It was
and is a way of life for a redeemed people and never a way to
life for the unredeemed.

The fourth assumption is that the significance of the law can
only be rightly understood in the light of Israel's role in the
purpose of God. Crucial to his understanding here is God's
covenant with Abraham which contains the promise that all the
nations of the earth would be blessed through him.[6] Wright
comments: 'There was a universal goal to the very existence of
Israel. God's covenant commitment to Israel served his commitment to humanity as a whole and therefore what he did in, for
and through Israel was ultimately for the benefit of the nations.'[7]
This was as true ethically, as in any other sense, since God clearly
links his promise of universal blessing with Abraham's obedience to his will expressed in his day-to-day living in the context
of his family.[8]

---

[5]   Tim. 3:15–17.
[6]   Gen. 12:1–3.
[7]   Wright, 'The Ethical Authority', p. 226.
[8]   Gen. 18:19; 26:4ff.

The fifth assumption is that God had rescued Israel from slavery in Egypt so that they could be 'his treasured possession', 'a kingdom of priests and a holy nation' among the nations of the whole world, which also belongs to God.[9] 'The law was given to Israel to enable Israel to live as a model, as a light to the nations, such that, in the prophetic vision, the law would "go forth" to the nations, or they would "come up" to learn it.'[10]

Following on from the fifth assumption the sixth is that Israel and its law is a paradigm for the nations. The term 'paradigm' is used in grammar and in the world of science and its use in both these spheres is relevant to the way Wright uses it in the biblical and theological context:

> A paradigm verb provides a pattern which you can recognize when reading other verbs in a new context, or which you employ in speech or writing to make sure that your own creative use of verbs in other contexts is grammatical. A paradigm can be recognized or applied in widely differing contexts. It enables you to check bad grammar in a speech or writing, and to use good grammar in fresh communication. In the world of science, paradigm can be used in two further ways. It can mean the overall set of assumptions, theories, beliefs and standards in any given field, within which the scientific community carries on its work. Or it can refer to a concrete example of experimental research which provides a model [for] problem-solving in other areas.[11]

The law was given to God's redeemed people Israel so that they would become a very distinctive type of society in their historical and cultural context. That they should become such a society was not an end in itself. Israel was brought into being for the sake of the nations as well as for the glory of God. In the scientific sense of paradigm Israel's theology was meant to provide a 'normative framework' for other nations and their way of life was meant to provide a specific model of how any society should function under God.

---

[9] Ex. 19:1–6; cf. Deut. 4:5–8.
[10] Wright, 'The Ethical Authority', p. 227.
[11] Ibid. p. 228.

In the method built on the assumptions outlined by Wright, his first step is to define the various general categories of law in the Old Testament. He is not satisfied with the traditional division into moral, civil and ceremonial and suggests at least five categories: criminal, civil, family, cultic and compassionate.[12] His main contention is that it is impossible to distinguish a category of 'moral' law from the mass of Old Testament legislation. He claims that all the laws are expressions of a moral motivation and principle. He does not accept the very reasonable argument that some laws are a more complete expression of the principles of the law than others. However, this weakness in his argument does not undermine his fundamental point that what needs to be done is to penetrate to the principle/motivation of the laws and to do so, as much as possible, from Israel's own social perspective.

The second step in Wright's method is to discover how specific laws and institutions function within the overall framework of Israelite society. By doing this it will be possible to see what is primary and what is secondary legislation. To do this involves drawing on all the advances that have been made in the modern era in understanding Israelite society. While accepting with Wright the value of much modern research there is also a need to re-emphasize the accessibility of the Bible to ordinary people. It is amazing how much the Holy Spirit is able to achieve when the Bible is placed in the hands of believers who have only the minimum skills to grasp its meaning! The fundamental prerequisite to understanding the Old Testament is the conviction that it is indeed the Word of God.

The third methodological step is to define the objectives of particular laws. Any law has an objective – it is meant to protect some interest or restrict someone's power, and so on. When this analysis has been done it will then be possible to move from the Old Testament to our contemporary world, preserving in the process the objective of the law while changing its context. 'At this point', Wright concludes, 'we are "descending the ladder of abstraction" into the realm of specific policy and action in our

---

[12]   See Wright, C.J.H., *Living as the People of God* (Leicester, IVP 1983), ch. 7, for an extended discussion of these categories.

world. But we are doing so, not merely with highly generalized principles, but with much more sharply articulated objectives derived from the paradigm of the society God called Israel to be.'[13]

The wider context of Israelite law in the purpose of God

Before looking at some examples of the application of Wright's method to specific laws it may be helpful to supplement the outline already made with a description of his view of the relationship between God's purpose in creation, in calling Israel and in renewing all things in Christ. This is found in his volume entitled *Living as the People of God*.[14]

Wright illustrates his thesis with a series of triangles which have God, people and the earth as its three points. In the beginning God created the earth and, having created the first human beings, he gave them authority to care for it in obedience to him. Sadly, they rebelled against God's authority and as a result the earth itself was cursed because of their sin. In due time God in his grace redeemed Israel from slavery in Egypt and gave them a part of the earth, the land of Canaan, in which they were to express God's will in their corporate life and in the way they handled the very land itself.

This phase in God's redemption of fallen humankind and their earth was preparatory to the next phase which was heralded by the coming of Christ. Now God's people were not to be one nation or confined to one specific part of the earth. They become a people drawn eventually from every nation. Though drawn from any nation these people of God are distinguishable because of the way in which they handle the resources of the earth which God gives them. The way they handle the earth's resources is best expressed in the term *koinōnia*, 'fellowship' or 'sharing'. These people look forward to the great day of the consummation when Jesus will be all in all, all evil will be

---

[13] Wright, 'The Ethical Authority', pp. 230–31.
[14] Wright, *Living as the People of God*.

banished and they will enjoy the glory of God forever in a new heaven and a new earth.

In this scheme God has only one purpose for humankind and the earth, which is expressed in different ways in different contexts. This being so, the law that was given to the Israelites looks back to the original purpose of God for people on his earth and also looks forward to the fuller revelation of that purpose in Christ and even to the final consummation of all things. The root of that purpose is found in the recognition of God's authority and grace. That is why it is so imperative that people should be brought into a living relationship with God in Christ. Yet the will of God as expressed in the law, which Jesus endorses, remains as a witness to and a demand upon all people. As such it constitutes a great challenge to Christians, as it was to Israel in ancient times, to show to the rest of the world that God's way is the best way.

Specific examples of Wright's approach at work

We shall look at Deuteronomy 15:1–18, which deals with various aspects of poverty. The passage divides into three sections, dealing with debtors (vv. 1–6), the poor (vv. 7–11) and slaves/servants (vv. 12–18).[15]

The main thrust of the legislation with regard to debtors is that when the sabbath year of the land arrived they were to be released from their debts. Some say that the release was to be only during the fallow year. That may have been the original intention of the law but Jewish tradition has taken the release as absolute. God gives three reasons for being generous in this context: a) he will provide enough for everybody so that there is no need to fear being generous. Generosity will not lead to poverty. If his people live in obedience to him the land which the Lord their God has given them will produce abundantly for everyone (v. 4). b) They have a responsibility to obey God's commands (v. 5). c) They must trust God's promise to provide.

---

[15] See Wright, C.J.H., *Deuteronomy* (Massachusetts, Hendrickson/Carlisle, Paternoster 1996), pp. 185–194.

Being generous to debtors may not seem very prudent, but God promises such blessing to those who take the risk that they will 'lend to many nations but will borrow from none' (v. 6).

The crucial question is how to 'descend the ladder of abstraction' from understanding this law in the context of Israel to where we are today. There are some obvious applications to the church at least. The picture that we have of the church at its inception in Jerusalem is of a community of people that was incredibly generous towards its poor. 'There were no needy persons among them.' Some of those who had property were happy to sell it so that the proceeds of the sale could be shared among the poor.[16] The theology behind this enthusiastic generosity is found in 2 Corinthians 8–9. There Paul underlines the fact that Christians have a responsibility to share with one another as he encourages the Corinthian church to give generously to his collection for the impoverished saints in Jerusalem. One of his arguments as he exhorts them is very reminiscent of Deuteronomy 15:1–6. He assures them that generosity is not a route to poverty but the opposite. The more generous we are the more God will give us so that we can be even more generous.[17]

If the application of the principles of Deuteronomy 15:1–6 are clearly applicable in the context of the church, what about society in general? In that they are an indication of how God intends people to behave in relation to one another they must be a valid paradigm for everyone. The major difficulty for people in general (and sadly, too often, for God's people as well), is that they demand a large measure of faith to be put into practice. The law under consideration here, when put together with other laws such as that of leaving the ground fallow in the seventh year, took a considerable measure of faith to obey. Obedience meant putting to one side the natural fallen instinct of people to seek security for their future in this world. God's laws cut across this desire and asked for self-denial but with the promise attached that abundant blessing would be poured out on those who obeyed. If faith is at the root of obedience, then the law can

---

[16] Acts 2:42–7; 4:32–6. Note, Acts 4:34 is almost a direct quotation from Deut. 15:4.

[17] 2 Cor. 9:6–11.

only become a paradigm to people in general when God's people obey it. It is when God's people take this law seriously that something of its benefit to the poor can overflow into society at large – when people see generous Christians and the blessing that flows to society as a whole when the poor are cared for.

When this happens an aspect of the kingdom is already manifested on earth, though only as a foretaste of what is to come when the kingdom will be fully revealed. At that time the saints, who will constitute the new humanity, dwelling in the reconstituted earth, will 'judge the world'.[18] Then, God's will that has already been revealed in the law will be fully obeyed.

Some of the broad principles already outlined in the case of the debtors also apply in the case of the poor and the servants/ slaves. But there are also some factors that are unique to these passages. For example, there is an obvious link between the statement that 'there will always be poor people in the land' (v. 11) and Jesus' statement that we will always have the poor with us.[19] Jesus praised Mary for her lavish love towards him as one who had chosen the path of voluntary poverty and bequeathed the poor to us as objects of the same type of love when he was no longer among us. The section on the poor is also very significant in that the main aim is not relief but empowerment. The poor are to be loaned what they need in order to be able to stand on their own feet. Here the Old Testament law is crucial to understanding the full meaning of almsgiving in the New Testament. It is not handouts but handups that the poor need.

Slavery was a consequence of poverty in Old Testament society. Destitute people could survive by selling themselves into slavery. But this type of slavery was not to be permanent. Its maximum period was to be six years unless the slave voluntarily chose to remain with the master. Even then the Jubilee would have provided a further opportunity of freedom. Added to this the released slave was to be sent away heavily laden with goods as a sort of payment in lieu of service. This would make

---

[18]　1 Cor. 6:2.
[19]　Mk. 14:7.

it possible for freed slaves to provide for themselves. The thrust of this law again is care for the poor in such a way as to encourage their economic independence.

The case of freeing slaves also graphically highlights the typological meaning of these passages, though that is also present in the sections on freeing from debt and on lending generously to the poor. The case of the slave choosing to remain with the master rather than going free is a particularly graphic illustration of Christian discipleship. To be a slave of Jesus is perfect freedom.

When passages such as Deuteronomy 15 are viewed in the broad context of the overall purpose of God for humanity and the earth it is necessary to appreciate that there are different levels of interpretation that are not mutually exclusive. To see Deuteronomy 15 as pointing typologically to salvation in Christ, while perfectly legitimate, does not mean that the very practical principles taught in the passage have no relevance. They are in fact perfectly consistent with the principles of salvation. They are, as always in the Scriptures, the evidence of the reality of redemption.

Not to abolish but to fulfil

In the Sermon on the Mount Jesus spells out his attitude to the Old Testament:

> Do not think that I have come to abolish the Law or the Prophets; I have not come to abolish them but to fulfil them. I tell you the truth, until heaven and earth disappear, not the smallest letter, not the least stroke of a pen, will by any means disappear from the Law until everything is accomplished. Anyone who breaks one of the least of these commandments and teaches others to do the same will be called least in the kingdom of heaven, but whoever practises and teaches these commands will be called great in the kingdom of heaven.[20]

---

[20] Mt. 5:17–19.

It is difficult to imagine a stronger endorsement than the one contained in this passage.

While claiming to fulfil the whole of the Old Testament Jesus focuses on observing and teaching others to observe even the least significant commandments that it contains. He does not say that those who ignore some of the commandments will be excluded from his kingdom but warns that an honoured place will be given only to those who display a high respect for all the commandments. He then takes us through a small sample and in doing so defines a righteousness that is superior to the 'righteousness' that flowed from the way in which the Pharisees and teachers of his day understood and applied the law.

Jesus and the law

Jesus deals with murder, adultery, divorce, oaths, retribution and love for enemies in his brief interpretation of the law in the Sermon on the Mount.[21] What is most striking in this section of teaching is the authority which Jesus takes to himself as an interpreter of the law. He begins his discussion of each command with either 'You have heard that it was said to the people long ago', or simply 'You have heard that it was said'. He then takes authority over the command when he says in each case, 'But I tell you'.

The law will stand until the end of the age but Jesus has become the key to its meaning. He fulfils the ceremonial law through his vicarious death and resurrection, as is made clear in the letter to the Hebrews in particular. He fulfils the ethical commands in his claim to be the authoritative teacher of their true meaning. What he does is to go behind the surface meaning of the command and show that it has to do with the attitudes and motivations of the heart.

The first two commands he deals with come from the Ten Commandments: 'You shall not kill' and 'You shall not commit adultery.' Jesus explains that obedience to these commands is not complete when we are able to refrain from actually commit-

---

[21] Mt. 5:21–48.

ting murder or adultery. Murder and adultery begin in the heart. People can by full of hatred and anger and even express their anger in hurtful words and never actually commit murder. Such are guilty of breaking the commandment, according to Jesus, and will be brought to judgment as surely as those who have performed the heinous deed of taking the life of another. The same is true of adultery. The man who looks at a woman and imagines how nice it would be to have sex with her has already committed adultery in his heart. There would be no adultery in fact without this adultery in intention. It is true that actually to murder or commit adultery is a greater sin but there is guilt in wishing to do something as well as in the actual doing. Jesus wants to deal with us at the deeper level of our wishes and intentions. As Stott says, 'There has been much talk since Freud of "depth-psychology"; the concern of Jesus was for a "depth-morality". Pharisees were content with an external and formal obedience, a rigid conformity to the letter of the law; Jesus teaches us that God's demands are far more radical than this.'[22]

The next command in Jesus' list concerns divorce. What is in view here is the law of divorce outlined by Moses in Deuteronomy.[23] He is not dealing here with a direct command, as in the first two cases, but with legislation framed to deal with breakdown in marriage. Even when originally given by Moses this law was meant to be a protection for women. A husband in Israel was not able to get rid of a wife at his slightest whim as was the practice among the surrounding nations. He first had to find 'something indecent in her'. It is not clear from the Hebrew precisely what Moses meant and the rabbis were still debating the issue in Jesus' day. Shammai and his school argued that it simply meant adultery while Hillel argued that it meant anything that displeased a husband – even ruining the dinner was an adequate reason for divorce. Jesus adopts a position similar to Shammai and forbids divorce on any ground other than adultery.

The next matter to be dealt with is swearing oaths. To swear an oath is 'to make a solemn declaration or statement with an

---

[22] Stott, J., *The Message of the Sermon on the Mount* (Leicester, IVP 1978), p. 75.
[23] Deut. 24:1–4.

appeal to God or a superhuman being, or to some sacred object, in confirmation of what is said'.[24] Added to this is the idea that those who swear invite all manner of curses on themselves if they fail to keep their word. The Old Testament recognizes the fact that oaths were made and lays down rules for their regulation. Those who swore oaths, particularly if the Lord's name was invoked, were commanded to keep their word. It is to such commands that Jesus refers here.[25] Is Jesus saying here that Old Testament commands about keeping oaths are no longer relevant because his followers are not to swear oaths at all? Jesus may be using hyperbole here, as he does in other places. He wants to emphasize strongly that the matter of oaths is really an issue of integrity and that the crucial thing is to be so transparently honest in our dealings with each other in community that oaths become unnecessary. The teachers of the law had become so taken up in the technicalities and trivialities of swearing oaths and the relative value of swearing by heaven, the earth, Jerusalem or even one's own head that they were failing to see the wood for the trees. The oath is not the important thing but the need to be honest and transparent before God and each other.

Jesus is not an unrealistic idealist but he wants to remind us that the law reflects the profound imperfection of the world in which we live. It is not at all certain that he abrogates the use of oaths in law courts in this passage. What he does is open our minds to the possibility of community at a level which transcends law. Perfection should be our aim. We should come at the murky waters of this world's imperfection from the vision of perfection and with faith in the possibility that human life can be transformed upwards through the working of the Spirit of Jesus in our lives.

The next law to come under consideration is that of retaliation. In the Old Testament context this law has to do with the level of punishment that should be meted out for a particular crime. The idea behind the legislation is that the punishment should be as equal as possible to the damage caused by the

---

[24] *Shorter Oxford Dictionary*, quoted by Morris, L., *The Gospel According to Matthew* (Leicester, IVP, 1992), p. 123.

[25] E.g. Lev. 19:12; Num. 30:2; Deut. 23:21.

criminal.[26] This principle that punishment should fit the crime is fundamental to any just legal system. It is inconceivable that Jesus is advocating the abandonment of justice in the courts. What he says to his followers is that they must not use the legal principle of retaliation to justify revenge against someone who has wronged them.

It is easy to understand that a disciple of Jesus should not hit back when assaulted. But is Jesus saying that it is not appropriate for his followers to press charges against someone who has assaulted them and that they should allow them to assault them again? Would this not be to condone evil and lead to moral anarchy? The situation is not made any clearer at first glance because this is precisely what the Lord himself did. He allowed himself to be unjustly tried, condemned and executed when he had the power to defend himself. But Jesus was persecuted for righteousness's sake, and the ultimate victory of righteousness was dependent on his submission to the will of his enemies. It is not impossible that Jesus was thinking of the response of his disciples to persecution at this point in his discussion of the law. Those who are persecuted for righteousness's sake are not to retaliate, though as Paul showed in Philippi, they can use the law of the land to defend themselves against unjust treatment.

This principle of non-retaliation is further underlined in a positive way in the next section which deals with attitude towards enemies. That the Old Testament taught love for neighbours is clear. The question is whether the Old Testament advocated hatred of enemies? God certainly commanded the Israelites to be very stern with the inhabitants of Canaan during the time of the invasion. As instruments of God's judgment on the wickedness of the Canaanites they were to show no mercy. It was also important for the purity of their theocratic community that those who were deeply attached to idolatry should be destroyed from among them. It is not surprising that, having lived through the centuries among enemies who would gladly destroy them, the Jews understood 'neighbour' as fellow Jew. The command to love neighbours was, therefore, the command

---

[26] The principle is outlined in three places: Ex. 21:23–7; Lev. 24:17–22; Deut. 19:15–21.

to love fellow Jews. Those who were not Jews were perceived as
a threat and were, therefore, enemies. Because they threatened
the integrity and purity of the Jewish nation, conceived as the
special people of God, they could legitimately be hated.

Jesus simply expands the meaning of 'neighbour'. For him
'neighbour' cannot be defined in terms of nation, family or any
other social grouping. Everyone we come into contact with is a
neighbour and is to be loved. This is to be the case even with
those who hate us. In fact, as he shows in a graphic way in the
parable of the 'Good Samaritan', neighbour is not to be defined
in terms of the worthiness or otherwise of anyone to receive love
but in terms of showing love.[27] A neighbour is the person who
shows love irrespective of who the person is to whom the love
is being shown.

The great commandment

In his teaching on love to enemies in the Sermon on the Mount
Jesus focuses on what he believes to be the key to understanding the law, which he makes explicit in other contexts.
When asked by a Pharisee, who is an expert on the law, which
is the greatest commandment, Jesus answers, ' "Love the Lord
your God with all your heart and with all your soul and with
all your mind." This is the first and greatest commandment.
And the second is like it: "Love your neighbour as yourself."
All the Law and the Prophets hang on these two commandments.'[28] As we have already seen, Jesus differs from his contemporaries in his understanding of 'love' and 'neighbour'. In
the light of Jesus' fresh understanding the purpose of the law
becomes intensely positive and relational.

More often than not the law is couched in negative terms. The
Ten Commandments is mainly a series of commands *not* to do
certain things. As human beings we find it easy to focus on the

---

[27] Lk. 10: 25–37.
[28] Mt. 22:37–40. Jesus quotes Deut. 6:5 and Lev. 19:18. In Mk. 12:28–34 he is
commended by a teacher of the law for his answer and in Lk. 10:25–8 a teacher
of the law says that these are the two great commandments and is commended
by Jesus for doing so.

process of not breaking the commandments so that we forget that they were given in order to preserve our relationship with God and with each other as a community of his people. Obedience to the letter of the law can easily become an end in itself rather than a means to an end.

In the light of Jesus' emphasis on love as the essence of the law the view that negative commandments also enjoin positive acts is justified. Calvin makes this point in his introduction to the Ten Commandments:

> In this commandment, 'You shall not kill', men's common sense will see only that we must abstain from wronging anyone or desiring to do so. Besides this, it contains, I say, the requirement that we give our neighbor's life all the help we can. To prove that I am not speaking unreasonably: God forbids us to hurt or harm a brother unjustly, because he wills that the brother's life be dear and precious to us. So at the same time he requires those duties of love which can apply to its preservation.[29]

Love and Old Testament law

The eighth commandment

Calvin develops this thesis in his extensive commentary on the law. Rather than examining Exodus through to Deuteronomy verse by verse he takes the Ten Commandments as the essence of the law and groups legislation from the four books under its ten headings. We shall take his exposition of the eighth commandment, 'You shall not steal', as an example of his approach.[30]

He begins by defining theft in the light of the principle, approved by Jesus, that love is the end of the law. This means that everyone's rights must be respected and that no one should do to another what they would not want done to themselves.

[29] *Calvin: Institutes of the Christian Religion*, McNeill, John T. (ed.), trans. F.L. Battles, vol. 1., Book 2:viii:9 (Philadelphia, Westminster Press 1960), pp. 375–6.
[30] Ex. 20:15; cf. Deut. 5:19.

This is another way, according to Jesus, of expressing the principle of love, which 'sums up the Law and the Prophets'.[31] On this basis Calvin concludes that

> not only are those thieves who secretly steal the property of others, but those also who seek to gain from the loss of others, accumulate wealth by unlawful practices, and are more devoted to their private advantage than to equity. For we know under how many coverings men bury their misdeeds; . . . Craft and low cunning is called prudence; and he is spoken of as provident and circumspect who cleverly overreaches others, who takes in the simple, and insidiously oppresses the poor . . . God wipes away all this gloss, when he pronounces all unjust means of gain to be so many thefts.
>
> We must bear in mind also, that an affirmative precept... is connected with the prohibition; because, even if we abstain from all wrong-doing, we do not therefore satisfy God, who has laid mankind under mutual obligation to each other, that they may seek to benefit, care for, and succour their neighbours. Wherefore he undoubtedly inculcates liberality and kindness, and the other duties, whereby human society is maintained; and hence, in order that we may not be condemned as thieves by God, we must endeavour . . . that everyone should safely keep what he possesses, and that our neighbour's advantage should be promoted no less than our own.[32]

In the light of this New Testament understanding of the commandment Calvin then goes on to expound a large number of laws that have to do with different types of theft.[33] He begins

---

[31] Mt. 7:12.

[32] Calvin, J., *Commentaries on the Four Last Books of Moses*, trans. C.W. Bingham, vol. 3 (Edinburgh, Calvin Translation Society 1844), p. 110.

[33] Lev. 19:11,13; Deut. 24:14–15; 25:4; Ex. 22:21–4 with Lev. 19:33–4; Deut. 10:17–19; Lev. 19:35–6 with Deut. 25:13–16; Deut. 19:14; Ex. 22:26–7 with Deut. 24:6,10–13,17–18; Ex. 22:25 with Lev. 25:35–8 and Deut. 23:19–20; Deut:22:1–3 with Ex. 23:4; Num. 5:5–7; Ex. 23:8 with Lev. 19:15 and Deut. 16:19; Ex. 23:3,6. Calvin also deals with a number of texts under the heading of 'Political Supplements to the Eighth Commandment' which he does not consider binding in

with theft in the broad sense in which it is defined and prohibited in Leviticus 19:11,13, 'Do not steal. Do not lie. Do not deceive one another . . . Do not defraud your neighbour or rob him. Do not hold back the wages of a hired man overnight.' Theft here means denying to somebody by deception the enjoyment of what is rightly theirs. This can be done by violently removing neighbours' property against their will ('rob'), or appropriating it in more subtle ways ('defraud'). An example of the latter would be the purchase of some good, from a neighbour very cheaply in the knowledge that an enormous profit can be made on the resale. The example given here is failure to keep a contract of employment. If an agreement had been made to hire a worker at a particular rate for the day then it is theft even to refuse payment overnight. Since day labourers even today live from hand to mouth, to refuse to pay their wages at the end of their day's work is tantamount to stealing their daily bread.[34]

This point is underlined in various other places in the law and extended to widows, orphans and immigrants/refugees. In the context of a world where the eighth commandment, understood in this sense, is very commonly broken, God's people need to expose themselves more to some of these laws that Jesus bequeathed to us.[35]

From the positive point of view keeping the eighth commandment means enhancing the quality of life of others, particularly if they are weak and vulnerable. Even the immigrant is to be loved as oneself. It means refusing to do anything that will increase the comfort and well-being of one party at the expense of another. To suggest that such law is not valid in the light of New Testament teaching would be ridiculous. The quality of communal life which Jesus and the apostles expect from disciples is very much in line with Old Testament law at this point.[36]

Footnote 33 (*continued*) detail because they are what he calls civil laws. They do, however, contain principles which are still valid and instructive. See Ex. 22:1–15; Lev. 24:18,21; Ex. 21:33–6; Deut. 23:24–5; Lev. 19:9–10 with Lev. 23:22 and Deut. 24:19–22; Deut. 15:1–11; Ex. 21:1–6 with Deut. 15:12–18; Lev. 25:23–34, 39–55; Deut. 20:5–8,19–20; 21:14–17; 25:5–10.

[34] James confirms the continuing validity of this law in the NT, e.g. Jas. 5:1–6.

[35] Deut. 24:14–15; Ex. 22:21–4; Lev. 19:33–4.

[36] E.g. Eph. 4:25. Many other passages could be cited at this point.

The Western lifestyle that has been developed in the twentieth century is fundamentally a lifestyle of luxury and self-indulgence. Its whole aim and ethos is this-worldly comfort. Many Christians everywhere, but particularly in the West, have embraced its ideal to a greater or lesser extent. So, there is a great need for rich Christians everywhere to ask themselves whether or not they are enjoying their very comfortable lifestyle at the expense of others. Unfortunately it is not always easy to do this. The commercial world which delivers the luxuries which the rich crave has become so complex and internationalized that there is only a very indirect and often tortuous link between the producer and the consumer. Yet since Scripture makes it so clear that the rich will be held accountable if they oppress the poor in their consumption, rich Christians have no option but to make sure that those who have produced anything that they consume have been justly rewarded for their labour. To neglect to do so could leave the rich facing a charge of murder at the judgment!

Usury

Having dealt with the exploitation of the weak, Calvin works his way through passages that illustrate six other types of theft: a) Theft that happens as a result of using means of measuring that are either shorter or lighter than they claim to be (Lev. 19:35–6; Deut. 25:13–24). b) The theft of land by moving boundary markers (Deut. 19:14). c) The matter of pledges from the poor. For example, to take tools, such as millstones, as pledges on a loan is theft. This is because the poor need such tools to sustain their life (Ex. 22:26–7; Deut. 24:6,10–13, 17–18). d) Appropriating a neighbour's lost property (Deut. 22:1–3; Ex. 23:4). e) Stealing a just judgment in court by bribing the judge. Calvin describes this practice as the worst kind of theft. Sadly all over the world this type of theft is still perpetrated daily in some form or other. Some corrupt judges accept gifts as payment for a favourable judgment while others are biased towards one party through social solidarity or the ability to hire good lawyers. Justice is almost always stolen from the poor and vulnerable, not from the rich and powerful (Ex. 23:8; Lev. 19:15; Deut. 16:19). f) The sixth form of theft is usury (Ex.

22:25; Lev. 25:35–8; Deut. 23:19–20). Since commercial activity almost everywhere is now dependent on a banking system that runs entirely on the charging of interest this legislation deserves closer scrutiny.

Since the Israelites were permitted to charge interest on loans to foreigners Old Testament law does not forbid the charging of interest absolutely. The law is more concerned with the way to help those that have fallen on hard times. So, it forbids the charging of interest on loans to the poor. The point of the law is to stop the rich taking advantage of the desperation of the poor to 'feather their own nest'. This is precisely what moneylenders are doing all over the world. From the positive angle the law is about using resources to help the poor rather than increasing the resources available for one's own use and pleasure. In New Testament terms it is doing to others with our resources what we would have them do to us. This principle is the central thrust of the law according to Jesus.[37]

Interestingly in Luke's account of Jesus' teaching on love of enemies there is reference to giving loans:

> If you love those who love you, what credit is that to you? Even 'sinners' love those who love them. And if you do good to those who are good to you, what credit is that to you? Even 'sinners' do that. *And if you lend to those from whom you expect repayment, what credit is that to you? Even 'sinners' lend to 'sinners', expecting to be repaid in full. But love your enemies, do good to them, and lend to them without expecting to get anything back.* Then your reward will be great, and you will be sons of the Most High, because he is kind to the ungrateful and wicked.[38]

Jesus is using the law on lending to the poor here as an illustration of how his followers ought to relate even to their enemies. Lending to the poor is not a particularly prudent investment in economic terms. It was not meant to enhance the economic well-being of the lender but to help the needy and preserve their place in the community of Israel. It is not impossible for the poor

---

[37] Mt. 7:12.
[38] Lk. 6:32–5.

to do well with a loan and succeed in paying it back but it is too much to expect the sort of profit that could be made with the same money if it was loaned to a rich person or a more viable commercial enterprise. But Jesus affirms the law that puts people before profit and relationships before the acquisition of wealth.[39] It is the good of all involved that should be the guiding principle in all commercial transactions and not the maximization of profit. In the case of an enemy peace may have to be bought at the expense of personal loss. God-honouring human relationships are more important than personal gain.

Resources

Books

Calvin, John, *Commentaries on the Four Last Books of Moses arranged in the Form of a Harmony* (Edinburgh, Calvin Translation Society 1852). These magnificent commentaries are still available and worth the effort of reading antiquated English.

In our day Chris Wright has done more than anyone to raise the profile of Old Testament law. His *Living as the People of God* (Leicester, IVP 1983) is superb. He has also published his doctoral thesis, *God's People in God's land* (Carlisle, Paternoster 1997) and, *Walking in the Ways of the Lord: The Ethical Authority of the Old Testament* (Leicester, Apollos 1995).

Walter C. Kaiser is the other major contributor to this topic, e.g. *Toward Old Testament Ethics* (Grand Rapids, Academie 1983).

Articles

There are two articles by Chris Wright that review approaches to Old Testament law and contemporary literature on the subject: 'The Ethical Authority of the Old Testament: A Survey of Approaches, Parts 1 and 2' in *Tyndale Bulletin*, vol. 43, nos. 1 and 2 (1992). 'Bibliography on Biblical Ethics', *Transformation*, vol. 10, no. 3 (1993).

---

[39] Cf. Storkey, A., *Transforming Economics* (London, SPCK 1986), p. 84.

See also Geisler, Norman, 'Dispensationalism and Ethics', *Transformation*, vol. 6, no. 1 (1989) and Moo, D.J., 'Law' in Green, J.B. and McKnight, S., *Dictionary of Jesus and the Gospels* (Downers Grove/Leicester, IVP 1992).

THREE

The King's People

Introduction

Some hearts drop when turning from thinking about the kingdom to looking at the church. For them the kingdom is such an exciting topic while the church is so depressing. They associate the kingdom with life, action and hope while the church conjures up images of death, inaction and despair. That the church is, even today, a glorious agent of human transformation is not apparent to them.

It has to be admitted that what is called the church has been guilty of many things which make Christians feel very ashamed. According to statistical evidence 80 per cent of the population of Rwanda were members of a 'church' at the time of the devastating events of 1994 which resulted in the senseless killing of up to 800,000 people. That this awful genocide was possible in such a churched country not only tarnishes the name of the God whom all Christians hold dear but also raises fundamental questions about the nature of the church.

In 1995 an American couple buried their baby, who had survived for only a few hours after birth, in the cemetery of a Baptist church. When the officers of the church found out that they had allowed a coloured baby to be buried in their all-white cemetery they initially demanded that the child should be exhumed and buried elsewhere! They did eventually relent and allow the body to rest where it had been laid but by then the racism of the church had been exposed for all to see.

In the summer of 1989 the participants of a conference of Orthodox Church leaders in Romania sent the following telegram to president Ceauşescu:

> [We] think with profound respect and great appreciation of You, the most beloved son of the Romanian nation, a hero among the heroes of our country, a brilliant founder of Socialist Romania and a remarkable representative of the world today, and express our profound devotedness and gratefulness to You for the grandiose work you have initiated and planned with a view to taking the nation to the highest peak of spiritual development ...

Patriarch Teoctist was one of the participants who sent this telegram and though he offered his resignation after the fall of Ceauşescu he has since been reinstated. That church authorities could come to such an accommodation with a man and a regime which can only be described as intensely wicked is frightening.[1]

The church – God's second-best?

One could go on and on telling stories such as these about the failings of the church. If we did, or if our experience of the church was predominantly an experience of such failings, then it would be surprising if we did not end up with a very negative view of it.

Such evidence has led some into making the hope of the kingdom and the disappointment of the church into a theological principle. This is particularly true of dispensationalists who believe that Jesus set out to establish the kingdom in his lifetime but changed his mind and decided to establish the church instead. The kingdom which he set out to establish according to them was a literal Jewish theocracy with its centre in Jerusalem

---

[1] Bordeaux, M., 'Response to Joseph Tson: Key Theological Themes Needing Attention in Post-Communist Europe'. An unpublished paper presented to a Consultation on Theological Education and Leadership Development in Post-Communist Europe, Oradea, Romania, 1994, p. 4. Ironically, Michael Bordeaux received the issue of *Romanian Orthodox Church News* containing the text of the telegram two weeks after Ceauşescu had been executed for murder and treason!

to which all nations would pay homage. But when he was rejected by the Jews, Jesus changed his mind and decided to postpone the establishment of the kingdom until his second coming. The dispensation that is added because of Jesus' disappointment is called the dispensation of grace during which Jews and Gentiles are rescued from the world to wait for the fulfilment of the kingdom. During this period the world, which includes the church as an institution, goes from bad to worse as it ripens for judgment. In this scheme the church has nothing in common with the kingdom. The church does have the task of proclaiming the gospel of salvation but it is not expected to be that successful. Christ will be much more successful when he returns visibly to establish his kingdom. To put it simply, the church in dispensationalism is not good news. It is second-best, provisional and expected to get more and more corrupt and ineffective as the time approaches for Jesus to return as king.

The Biblical foundation for this dispensationalist view is not well founded. Though dispensationalists differ among themselves, the earliest point at which they maintain the crucial transition from kingdom to church took place is Matthew 11:20. But in the story of the centurion's servant recorded in Matthew 8:5–13 Jesus had already commended a Gentile for his faith and proclaimed that many Gentiles would enter the kingdom before the children of Israel. The story of the conversion of the Samaritan woman, and many others in her village of Sychar, recorded in John 4, also preceded the events recorded in Matthew 11. Neither did Jesus abandon his proclamation of the kingdom after Matthew 11 as dispensationalists claim. Matthew 13 contains a whole series of parables of the kingdom. Dispensationalists resort to the very implausible theory when interpreting this chapter that, when Jesus says 'the kingdom of heaven is like . . .' when introducing the parables, he actually means 'the dispensation of grace which I have been forced to resort to before establishing my kingdom is like . . .' Jesus did not preach two gospels. He did not set out to re-establish a Jewish theocracy. What he proclaimed consistently was the fulfilment of the spiritual reality typified in the Old Testament kingdom, in him. Because the kingdom is so inextricably bound up with his person, the kingdom was present when he was present, has been present by his Spirit since his ascension and will come in all its glory when he returns. So, if the church belongs to Jesus, as the New Testament teaches so clearly, there can be no essential contradiction between it and the kingdom.

Darby, one of the pioneers of dispensationalism, who founded the Plymouth Brethren movement, was certainly disillusioned with the church of his day and refused to call his movement a church. The place where the Brethren met was called a Gospel Hall and the groups that met were 'assemblies'. They tried to avoid the trappings of institutionalism as much as possible. There was no doctrinal framework, no formal offices to which people were chosen by the congregation and certainly no officer employed by the assembly to lead. Yet, despite this vigorous attempt to avoid institutionalism, the Brethren were not able to escape the weaknesses that can be seen in other Christian denominations. Their non-institutionalized assemblies can also be riddled with ambition for power and prominence, traditionalism and formalism. Even non-institutionalism can be institutionalized!

Sunand Sumithra is correct, therefore, when he says that 'the church is limited by all the sociological (status), economical (possessions), political (power), cultural (values and institutions) conditioning of an institution'.[2] But he is wrong in advocating the abandonment of the church in favour of the kingdom. He is right to emphasize the provisional nature of the church in some respects but wrong in claiming that the church was not a part of God's intention. Paul says of God that, 'His intent was that now, *through the church*, the manifold wisdom of God should be made known to the rulers and authorities in the heavenly realms' (Eph. 3:10). The church is such a glorious community that even the great powers of heaven will marvel at the multi-coloured wisdom of God manifested through it.

It is right to be very sceptical about many of the institutions that call themselves 'church'. But that should not lead to a rejection of the church altogether. What is needed is a renewed biblical vision of what the church could be and the power of the

---

[2] Sumithra, S., *Holy Father, A Doxological Approach to Systematic Theology* (Bangalore, Theological Book Trust 1993), p. 367.

Spirit to make the vision a reality: 'What we need to do is wash
the face of Jesus, that beautiful face that has been dirtied by so
many compromises our churches have made with the culture
through the centuries.'[3]

A biblical vision of church

It would be a great mistake to abandon the church because it has
covered the face of Jesus with dirt. Any precious item that is
buried in dirt will inevitably become disfigured and tarnished.
But it would be folly to throw a precious item away when what
it needs is a good clean. Any work of restoring a disfigured
antique is made much easier if a picture or detailed description
or another example of the object exists. Where the church is
concerned we have the biblical blueprint and pristine contemporary and historical examples to help us in the task of restoration.

It is unfortunate that the translators of the Authorised Version of the Bible used 'church' to translate *ekklēsia* rather than
follow Tyndale and use 'congregation'. 'Church' has a strong
flavour of place, while *ekklēsia* means a particular group of
people gathered together – a congregation. In the Septuagint
ekklēsia is often used to translate *qahal*, the 'congregation' of
Israel, 'the nation in its theocratic aspect, organized as a religious community'.[4] 'Church' in the New Testament, therefore,
does not refer to buildings or hierarchical structures but simply
to people whose life is focused on Jesus Christ. The whole body
of those who believe in and worship Jesus wherever they may
be are the 'church'.[5] The whole body of those who are followers
of Jesus in a particular locality are the 'church'.[6] Those who
gather together to worship the Lord Jesus in certain people's

[3] Volf, M., 'Eastern European Faces of Jesus: Theological Issues Facing Chris-
tians in Eastern Europe'. An unpublished paper presented at a Consultation on
Theological Education and Leadership Development in Post-Communist
Europe, Oradea, Romania, 1994, p. 2.

[4] Bruce, F.F., *The Acts of the Apostles* (Leicester, IVP 1952[2]), p. 136.

[5] 1 Cor. 12:28; Eph. 1:22; 3:10; Phil. 3:6.

[6] Acts 11:22; 13:1; Rom. 16:1; 1 Cor. 1:2.

houses are the 'church'.[7] When Christians assemble together to honour Jesus and to praise God there the 'church' is.[8]

The community of Jesus

The term *ekklēsia*, therefore, has a strong communal element rooted firmly in the Old Testament. It implies that it is God's intention to assemble together from the generality of the world's population a special people who would be devoted to him in a unique way.

Communal devotion is expressed in different ways. There is the cultic or ritual dimension. In the Old Testament God's special people gathered together at the central shrine to offer sacrifices and to rejoice together 'before the Lord'.[9] There were also special times when they came together to listen to the word of God[10] or to renew their commitment to him.[11] In the New Testament the followers of Jesus gathered together to pray, to listen to the apostles teaching and to break bread.[12] The picture that we get of the followers of Jesus in those heady days in Jerusalem after the Spirit had come with power was of a people who loved to spend time together. They loved to learn together, to pray together and to eat together. Even from the ritual or cultic angle they quickly became a people that could easily be distinguished from others.

That they soon became a distinguishable community was not at all surprising because all the seeds of such a development had been planted among the body of intimate followers that Jesus had gathered around himself. Jesus spent a considerable amount of time teaching[13] his disciples as well as praying[14] and eating with them. Many significant events in Jesus' ministry actually

---

[7] Rom. 16:5 (referring to Aquila and Priscilla); Col. 4:15.
[8] Cor. 11:18; 14:19.
[9] Deut. 16:9ff.
[10] Neh. 8.
[11] 1 Sam. 7:5ff.
[12] Acts 2:42,46.
[13] Mt. 5:1ff.
[14] Lk. 11:1–4; Jn. 17.

occur at the meal table. The meal in Matthew's house was an example of rejecting the rules of ritual uncleanness that the rabbis had created to hinder recreative community.[15] It was during a meal that Mary poured an alabaster jar of precious ointment all over Jesus in expression of her love and devotion.[16] Then shortly before his death Jesus celebrated the Passover meal with his disciples in a way that left an indelible mark on their memory and led to their putting a special meal, the Lord's Supper, at the heart of his community's life.

In bringing into being at Mount Sinai a people devoted to himself, God did not just prescribe a unique way of worshipping. He also prescribed a unique way of living in community and a community in relationship with those outside. God expected his people to reflect in the way they lived the fact that they belonged to him. Jesus was no different. He did not claim to abrogate what God had revealed in the Old Testament but claimed to fulfil it. What he did was to open out in all its fullness the meaning of God's law.[17]

The church: God's people

Those who gather around the feet of Jesus and look to him as their Saviour and Master, will be distinguishable from other communities. Like the Israelites of old they are meant to be a special 'people'. In 2 Corinthians Paul takes up the Old Testament theme of Israel as God's people and applies it to the church. 'What agreement is there', he asks, 'between the temple of God and idols? For we are the temple of the living God. As God has said: "I will live with them and walk among them, and I will be their God, and they will be my people." '[18] Paul emphasizes the unique worship of the followers of Jesus. They are distinguished by the object of their worship. The reason for their communal existence is to worship the true God as revealed in Jesus, which

---

[15] Mt. 9:9–12. See also the very significant meal in the house of Zacchaeus, Lk. 19:1–10.

[16] Mk. 14:1–9.

[17] Mt. 9:13; 12:7; Jn. 15:12.

[18] 2 Cor. 6:16.

rules out being united with the community of unbelievers in the worship of their idols.[19]

The people of Jesus will also be distinguishable because of the quality of their lives. Jesus warns the Jews that the kingdom would be taken away from them 'and given to a people who will produce its fruit'.[20] The church is a people who produce fruit that is characteristic of the kingdom of God. This point, where Jesus brings together the idea of the kingdom, his special people and bearing fruit, is as good a place as any to dwell a little on the relationship between the kingdom and the church. In fact, the relationship is much clearer when viewed in the context of the identification of the concept of 'church' with that of the 'people of God'.

Just about everyone who writes about the kingdom of God is quick to emphasize that the kingdom cannot be identified with the church. The primary idea where the kingdom is concerned is the rule of God. But the idea of rule without anyone or anything to rule over is a nonsense. As I. Howard Marshall puts it:

> The concept of the kingdom of God implies a community. While it has been emphasized almost *ad nauseam* that the primary concept is that of the sovereignty of God and not of a territory ruled by a king, it must be also emphasized that kingship cannot be exercised in the abstract but only over a people. The concept of the kingship of God implies both the existence of a group of people who own him as king and the establishment of a realm of people within which his gracious power is manifested.[21]

God's rule in providence is part of his 'kingdom' so that what is meant by 'kingdom' is not exhausted by what is meant by 'church'. But given the central importance of human beings in God's creative and redemptive work the rule of God in human hearts and lives must be crucial in what is meant by his kingdom. In fact, the church, as the distinguishable people of God, is the

---

[19] Paul quotes Lev. 26:16 here. See also Heb. 8:10.

[20] Mt. 21:43.

[21] Marshall, I.H., 'Church' in Green, J.B., McKnight, S. and Marshall, I.H. (eds.), *Dictionary of Jesus and the Gospels* (Leicester, IVP 1992), p. 123.

supreme manifestation of the kingdom in any generation. The crucial question, therefore, is what distinguishes the church as a manifestation of the kingdom. Some of the images used to describe the church will help to make this clear.

A brotherhood/sisterhood

Both Peter and Paul refer to their fellow Israelites as 'brothers'.[22] This Jewish idea was soon transferred by the apostles to the followers of Jesus. Initially, Jesus' community was but a sub-group within the community of Israel. But it was not long before the situation changed and significant numbers of Gentiles who had attached themselves to Jewish synagogues also believed in Jesus.

The first major influx of Gentiles occurred in Antioch. Eventually the leaders of the community of Jesus, who were at that time still based in Jerusalem, were forced to meet together to decide whether or not one had to be a Jew in order to follow Jesus. They came to the conclusion that it was not necessary. All they required from the Gentiles was that they should be sensitive to Jewish culture in certain areas. They decided to write a letter to the churches with Gentile members to inform them of their decision. The initial greeting in that letter is full of significance: 'The apostles and elders, your *brothers*, to the Gentile believers in Antioch, Syria and Cilicia.'[23] Gentile believers in Jesus were brothers even though they were not Jews and had no need to become Jews. This was a critical point in the history of the church, when it was recognized that the New Testament people of God was not to be one ethnic group but an international brotherhood gathered eventually from every nation on earth. From this point 'brother/s'[24] became a favourite greeting among Christians.[25]

---

[22]   Acts 2:29,37; 23:1; Rom. 9:3.

[23]   Acts 15:23.

[24]   The New Testament nowhere refers to a sisterhood but it is assumed that since Jesus had female disciples who were crucial to his ministry sisters are included when the Christian community is referred to as a 'brotherhood'.

[25]   There are whole pages of references to 'brother/s' in any full concordance of the New Testament and the term is used by all the apostolic authors.

Jesus himself had taught his followers that they were brothers and sisters. He taught a crowd, which included his disciples, that those who obey God's revelation were not to be like their religious leaders at that time who used their religion as a means of satisfying their lust for power. To the contrary, Jesus says to them, 'you are all brothers'.[26] In his comment on this verse Leon Morris says, 'Brothers are equal, and they cannot be arranged in a hierarchy. Over and against Jesus they all hold inferior rank, and none of them is in a position to lord it over the others.'[27]

The extent to which this clear teaching of Jesus has been ignored in the church is amazing. Jesus forbids explicitly the creation of positions of authority among his followers which would flame the fire of human lust for power, domination and human adulation. But churches that claim to follow him have created a host of positions of power and influence with the titles to go with them: Reverend, Very Reverend, Most Reverend, Lord Bishop, His Eminence, Doctor, Father. Godly and humble men sometimes occupy the positions that carry these titles, but that does not undermine the truth that their creation, and the creation of the hierarchy which they reflect, seems to be a case of direct disobedience to Jesus.

One of the great tragedies of the modern Protestant missionary movement is that it led not only to the spread of the gospel to many countries but also to the establishment of Western church structures. Significantly, the missions sent by the most hierarchical Western churches were the slowest to hand over the hierarchy to indigenous leadership. This denial in itself was a tremendous temptation because church leadership was identified with the colonial power structure which was shutting out indigenous leadership from exercising authority. When the scarcity of opportunity to get on in the world because of poverty is added to the denial of self-determination, it is almost inevitable that the church came to be seen as a place to carve out a good career. After all bishops could afford to send their children to smart schools in England or be chauffeur driven around in very

---

[26] Mt. 23:8–12.
[27] Morris, L., *The Gospel According to Matthew* (Leicester, IVP/Grand Rapids, Eerdmans 1992), p. 576.

smart vehicles with a flag on the front announcing their importance.

Even in less hierarchical 'churches' there is a very real danger when office in the church is viewed as a way out of poverty, with the added bonus of respect which comes with position. In early twentieth-century Wales, for example, becoming a minister of a Baptist, Presbyterian or Congregational church was often viewed as a way to a comfortable life with the added bonus of public respect. This was much better than the rigours of coal mining or factory work. But it could also lead to bitterness and the rejection of the Christian faith.

The author's grandfather was a clerical worker in a slate quarry in North Wales and a member of a Congregational Church. He died of kidney failure aged thirty-five leaving a widow and four children under eight years of age with hardly any pension or welfare benefit to sustain them. Times were very hard for the family. It was during this time that the minister of the Congregational church became the first man in the village to have a bathroom fitted in his house. That the minister was able to live in what was perceived to be such luxury, while many of the congregation who supported him from their meagre earnings were struggling to make ends meet, still rankled with the author's father 50 years later. Such behaviour, which was not uncommon, drove many from the churches into left-wing politics which was seen as a better way to address the issues of poverty and injustice. That is what happens when the structure of church leadership becomes conformed to the pattern of worldly ambition.

The pentecostal/charismatic movement, which is the most vigorous branch of Christianity at the moment, is probably still more of a brotherhood than many other churches. At this stage in its development the emphasis is still very much on leadership by means of the extraordinary gifts that are endowed by the Spirit. But the situation can change very quickly. This is particularly the case where there is rapid church growth which makes it possible even for the poor to support leaders in full-time ministry. Leadership can very quickly become a position that is coveted for the wrong reason. This is one area of church life that calls for continual reformation and constant vigilance.

A family

When Jesus says that his followers are brothers he implies that they are members of the same family. Fairly early on in his ministry, when people were very keen to hear him, his family came to the conclusion that he was out of his mind. They went together to take him home but were unable to get into the house where he was teaching because of the crowd. They managed to get a message to him to say that they were waiting to speak to him outside the house. When he heard their message Jesus said, ' "Who is my mother, and who are my brothers?" Pointing to his disciples, he said, "Here are my mother and my brothers. For whoever does the will of my Father in heaven is my brother and sister and mother." '[28]

The phrase 'my Father in heaven' is unique to Matthew. What is interesting about the reference is that 'father' is absent from the list of those who belong to the Father's household. Mothers, brothers and sisters are included but not fathers. Is it possible that Jesus is making a statement about the nature of authority in his family by omitting 'father' from the list? It is certainly true that household government in the time of Jesus was patriarchal. The father was the authority in the home and all the members of the household were in different degrees of subservience to him. But in the household of Jesus the father is his Father in heaven and all other members are on the same level as mothers, brothers and sisters. This could also be the reason why Jesus forbids his followers to call anyone 'Father' in the discourse in Matthew 23.[29]

The dignity which Jesus gave to mothers, sisters and particularly small children, who were accorded a very low status in the family in New Testament times, is further confirmation of this thesis. His kindness to the repentant prostitute, his friendship with Mary and Martha, his view of divorce which gave equal rights to women and the fact that it was to women that he first showed himself after the resurrection witnesses to the respectful way in which he treated them.[30]

---

[28] Mt. 12:48–50.
[29] Mt. 23:9.
[30] Lk. 7:36–50; 10:38–42; Jn. 11–12:11; Mt. 19:1–12; 28:8–10; Jn. 20:10–18.

When mothers brought their infants to be blessed by Jesus and were hindered by the male apostles Jesus was indignant and commanded that the little children should be allowed to come to him.[31] This is the only place in the gospels where indignation is directly attributed to Jesus. His teaching about service and the way he uses children to illustrate what it means to belong to the kingdom in other places helps us to understand his indignation.

Jesus' answer to the question about who is greatest in the kingdom was to call a child to him and say that unless his followers were prepared to become like children they could not enter the kingdom.[32] The concept which he was emphasizing was dependence rather than innocence or simplicity. Children had a very low status and were very dependent on others. Jesus says that his followers must humble themselves and become dependent on God. To enter the kingdom we must lose our powers of self-determination and surrender our wills entirely to God. The proof that this has happened is readiness to serve those of low status.[33] In the worldly thinking of the disciples, to be great in the kingdom would distance the great one from those of low status. For Jesus the opposite is true. Kingdom greatness is to serve the servant, which is the same as saying to serve the poor.

Jesus' response to the indignation of the other disciples when they heard about the request by the mother of James and John that they should sit on his right and his left in his kingdom is in the same vein.[34] The apostles were indignant that James and John had grasped at the positions which many of them coveted; Jesus was indignant at the apostles' perception that he was too important a figure to bother with the weak and marginalized represented by children. Any reading of church history and any knowledge of the contemporary church scene highlights the desperate need for a continual return to the teaching of Jesus at this point. ' "Whoever wants to become great among you," Jesus says, "must be your servant, and whoever wants to be first must

---

[31] Mk. 10:13–16.
[32] Mt. 18:1–6.
[33] Mt. 18:5.
[34] Mt. 20:20–8.

be your slave – just as the Son of Man did not come to be served, but to serve, and to give his life as a ransom for many." [35]

Status has no place whatsoever within the 'family' that Jesus came to establish. His community is made up of brothers, mothers and sisters who are equals and who vie with each other to do good to the weaker members within their community and also to the weak and marginalized in the society outside. The Lord himself is the supreme example in that he gave his life to redeem weak and helpless sinners. A church that has this principle at its heart will be a transforming community that will effect real and meaningful development in the lives of individuals and society at large.

In Matthew 25 Jesus gives us a very striking picture of the last judgment. He imagines the shepherd returning home at the end of a day with his mixed flock of sheep and goats and sorting them out into different pens before retiring for the night. The sheep, the helpless and harassed ones who were in such need of someone to look after and protect them, represent the righteous who are ushered into the glory of the everlasting kingdom. The resourceful and independent-minded goats represent those on the left who are sent away to their eternal punishment. The heart of the story is the reason given by the shepherd for identifying some as sheep and others as goats:

> Then the King will say to those on his right, 'Come, you who are blessed by my Father; take your inheritance, the kingdom prepared for you since the creation of the world. For I was hungry and you gave me something to eat, I was thirsty and you gave me something to drink, I was a stranger and you invited me in, I needed clothes and you clothed me, I was sick and you looked after me, I was in prison and you came to visit me.' Then the righteous will answer him, 'Lord, when did we see you hungry and feed you, or thirsty and give you something to drink? When did we see you a stranger and invite you in, or needing clothes and clothe you? When did we see you sick or in prison and go to visit you?' The King will reply, 'I tell you the truth,

---

[35] Mt. 20:24–8.

> whatever you did for one of the least of these brothers of
> mine, you did for me.'[36]

This is not an easy passage to understand in detail but some
things are very clear. It is clear that those who belong to the
family or household of Jesus share their resources with the
needy. If we are true members of Jesus' family we will all stand
before him in the judgment convinced that we are the least of
his brothers and sisters. As such we will be able to point out
those who stretched out a hand of mercy to us: those who spent
the resources given them by God to do good to us. In our turn
we will be surprised to find that our humble service will also
be valued by the Lord. We may also be surprised to find that
that poor person whom we fed or clothed or welcomed into
our home was also a brother or sister. It is those who took
seriously the invitation of Jesus to make everything that God
had given them available for his family, that take their place in
'the kingdom prepared' for them 'since the creation of the
world'.[37]

A body

Jesus' favoured picture of his church was a family or household.
Paul also calls the church 'God's household',[38] but his favourite
picture of the church is a 'body'. Paul develops this theme
extensively in Romans 12, 1 Corinthians 12 and Ephesians 4 and
refers in a number of other places to the church as the body of
Christ.[39]

In comparing the church to a body Paul highlights its unity
and diversity. It is interesting in the light of Jesus' teaching on
the essential nature of his community that in both Romans and

---

[36] Mt. 25:34–40.

[37] Mt. 25:34. For further exploration of these themes see Crosby, M.H., *House of
Disciples, Church, Economics and Justice in Matthew* (New York, Orbis 1988). There
are no direct quotations from this volume in the section on the family/household
of Jesus. Though the author cannot accept the critical method adopted by Crosby
he provided many stimulating leads and much illumination on some of the key
passages that were considered in this section.

[38] 1 Tim. 3:15.

[39] Eph. 5:23; Col. 1:18,24; 3:15.

Ephesians Paul places his discussion of the church as a body in the context of an appeal for humility.[40] Humility is the first step to a real experience of unity in the context of the church. After all, the church is a collection of very different people from diverse backgrounds with a whole range of endowments. Yet there is no difference that is able to keep them apart – nationality, colour, social and economic status and gender are all irrelevant. In the community of the church 'there is no Greek or Jew, circumcised or uncircumcised, barbarian, Scythian, slave or free, but Christ is all, and is in all'.[41] Spiritual unity transcends any earthly diversity that can and does push people apart.

What Paul has in mind when discussing the diversity of gifts in the church are those divine endowments that, even though they highlight the difference between people, have been given in order to create unity. The gifts that the Holy Spirit gives are not given for individual satisfaction but for the good of the church and of society at large. They are what individual members use in order to build up the community and to bless those who do not belong to it. It is also clearly implied in those passages that focus on gifts that every member of the body has some gift/s to offer that will benefit the whole. This is one reason why humility is so important, since it is so easy for those who have public gifts to fall into the temptation of thinking that their gifts are the only ones with any significance. In fact, says Paul, those gifts which are hidden from view, like our private parts, are still very important members of the body!

Different attempts have been made to put together a full list of gifts mentioned in the New Testament. There are at least 25 of them, though it is not always clear precisely what the gift entailed. The apostles themselves seem to divide the gifts into two main categories: those that have to do with speaking a word from God in some way or other, and those that have to do with giving practical assistance to those in need. This seems to be the case in 1 Peter 4:10–11, for example: 'Each one should use whatever gift he has received to serve others, faithfully administering God's grace in its various forms. If anyone speaks, he should do it as one speaking the very words of God.

---

[40] Rom. 12:3; Eph. 4:2–3.
[41] Col. 3:11.

If anyone serves, he should do it with the strength God provides, so that in all things God may be praised through Jesus
Christ.'

'Faithfully administering' literally means 'ministering as
good stewards'. The *oikonomos* (steward) was the person who
was put in charge of a household by its patriarchal head. This
reference by Peter echoes Luke 12:42ff. where Jesus refers his
teaching about the responsibility of the steward in his house
directly to Peter, though it is clear from this passage in Peter's
letter that Jesus was making a general point.[42] What is interesting
here is the link between Jesus' view of his household and the
idea that there are stewards in the house who have gifts of
instruction and of making sure that the resources of the house
are equitably divided. There are those who can speak and those
who are able to serve the physical needs of the community.
Those with either type of gifting need all the strength they can
get from God to fulfil their role.

Body gifts for meeting practical needs

In a volume focusing on the poor the emphasis needs to be on
those gifts which have been given with the meeting of physical
human needs in view. But, before looking in some detail at these
gifts, we need to remember that they are body gifts. Christian
community, as envisaged by Jesus and the apostles, will not
function properly without gifts which serve both its spiritual
and physical needs. It is also worth emphasizing that all the gifts
are spiritual gifts and not natural endowments.

While it is not always easy to define precisely what some gifts
are, the following have a clear orientation to the practical and
physical needs of the community:

1. Healing (1 Cor. 12:9,28,30)

Paul in Corinthians is definitely thinking of miraculous healing
which was an aspect of the ministry of Jesus and the early

---

[42] See also Mk. 13:37.

church. This gift was used to heal those outside the community as well as those inside. Interestingly, compassion for the sick is one among a number of motives for healing in the New Testament.[43] More significant are the links between healing and faith and the coming of the kingdom of God. Some are healed as a *result* of their faith but more often than not the sick are healed in order to *produce* faith. Jesus' miracles are proof that the kingdom has come in him. Some of Jesus' healings also break down social barriers. He touches a leper, praises the Samaritan leper who returned to give thanks for his healing and heals the daughter of a Syro-Phoenician (Gentile) woman.

There is no adequate reason to believe that the Spirit of God is incapable of granting this gift to Christians today. Miraculous healing has always been a part of the church's experience though it may not be quite as common as some Charismatics and Pentecostals claim. Where there is a genuine manifestation of this gift we should expect it to have the same significance as in the New Testament. It should produce faith in the reality of the kingdom and break down barriers between people as well as bringing health to the sick.

It is also valid to ask whether healings by means of modern medical practice can be included within the category of gifts of healing. That they can is not immediately apparent. Yet a number of the gifts, such as teaching, can be seen as natural endowments that are enhanced by the Holy Spirit. There is no reason why the Spirit cannot take hold of a gift of healing that has been fashioned by modern medical practice and use that to bring blessing to the sick within and outside the Christian community. The world is crying out for those with such gifts to forsake the opportunity for worldly wealth and advancement, which their gift makes possible, and to devote themselves to the healing of the needy. It is not surprising that care of the sick and use of the healing qualities that have been discovered in various substances, as well as the occasional miraculous healing, have characterized the life of the church throughout the ages. The meaning of healing can also be consistent with the teaching of the New Testament, whether miraculous or not.

---

[43] E.g. Mt. 14:14; 20:34.

2. Helping (1 Cor. 12:28)

Since this is the only reference to this gift and the only use of this particular word in the New Testament any attempt to penetrate its meaning has to be somewhat speculative. In the opinion of lexicographers it refers to the service of those who care for the poor and the sick.[44]

3. Serving (Rom. 12:7; cf. 1 Pet. 4:11)

Diakonia (service), is a generic term which has to be qualified in order to indicate the type of service which is in view. So, Paul speaks of his own apostolic service, or of the service that 'brings righteousness', or of the service of reconciliation.[45] But it is also used specifically of the service of giving alms and seeing to the physical needs of the poor.[46] It is the opinion of commentators that Paul is referring to giving alms in Romans 12:7. What he is saying is that if someone has the gift of caring for the poor they must not slacken in their resolve to get on and do it.

In many churches this gift has become an office of deacon which has lost its significance of caring for the poor. There is a desperate need, particularly in Western churches, to rediscover this supernatural gift of the Spirit that is devoted to the redistribution of wealth. There can be no real community/body of Christ without it.

4. Sharing (Rom. 12:8; cf. Lk. 3:11; Rom. 1:11; Eph. 4:28; 1 Thess. 2:8)

Here again, as in the case of serving, Paul seems to make a special gift out of something that should characterize all believers. Yet we should expect to find those in the body of Christ who have a special gift of sharing. Their special charism is to channel their own resources to those in need. The way this gift is to be exercised is 'in simplicity' or 'in liberality'.[47] Any sharing has to

---

[44] Thayer, J.H., *A Greek-English Lexicon of the New Testament* (Edinburgh, T. & T. Clark 1901⁴), p. 50. Abbott-Smith, G., *Manual Greek Lexicon of the New Testament* (Edinburgh, T. & T. Clark 1937), p. 50.

[45] Rom. 11:13; 2 Cor. 3:9; 2 Cor. 5:18.

[46] 2 Cor. 8:4.

[47] Simplicity: 2 Cor. 11:3; Eph. 6:5; Col. 3:22. Liberality: 2 Cor. 8:2; 9:11, 13.

be done without any duplicity of motive but simply out of a pure desire to use one's resources to bless the needy.[48] On the other hand, sharing of any sort is to be generous and liberal.

5. Showing mercy (Rom. 12:8)

There are many causes and manifestations of human wretchedness rooted in the pervasive influence of sin. We are very good at getting into trouble in every area of our life – spiritually, emotionally, physically. What we need in our wretchedness is someone to come alongside to help us on to our feet again. Mercy is at the heart of the gospel and poverty is a condition which cries out for mercy. Interestingly, the New Testament term for alms is derived from the verb 'to show mercy'. All who follow Jesus are expected to show mercy in this sense of giving alms but some have a special gifting in this area. What Paul says about such is that they are to do their work cheerfully. To take the love and mercy of Jesus into a situation of poverty can make heavy demands even on those who are especially gifted. But the cheer with which alms are administered can be as much of a blessing to the poor as the alms themselves.

Examination of these gifts helps to create a picture of a church community that is concerned for the physical as well as the spiritual needs of its members. The point emphasized here is that care for the poor is fundamental to the internal life of the church which is the body of Christ. Since the 'body' of Christ can refer to the visible church in one locality or universally we should expect care for the poor to characterize the church at every level of its existence.

It is also significant that most of the New Testament teaching on the issue of poverty focuses on its relief within the church. This is not to deny that Christians should reach out in love and mercy to those outside.[49] What is highlighted by the focus on care of the poor within the church is the fact that its calling is to be an alternative community. The world is characterized by pride and injustice. It is the sphere where human beings are out to get the most for themselves and their kind, no matter what that may

---

[48] Mt. 6:1–4.
[49] Gal. 6:10.

mean for others. In the church all distinctions are broken down and we become members of one family/household. The resources of individuals cease to be their own property and become the resources of the family. This happened literally and extensively in the early days of the church's life in Jerusalem and beyond.[50] Paul was just extending this principle of action on to a wider international plane when he organized the collection from Greece and Macedonia for the poor Christians of Palestine.[51]

It is all too obvious that the contemporary church often ignores this clear biblical teaching on community. There is some movement of resources from the rich to the poor in individual congregations and from rich churches to poor churches within countries and internationally. However, the movement is nothing like on the scale demanded by New Testament teaching. Some attention is given to gifting that is particularly orientated towards redistribution of wealth on behalf of the poor in some churches but very few seem to take this matter really seriously. In the UK, for example, a biblical view of the 'diaconate' is all but dead. Very few churches recognize and support the service of those with gifts of service, helping, etc. Most Western Christians would find any serious encouragement of wealth redistribution a threat to be vigorously resisted. The examination of what Jesus says about wealth in the next chapter should help to break down such resistance.

Resources

Books

Watson, David, *I Believe in the Church* (London, Hodder & Stoughton 1985), is a good introduction to the subject.

Snyder, H.A., *New Wineskins, Changing the Man-Made Structures of the Church* (London, Marshall, Morgan & Scott 1975), still provides a fresh look at what the church should be.

Shenk, D.W. and Stutzman, E.R., *Creating Communities of the Kingdom* (Scottdale, Herald 1988).

---

[50] Acts 2:42–7; 4:32–7.
[51] 1 Cor. 16:1–3; 2 Cor. 8–9.

Stibbe, Mark, *O Brave New Church, Rescuing the Addictive Culture* (London, Darton, Longman & Todd 1995), is a strong challenge to the Western church.

Crosby, Michael H., *House of Disciples, Church, Economics and Justice in Matthew* (New York, Orbis 1988), is a very stimulating and fresh look at Matthew by a Roman Catholic author.

Articles/Chapters

Marshall, I. Howard, 'Church' in Green, J.B. and McKnight, S., *Dictionary of Jesus and the Gospels* (Downers Grove/Leicester, IVP 1992).

Section 6 of Perkins, John, *A Quiet Revolution* (London, Marshalls 1976), is a wonderful description of a real church coming into being in the midst of the black struggle for justice in the USA.

Adams, Jerry, 'Transforming by Participation: A Model for Community Development in the Republic of Belarus', (Teddington, Tearfund Case Studies 1997).

FOUR

The King's Wealth

There is a lot of material in the New Testament that is directed at the 'haves' rather than the 'have-nots'. Many passages warn of the great danger of acquisitiveness. This focus is surprising given that probably most of the people who heard the words of Jesus were poor, as were most of those who received the letters of the apostles. Why did they need to hear of the dangers of wealth? Part of the explanation is that the desire to possess and experience increasing material comfort is a danger for rich and poor alike when it distracts from God. Also, Jesus has compassion on all human beings including the minority of rich people that he meets. He sees them as in particularly grave danger. Furthermore, it is Jesus' passionate concern for the poor that leads him to address the rich who are in a position to help them.

The New Testament, therefore, forces us to look carefully at the rich. In so doing it questions the tendency of some thinking on poverty which focuses primarily on how the poor can get richer as the rich also continue to get richer. In some circles it is believed that the beneficent, invisible hand of the free market will cause all, rich and poor, to grow richer. There is no question of the rich voluntarily sacrificing their riches for the poor because this would be a denial of the ethos of the capitalistic system that is believed to offer most hope for the poor. Similarly there is little discussion of the dangers to the rich of the endless search for more wealth.[1]

---

[1] For an incisive exception written from a non-Christian perspective, see for example Giddens, Anthony, *Beyond Left and Right: The Future of Radical Politics* (Cambridge, Polity Press 1994).

This is not to say that the focus of the New Testament is against the free market. But the fact that Jesus focuses so much on the rich in a society where the overwhelming majority were poor suggests that he did believe in a direct link between the plenty of the few and the lack of the many. For him the rich must be got on board if the rights of the poor are to be met, and this will involve some sacrifices on the part of the rich. Those who live in the rich West have become accustomed to viewing poverty in Third World countries as a problem which they need to solve. The focus has been on the poor South not the rich West. This is not the perspective of Jesus who focuses on the rich.

The minority rich in first-century Palestine, whom Jesus repeatedly challenges, are clearly equivalent in terms of relative wealth, status and power to the majority of Western Christians in the world today. They too have access to great wealth which they are very reluctant to share. According to Ron Sider, 'U.S. evangelicals have roughly $800 billion in after-taxes income. We spend $8 billion on weight-reduction programs and only one fourth as much (a mere $2 billion) on missions.'[2] The $2 billion referred to here includes the money given to the type of Christian mission that is involved in ministering to the poor. Os Guinness similarly identifies theologically conservative evangelicals as the self-seeking rich of today, 'Christendom's ultimate worldling today', he claims, 'is not the Christian liberal but the Christian conservative.'[3]

The same statistics show clearly that obedience to Jesus with reference to possessions could make a very significant difference to the economic imbalance between rich and poor in the world. If evangelicals in the USA shared a mere 1 per cent of their disposable income with the poor annually it would amount to $8 billion. Norm Ewert[4] estimates that it costs around $1000 to create one job in small-scale industry in a Third World context. $8 billion could create 8 million jobs which would bring blessing

[2] Sider, R., *Evangelism and Social Action* (London, Hodder & Stoughton 1993), p. 191.
[3] Guinness, O., 'Mission modernity', in *Transformation*, vol. 10, no. 4 (1993), pp. 3–13.
[4] Ewart, N., 'The role of business enterprise in christian mission' in *Transformation*, vol. 9, no. 1 (1992), p. 11.

into the lives of at least 40 million people. That is no small figure! Ron Sider's statistic just happens to refer to evangelicals in the USA but the situation is the same in other Western countries and is very probably the same for rich Christians in Third World countries as well.

Clearly, therefore, Western Christians as well as the increasing minority of very prosperous Christians in the Third World need to hear the New Testament teaching that is aimed particularly at those who are, or are aspiring to be, rich. We shall concentrate on Luke where much of the Gospel teaching on wealth is found, although the focus is maintained with complete unanimity throughout the New Testament.

The background to Luke's concern for the rich

Luke, when he came to write Luke and Acts, had at least three experiences which may have alerted him to the significance of Jesus' teaching and example for the rich.

Firstly, Luke had been a close companion of the apostle Paul while the latter was organizing collections from Asia Minor and Greece for the impoverished Christians of Palestine. In some places, like Corinth, Paul had found it quite difficult to get Christians to release funds for international aid even though he knew that they were in a position to do so.

Secondly, there was the sad experience of Demas' defection. In his letter to the Colossians Paul writes that 'Our dear friend Luke, the doctor, and Demas send greetings.'[5] By the end of his second letter to Timothy he writes that 'Demas, because he loved this world, has deserted me.' He then goes on to say almost immediately, 'Only Luke is with me.'[6] It may well be that Luke and Demas were friends as well as co-workers with Paul. Watching his friend and colleague being lured into worldliness may have been another motivation for Luke to focus on the Lord's teaching on the issue of wealth and the love of comfort. Luke saw the awful truth of Jesus' teaching that the desire for this

---

[5] Col. 4:14.
[6] 2 Tim. 4:10.

world's goods is a great danger even for those who are intensely committed to the propagation of the gospel.

Thirdly, Luke had witnessed the tremendous freedom from the desire to possess things that was so characteristic of the early history of the church.[7] Such a vivid experience demonstrated the reality of the hope which Jesus could offer even for the rich that, through the power of the kingdom of God, they too could conquer greed and draw near to God.

Jesus and the rich according to Luke

The dangerous magnetism of wealth

Jesus sees possessions, riches, wealth or money, for which he uses the term 'Mammon', as the focus of a magnetic spiritual force operating in opposition to God and against the poor. People can find themselves in its service. People can live for money or possessions just as they can live in order to serve God. In fact we have to choose between living in order to multiply 'possessions' on earth or 'treasure in heaven'. We have to choose between living to enjoy our money ourselves or living to bless the poor with it.[8] We can either invest our lives in acquiring the visible possessions of earth or in grasping the invisible things of heaven while benefiting the poor in the meantime. The choice is simple because it is impossible to 'serve both God and mammon'.[9] Material comfort, Jesus teaches, contains its own reward that does not take us beyond the limitations of earthly existence; 'Woe to you who are rich', says Jesus, 'for you have already received your comfort.'[10]

Jesus also illustrates the dangers of wealth through a number of his parables. The dangerous, distracting magnetism of the desire for material possessions is underlined in the parable of 'The Rich Fool' in Luke 12. The rich farmer of the parable, faced with the possibility of being even richer, was totally preoccupied

---

[7] Acts. 2:42–7; 4:32–7.
[8] Lk. 12:33.
[9] Lk. 16:13. See also Mt. 6:24.
[10] Lk. 6:24.

with schemes to keep everything for himself so that he could have a wonderful retirement. There was no question of a life that was more than the enjoyment of his possessions and certainly no suggestion of sharing them with the needy. So, when he was hastily ushered into the presence of the invisible God he arrived there empty-handed because he had not used his possessions to build heavenly capital.

This point is underlined again in the parable of 'The Rich Man and Lazarus'.[11] In the parable of 'The Rich Fool' Jesus had focused entirely on the rich farmer and only when he teaches the disciples immediately afterwards, does he get to the poor. In this second parable the poor man is part of the plot. This rich man enjoys his life of luxury, with the suffering poor man sitting just outside his house. Then they both die and enter the afterlife. The poor man goes to heaven and the rich man to Hades. The rich man can see Lazarus in heaven with Abraham so he asks the latter to send Lazarus to relieve his torment: 'But Abraham replied, "Son, remember that in your lifetime you received your good things." '[12] Jesus reaffirms that those who serve mammon get what joy they are going to get in what is but the brief interlude of their earthly existence. Having enjoyed themselves briefly, the rich then leave their wealth behind them, find themselves as paupers in Hades with an eternity of torment in which to remember and regret. Lazarus offered to the rich man the opportunity of proving the reality of another world. However, the rich man remained too preoccupied with this world to notice.

In the third parable, of 'The Sower', the magnetic danger of mammon even for those who have heard and received God's word is highlighted. The word or message from God, which is the good news of the gospel of Jesus Christ, comes to different types of minds and hearts. Some are like seed that falls among thorns, 'who hear, but as they go on their way they are choked by life's worries, riches and pleasures, and they do not mature'.[13] It is possible even for those who seem to welcome the word of

---

[11]   Lk. 16:19–31.

[12]   Lk. 16:25.

[13]   Lk. 8:14; Mk. 4:18–19.

the gospel to be drawn away through love of money and the things of this world.

The rich young ruler

Luke records one incident in the life of Jesus which particularly illustrates the themes that have emerged in Jesus' parables. It is the story of a rich young ruler who came to Jesus inquiring about eternal life.[14] The encounter gives a tragic account of the crippling power of wealth.

In the time of Jesus there was a very small landed class in Palestine, most of whom were linked either to Herod's family or to those responsible for running the religious life of Israel centred on the temple. We are not told which group this ruler belonged to. We learn from Luke 18:23 that he was very rich and Matthew's account tells us that he was a young man.[15] Some think that his youth would have precluded him from belonging to Israel's ruling council, the Sanhedrin. Others think not, so that 'ruler' means 'member of the Sanhedrin'. What is clear is that he belonged to the class of society that had power to order others around and that, despite his youth, he already had large material resources at his disposal.

It is also clear that he came to Jesus with a genuine request. He really did want to know the way to eternal life. This was not a case of someone from the ruling class trying to trip Jesus up. Mark says that he ran up to Jesus and fell on his knees before him.[16]

That the conversation about the way to eternal life initially focused on keeping the law is not at all surprising in the Jewish context. The law had been given as a way of life for a redeemed people.[17] The young ruler had obviously not understood the commandments in the way which they had been meant by God. So, like Paul before his conversion, he was happy to claim that he had kept all the prescriptions of the law since he was a little boy. There may be a hint of disappointment in the young ruler's

---

[14] Lk. 18:18–30.
[15] Mt. 19:20.
[16] Mk. 10:17.
[17] Deut. 32:47.

response at this point. He had come to Jesus for some new insight. The Pharisaic way of keeping a whole pile of minute regulations had not brought satisfaction into his life. We can almost feel his disappointment when Jesus refers him to the commandments.

What he had not understood was that what *Jesus* meant by keeping the commandments and what *he* meant was different. To make this quite clear Jesus throws a verbal grenade into this rich young man's life that left him reeling. It is as if Jesus says to him, 'Do you really want to know what loving your neighbour is about?' In referring to the law Jesus had gone to what is known as the Second Table of the Law, the commandments that have to do with human relationships, rather than the relationship between human beings and God. 'For you', Jesus in effect says to the ruler, 'it will mean getting rid of all your wealth. You must sell your land, share the proceeds among the poor and then come and be one of my closest followers.'

In this invitation Jesus repeats a number of themes that are central to his message: treasure in heaven, following him, sacrificing oneself for others, and selling possessions in order to give to the poor.[18] He could see that this young ruler was firmly tied to his wealth and position, so he hits at the root of his problem. 'If you really want to live', Jesus in essence says, 'get rid of it all and follow me.' This was too much to ask and the young ruler with sadness written all over his face turns his back on Jesus.

Jesus loved the young ruler, so he would have been sad to see him turn his back on real life.[19] As the young man walks away Jesus takes the opportunity once again to warn his followers about the great danger of riches. Using the common rabbinical device of hyperbole, he says that it is as impossible for a rich person to enter the kingdom as it is for a camel to go through the eye of a needle. To Jesus, attitude to wealth is a matter of eternal salvation. His invitation to the rich young ruler to dispose of his possessions and follow him was not a response to a question about economic ethics. Rather, it was a response to a question about inheriting eternal life. Jesus out of love was offering

---

18   Lk. 12:32–4.
19   Mk. 10:21.

eternal life to the rich young man. Not that sharing his possessions with the poor alone would save him. The key to salvation
is the invitation to follow Jesus. What Jesus is saying is that
following him is an absolute demand. He wants to be Lord over
the whole of life. He can give the rich young ruler the eternal life
he craves but Jesus must have control of his wealth as well as
every other aspect of his life. In this case the distribution of his
wealth among the poor would be essential to prove the young
ruler's genuine desire for eternal life.

In Jesus' teaching, therefore, the redistribution of wealth is a
matter of eternal life or death. This emerges particularly strongly
in the parable of 'The Sheep and Goats' in Matthew 25:31–46.
Jesus makes it quite clear here that those who had it within their
power to relieve the suffering of his poor brothers and sisters,
but neglected to do so, will go to hell.[20] Rich Christians who see
brothers and sisters in need and refuse to use their excess resources to relieve them cannot have the love of God dwelling in
them.[21] So, when they appear before Jesus in the judgment they
will be empty-handed. On the other hand, those who have really
appreciated the self-denying love of God in Jesus and replicated
it in a life of service to the needy will be welcomed into the
kingdom. They will have spent their life spontaneously serving
Jesus himself in the form of his poor and needy.

Significantly, the severe warning about the danger of riches
that emerges from the encounter with the rich young ruler
confuses the disciples who were tied in to a 'prosperity' type of
theology. They assumed that riches in the hands of devout
people like the rich young ruler were a blessing. It was this type
of thinking that lay behind the request of James and John, which
was made soon after this event, for the top positions in the
kingdom.[22] They were unable to see that kingdom people may
have to go without wealth and power in this world – that riches
and blessing were not necessarily linked. So they wonder who
can be saved if the upright rich are lost.

---

[20] Mt. 25:31–46.
[21] 1 Jn. 3:17.
[22] Mk. 10:35–45.

God's power over the magnetism of wealth

Jesus' immediate answer is that even if it is 'impossible' for rich human beings to enter the kingdom of God, 'What is impossible with men is possible with God'.[23] Luke vividly illustrates this point in the encounter with Zacchaeus which soon follows and contrasts with Jesus' encounter with the rich young ruler.[24]

In the eyes of devout Jews Zacchaeus was seen as a 'sinner', which means something like 'heathen'. He had put himself outside the community of Israel by collaborating with the Romans in raising taxes. We can surmise that at some point he had decided that it was worth forsaking his religious heritage for the material gain that would come from serving the Romans. He had succeeded in his chosen career and was now rich.

Zacchaeus finds out that his desire to see Jesus, albeit from a distance, was matched by Jesus' desire to see him at close quarters. Jesus invites himself into Zacchaeus' home and heart. The people are very critical of Jesus for being so friendly with a sinner, but in Zacchaeus' house we arrive at the climax of the story that started when the rich young ruler fell at Jesus' feet, asking what he had to do to inherit eternal life. A rich man stands up in the middle of the large company gathered in his house and calls Jesus 'Lord'. To prove it he says, 'Here and now I give half of my possessions to the poor, and if I have cheated anybody of anything, I will pay back four times the amount.'[25] Here is proof that something very dramatic has happened to this particular sinner. God's impossible has happened. A rich man has been freed from his attachment to his possessions. Because Jesus is now Lord in his life he is free to give away his wealth in order to bless the poor and make restitution for past exploitation. What he says may have meant getting rid of everything in order to follow Jesus. We don't know precisely. In fact, whether he did so or not is not crucial. The crucial point is that he had been freed from the tyranny of wealth and was now intent on using his resources in the service of the kingdom. Doing good to the poor is at the heart of kingdom activity.

---

[23] Lk. 18:27.
[24] Lk. 19:1–10.
[25] Lk. 19:8.

Zacchaeus' confession and statement of intent is seen by Jesus as clear evidence that salvation had come into his house. 'House' in this context probably means 'family'. Jesus is not individualistic in his teaching. Zacchaeus' family, which would include his servants, would certainly be poorer from now on but they had the opportunity to share in something far more valuable than material wealth. The story ends with the declaration that the Son of Man has come 'to seek and save what was lost'. Rich Zacchaeus was lost but even he has been saved. Zacchaeus has been gripped by a relationship with Jesus that far outshines his previous dedication to making money. The result of his awakening to spiritual reality is the release of resources desperately needed to bless the poor. In Christian economics, the salvation of the rich must be a fundamental aim.

The practical outcomes of breaking the magnetism of wealth

Leaving it all
Peter's response to Jesus' encounter with the rich young ruler is to state that he and the other apostles had left all in order to follow Jesus.[26] It is important to understand how this sacrifice expressed itself in practice.

Peter, Andrew, James and John had given up working as fishermen in order to accompany Jesus in his itinerant ministry. Matthew/Levi also left his work as a tax collector. Jesus and his band of followers had a common fund with Judas Iscariot in charge.[27] The fund was replenished by gifts, particularly from wealthy women, or women with wealthy husbands, who also accompanied the band of disciples.[28] The family of Lazarus, Martha and Mary were also well off and unquestionably supported the Lord in his work. Jesus obviously approved of these people who made their resources available to him and to the poor but who had not 'left all' to follow him.

---

[26] Lk. 18:28.

[27] Jn. 13:29. This verse is very interesting because it proves that gifts to the poor were regularly made from this common fund.

[28] Lk. 8:1–3.

While Peter, Andrew, James and John had given up normal employment, there are indications that other parts of their life in effect remained constant. We know that Peter had a home where his wife and mother-in-law lived even after he had left his nets.[29] The implication is that Peter owned the house with the suggestion that he may have shared it with Andrew. We don't know whether or not their fishing business was kept up by other members of the family, although we do know that Peter had a boat and gear to go back to after the resurrection. We also know that Peter's wife travelled with him as he carried out his work as an apostle later on.[30]

Where John and James are concerned, the fact that their father Zebedee had hired servants suggests that they were from a fairly well-to-do family.[31] The business would certainly have carried on without the brothers and it is not impossible that they would eventually have had a private income to support their work as apostles. It is also possible to surmise on the basis of a comparison of Mark 16:1 and Matthew 27:56 that the mother of John and James was one of the women listed in Luke 8:1–3 as financial supporters of Jesus' mission. It is also unlikely that Jesus would have entrusted his mother to someone who did not have the means to care for her when from the cross he entrusted her to John. John certainly had a home where Mary could take up residence.[32]

When Peter says of the apostles, therefore, that they had left all, what he means is that they had turned their back on the whole process of acquiring wealth for themselves. That does not mean that they were not plugged into strong family networks of support, or that they had got rid of their property, or that they had given up any prospect of inheriting wealth in the future. Furthermore, while the emphasis in Luke is very much on the disruption to family life that following Jesus sometimes causes, a reward is to be found in the fellowship of the community of believers who support each other.

---

[29]   Mk. 1:29–30.
[30]   Jn. 21:3; 1 Cor. 9:5.
[31]   Mk. 1:20.
[32]   Jn. 19:26–7.

This is not to minimize the extent of the sacrifice required to follow Jesus. Immediately after Peter's confident assertion that he and the other disciples had given up everything, Luke shows, yet again, that the disciples had not understood the extent of the self-sacrifice at the heart of Jesus' way. For the third time since Peter made his great confession in Caesarea Philippi Jesus predicts his passion.[33] What Jesus had asked of the rich young ruler was an act of great self-sacrifice. He now reminds his followers that self-sacrifice is at the heart of his ministry. He is going to Jerusalem to die, to give his life a ransom for many. But even after telling them this for the third time the apostles' minds are completely closed to what Jesus is saying. They find it impossible to grasp the idea that the Messiah is the Suffering Servant. In Mark's gospel this third prediction of Jesus' passion is immediately followed by James and John's request for the top positions in the kingdom.[34]

Using what you have

Jesus' focus is on the dangers of the love of mammon, not of wealth creation. Jesus sees nothing wrong with making money – how that money is used, is where things can go wrong. The parable of 'The Shrewd Manager' makes this clear.[35]

Jesus tells a parable about a manager who had got into trouble with his boss for wasting his possessions. Seeing that he is likely to lose his job he immediately sets about arranging things so that when he is dismissed there will be people who will be glad to know him and who will see to it that he is not destitute. So, he quickly calls some of his master's debtors and reduces their debt. We are not told whether the rather bent manager was sacked or not, but when the master heard about what he had done he was impressed with his shrewdness. Worldly people are impressed with the way they are able to get away with murder, literally, at times, in order to preserve their own skin. Jesus comments that 'the people of this world are more shrewd in dealing with their own kind than are the people

---

[33] Lk. 18:31–4. See also Lk. 9:21; Mk. 9:30–32.
[34] Mk. 10:35–45.
[35] Lk. 16:1–15.

of the light'. 'I tell you', he goes on, 'use worldly wealth [literally 'Mammon of unrighteousness'] to gain friends for yourselves, so that when it is gone, you will be welcomed into eternal dwellings.'[36]

The fact that Jesus uses a rather unprincipled individual to illustrate a point has caused a lot of problems for many theologians and commentators. Even the title of the parable in the NIV plays down the fact that he was a typical worldly man driven by the desire to feather his own nest. But Jesus' point is quite clear. He invites us to look at the endless cleverness which the worldly employ in making sure that they remain comfortably supplied with earthly goods. They use wealth so well to gain more wealth for themselves. Jesus then compares this worldly wisdom with the lack of wisdom of those who belong to the light. Those in the light do not use their money to bring material and spiritual blessings to others – to make friends that will welcome them, not to earthly houses, but to the eternal dwellings of heaven.

John Wesley has three headings in his sermon on the point of the parable of 'The Shrewd Manager' made in Luke 16:9: a) Earn all you can. b) Save all you can. c) So that you can give all you can.[37] In sermon 87, 'The Danger of Riches', on 1 Timothy 6:9[38], he applies the points of the earlier sermon specifically to himself: '*I gain all I can* [namely, by writing] without hurting either my soul or my body. *I save all I can*, not willingly wasting anything, not a sheet of paper, not a cup of water . . . Yet by *giving all I can*, I am effectually secured from "laying up treasures upon earth" . . . And that I do this, I call all that know me, both friends and foes, to testify.'[39] John Wesley undoubtedly lived according to his exposition. He was one of the most successful church leaders ever at making money. He wrote books and pamphlets which sold very well and made him an enormous fortune by any standard. But being free from the worship of Mammon he was

---

[36] Lk. 16:9.

[37] Wesley, J., *Wesley's Sermons*, vol. 2 (London, John Mason 1850), pp. 124ff. Wesley's sermons constitute the official doctrine of the Methodist Church so they appear in a host of different editions.

[38] Ibid. vol. 3, pp. 1ff.

[39] Ibid. p. 9.

very careful to take for himself only what he needed to sustain his life with some dignity and gave most of his fortune to the poor. In this attitude he reflected the teaching of the apostle Paul that using leadership in the church in order to make oneself rich is an abomination.[40]

Jesus goes on naturally from the story of 'The Shrewd Manager' to teach about stewardship of material things in the verses that follow. If God cannot trust you to use your material possessions for the sake of his kingdom, he implies, how can he trust you with heavenly riches. If you refuse to share what you have and spend it on your own lusts; if you ignore the poor who are suffering terrible deprivation outside your door or on your screen, how can God entrust you with the glorious riches of heaven. He says again, 'You cannot serve God and Money [Mammon].'[41]

Money, which is a good translation of 'Mammon', is one of the high gods of the Western secular world and his cult is steadily making more and more proselytes all over the world. In the world of international banking and high finance money is now so totally dissociated from anything of value that it can be worshipped in its complete impurity.[42] Given God's power over the magnetism of wealth, it is time for Christians to resist this worship which is already the cause of terrible destruction in the lives of those who are subject to Mammon as well as in the lives of the poor who are deprived by the headlong pursuit of self-interest on behalf of the rich. How is this to be done?

The power of vision

The rich are good at ignoring the poor and rich Christians are not very different from unbelievers in this respect. Wealth can be enjoyed so much better if the suffering of the poor can be pushed from the mind. Just the act of seeing the needy creates a

---

[40] 1 Tim. 6:5–16.

[41] Lk. 16:13.

[42] For more on this theme see Korten, David, *When Corporations Rule the World* (London, Earthscan 1995), pp. 185ff.

new situation for the rich Christian.[43] Those practical gifts of
service that have been given to the church by the Holy Spirit
have the crucial function of making sure that the needy brother
or sister is seen by those who have the means to help. These gifts
are seen today in many para-church organizations devoted to
serving the poor.

If we have any compassion for those who have more than
what is necessary to sustain life then they must be shown the
means by which they can provide evidence of their salvation in
the day of judgment. What is in mind here is not the use of
terrible pictures of suffering in order to shock people into action,
or the public embarrassment of someone poor in any congregation by placarding their need before everyone. It is rather the
stubborn determination to refuse to let the haves forget the
have-nots, so that the haves are being continually shown ways
in which they can bring blessing into the lives of the needy.

The power of the heavenly

Being convinced of the value of the heavenly is crucial to this
whole process. If the choice is between God and Mammon the
poor will not be blessed by the rich until the rich have committed
themselves to God. At root the struggle is not for the wealth that
the rich have, but for their heart. It is a matter of committing
oneself to values which cannot be purchased and to a treasure
that will only be fully enjoyed in a future existence. It is an idea
that has been vigorously rejected and mocked by many modern
thinkers, but Christianity really is about 'pie in the sky when you
die'.

For the Christian the heavenly is focused in the person of
Jesus. 'Since . . . you have been raised with Christ', says Paul,
'set your hearts on things above, where Christ is seated at the
right hand of God. Set your minds on things above', he continues, 'not on earthly things. For you died, and your life is now
hidden with Christ in God.'[44] It is this conviction and experience

---

[43] 1 Jn. 3:17.
[44] Col. 3:1–3.

of being united with Jesus who is in heaven that enables the Christian to 'put to death . . . whatever belongs to [the] earthly nature'.[45]

Paul describes the various characteristics of this 'earthly nature' and the list includes 'greed, which is idolatry'. In Colossians and Ephesians Paul identifies greed with idolatry.[46] 'Greed' translates the Greek *pleonexia* which describes the character of those who want to grasp as much as possible for themselves. Other possible translations would be 'grasping', 'aggression', 'covetousness'. What Paul says is entirely consistent with the teaching of Jesus on Mammon as a very real alternative to the true God as an object of worship and service.

The teaching of the New Testament is powerfully relevant to the present world which is succumbing increasingly to the allurement of the secular materialism of the Western way of life. Not that Westerners have the monopoly of Mammon worship. That human tendency is universal. The genius of the West is that it has made possible a great explosion in this particular type of idolatry. For those who live in the West the power of Mammon is awesome and calls for supernatural energy to resist and overcome. This energy is precisely what Jesus gives to his followers through his Holy Spirit as witnessed in the tremendous freedom from greed and heavenly-mindedness that characterized the early history of the church.[47]

The power of Christian community

It is so clear from the teaching of Jesus and the example of the early church that the church should be a community. This should be true on a local, national and international level. The church exists to show the world the reality of self-denying love in the way its members share their life together, and sharing life necessarily involves sharing possessions.

This happened spontaneously in Jerusalem when the Spirit

---

[45] Col. 3:5.
[46] Col. 3:5; Eph. 5:5. In Colossians he calls greed idolatry and in Ephesians he calls a greedy person an idolater.
[47] Acts. 2:42–7; 4:32–7.

was poured out on the church for the first time. It happened again, internationally this time, when the Christians of Syrian Antioch sent money, in response to prophecy, not news, to relieve the expected famine in Palestine.[48] It happened again on a much wider international scale when Paul made his collection in many churches in Asia Minor and Greece to relieve the suffering of Palestinian Christians once again.[49]

That the Spirit should give gifts within the church to make sure that the community of possessions was expressed is not at all surprising. There is desperate need at present to look for such gifts and stir them up. Every church that is a real church needs those with the gifts of serving the poor, contributing to the needs of others and showing mercy. Without them rich Christians are in mortal danger.

Resources

Books

Ron Sider has done more than anyone to awaken Western Christians to their responsibility to use their wealth to bless the poor. *Rich Christians in an Age of Hunger* (London, Hodder & Stoughton 1990[3]) is now a classic. He has also edited a volume entitled *Lifestyle in the Eighties: An Evangelical Commitment to Simple Lifestyle* (Exeter, Paternoster 1982). Its principles are still relevant to the nineties.

White, John, *Money isn't God – So Why is the Church Worshipping it?* (Leicester, IVP 1993) is a more recent title by White on the same theme.

Perkins, John M., *Beyond Charity: The Call to Christian Community Development* (Grand Rapids, Baker Books 1993).

Griggs, Viv, *Companion to the Poor* (Sutherland, Albatross 1984), is a strong challenge to materialistic complacency, as are Wesley's sermons, nos. 50 and 87. (For those not familiar with Methodism, Wesley's Sermons are the official doctrine of the

---

[48] Acts 11:27–30.
[49] 1 Cor. 16:1–4; 2 Cor. 8–9; Rom. 15:25–7.

Methodist denomination. They come in many different editions so it is convenient just to mention the number.)

Blomberg, Craig L., *Neither Poverty nor Riches. A biblical theology of possessions* (Leicester, Apollos 1999). This challenging and scholarly volume is the best starting point for anyone who is serious about finding out what the Bible says about possessions.

Articles/Chapters

Guinness, Os, 'Mission modernity' in *Transformation*, vol. 10, no. 4 (1993). Ch. 14, 'The Money Game' in David C. Korten's brilliant book, *When Corporations Rule the World* (London, Earthscan 1995), shows how pure the worship of money/Mammon has now become.

Davids, P.H., 'Rich and Poor' in Green, J.B. and McKnight, S., *Dictionary of Jesus and the Gospels* (Downers Grove/Leicester, IVP 1992).

FIVE

The King's War

That the world has insisted on continuing in its wicked ways since the coming of Jesus is a mystery. How can it be that people, on the whole, prefer the rule of those whose best efforts are undermined by their selfish desires and pride, to the rule of the Lamb? How is it that the laws of the king, who as creator should know best what makes for the happiness of his creatures, are rejected in favour of laws framed by those who understand neither the true origin, nature nor destiny of human beings? Why is it that many of those who claim to bow the knee to the King of Kings are so reluctant to share their abundant resources with the poor? And finally, there must be some explanation for the fact that the visible church is often such an awful witness for the one it claims as its head?

Part of the answer to this mystery is found in the very deep depravity of the human heart. But that is not the whole story. Humans also live in a 'world' that represents the accumulated rejection of God over the centuries. Then behind this 'world' lies the supernatural powers of darkness dominated by Satan or the Devil. In biblical terms the righteous rule of God through Christ over people's lives has to contend with the world, the flesh and the Devil. This evil trinity represents everything that is contrary to God and his purpose. They are all spiritual forces opposed to God so that to resist any member of this trinity is to engage in 'spiritual warfare'.

A developing understanding of spiritual warfare

When the Protestant missionary movement really got under way at the end of the eighteenth century the remnants of pre-Christian beliefs in spirits, which were common in 1700 in Europe and North America, had been well and truly vanquished. The fathers of the great Evangelical Awakening were very conscious that the gospel was sweeping away a whole raft of superstitious beliefs and practices. When their children, fired by the same evangelical ardour, started taking the gospel all over the world, they fully expected its irresistible light to chase away the darkness of superstition as it had done in their home country. There was no need to study the stratagems of Satan and his servants, since they were believed to be defeated and in headlong retreat.

In many places the victory of the gospel did not come as quickly or as easily as had been anticipated. It had to be recognized that the Devil/Satan had great power to mislead people and to hinder them from accepting the truth of the gospel. Even so, not much attention was paid to precisely how the Devil was at work in the world and there was little concern with identifying his agents. Missionaries continued to dismiss animist beliefs in spiritual forces as superstition. Did not Paul after all write that 'We know that an idol is nothing at all in the world and that there is no God but one.'[1] Missionaries increasingly had also been brought up in a culture that did not commonly talk about spirits, spirits of the dead, omens, curses, sorcery, magic, witchcraft, divination, demons or angels. When it did such beliefs were ridiculed. This post-revival and post-Enlightenment culture inevitably affected the beliefs of missionaries.[2] Admittedly there was often a theoretical belief in the angels and demons of the Bible but in line with the

---

[1] Cor. 8:5.
[2] The effect of Enlightenment thinking on Christians was invariably to remove God and other supernatural beings from the physical world. God could not be scientifically tested because he occupied a supernatural plane. He was thus immune to the challenges of science. Slowly, therefore, the natural world was left to the scientists who could define its laws and patterns. The world gradually became defined as a place that operated according to testable rules. God may well have set up those rules in the first place, but he did not now intervene within them. Science and faith in God therefore learnt to live with each other by concerning themselves with different questions; as the old Sunday school

assumptions of their culture there was little expectation of actual encounter with them. Consequently there was little conscious engagement with the gods and spirits of indigenous religion other than to debunk them.

However, some missionaries have been forced into a drastic shift of world-view by their experiences within different cultures. They claim to have experienced things that their training could not provide the vocabulary to adequately describe. Such things include miraculous powers exercised by various specialists in indigenous religions, people possessed by some external force, geographical areas in which missionaries experience great physical, emotional or spiritual oppression, the reality and effectiveness of curses and objects that were possessed by some peculiar force. In short, they claim to have experienced things that are best explained by a belief in the reality of satanic supernatural powers at work in the world.

The following account of the experience of a Tearfund supported worker in Nepal is a good example:

> Close to our house there is a large deciduous tree at whose foot is a small shrine to the local earth spirit ... A local child contracted a skin disease which none of our medical kit could heal. The local spiritual healer (for want of a better term; in Nepal they are called either 'dhami' or 'jhankhri') was consulted and discovered that the child had urinated in the area of the shrine, thus bringing down a curse upon herself. The healer dealt with the curse through a process of all-night drumming and chanting ... and the skin disease subsequently cleared up.[3]

Footnote 2 (*continued*) saying goes, 'Science answers the "how" questions and religion answers the "why" questions'. This sort of thinking protected Christianity from the atheistic attacks of some scientists, but it also made it difficult to conceive of how the supernatural might act within the world of natural causes and effects. Some evangelical Christians: in effect, became believers in a sort of 'clockwork' universe God set up the physical universe with its own rules and patterns and provided the sustaining power for the universe, but he never intervened in the structures and patterns of that stable system. If God and angels did not intervene in the physical world then there was even less chance of the Devil and demons being able to intervene in physical and tangible ways that differed from the natural running of the system.

[3] Clare Crawford writing on behalf of herself and her husband, Dick. Virtually all Tearfund workers overseas who were interviewed in preparing this book recounted similar experiences.

Many bemoan the lack of training to handle and understand such experiences. Frustrations have been expressed in the following terms: 'During my years in Asia, I was often frustrated by the inadequacies of my Western Reformed theological training . . . scarcely a line of our theology books that addressed the reality of demon possession, the role of shamans, belief in ancestral spirits and the practice of exorcism.'[4] 'We wondered if the time we have had the Gospel in the West has made us less conscious of the powers of darkness in recent centuries. We noted also that the influence of the Enlightenment in our education, which traces everything to natural causes, has further dulled our consciousness of the powers of darkness.'[5]

As a result of experiencing what is believed to be demonic powers many are now seeking to find a biblical framework in which to understand their experiences.[6] There has also been a greater willingness among Western-trained missionaries to see God and Satan intervening miraculously in the natural realm. A whole literature has developed which seeks to do justice to this sphere of spiritual warfare.

---

[4] Greenway, R., 'Missions as spiritual warfare: An historical sketch of recent thinking', in *Urban Mission*, vol. 13, no. 2 (1995), p. 20.

[5] From the 'Statement on Spiritual Warfare' (1993) by the Intercession Working Group Report, Lausanne Committee on World Evangelisation. This statement is reproduced in *Urban Mission*, vol. 13, no. 2 (1995), pp. 50–3.

[6] Many writers are quite candid about the movement from experience to biblical doctrine. For example, 'I have come to believe that Satan does indeed assign a demon or corps of demons to every geopolitical unit in the world . . . This concept first came up in the missionary context when I read of a new missionary going into an American Indian village . . .' Warner, T., 'Dealing with Territorial Demons' in Wagner, P. (ed.), *Territorial Spirits Insights on Strategic-Level Spiritual Warfare from Nineteen Christian Leaders* (Chichester, Sovereign World 1991), p. 52.

Similarly, in the same book T. Warner retells a true story he first heard told by Ralph Mahoney of World MAP. In this incident a missionary was passing out tracts in a town which straddles the borders of Brazil and Uruguay. One particular street in the town straddled the border. On the Uruguay side of the street people were very unresponsive to the tracts. However when the evangelist crossed over to the Brazil side a person who had refused a tract on the Uruguay side of the street now received the tract. This pattern repeated itself. P. Wagner comments on how this experience coupled with further prayer led to a particular understanding of Mk. 3:27, 'Could it be that the "strong man" on the Brazilian side had been bound while the "strong man" on the Uruguayan side was still exercising power', Wagner, *Territorial Spirits'*, p. 53.

Within much of this literature a number of key concepts have emerged. The concept of 'territorial spirits' is a good example. This is the belief that particular territories are dominated by particular evil supernatural beings who have been given a stranglehold over an area because of past idolatry.[7] These territorial spirits need to be confronted and defeated through warfare prayer if blessing is to be released into the lands that they dominate. The result of this type of thinking is that Satan and his forces are becoming the object of considerable theological and popular definition.[8] This definition of and engagement with evil spiritual beings is deemed crucial to evangelistic success.

Spiritual warfare and service among the poor

Whilst there has been growing awareness of the supernatural dimension in evangelism, Christians involved in development work among the poor have rarely considered Satan to be interested in disrupting social transformation. There is an assumption that while the Devil is interested in maintaining spiritual blindness, he gets little pleasure from maintaining people in physical or emotional poverty. Indeed it is argued that the prosperity of the Western world serves Satan's purposes very well since people are too content with wealth to think about God.[9] Just as in some sections of the church God is thought to be only interested in the salvation of souls, Satan is

---

[7] The concept of territorial spirits lies at the heart of the growing discipline of 'spiritual mapping'. George Otis defines this discipline as 'superimposing our understanding of forces and events in the spiritual domain onto places and circumstances in the material world', Otis, G., 'An Overview of Spiritual Mapping' in Wagner, P. (ed.), *Breaking Strongholds in your City: How to use Spiritual Mapping to make your Prayers more Strategic, Effective and Targeted* (Tunbridge Wells, Monarch 1993), p. 32.

[8] See the hugely popular novels of Frank Peretti, *This Present Darkness* (Westchester, Crossway 1986), and *Piercing the Darkness* (Westchester, Crossway 1990).

[9] Prosperity is here defined according to the ideology of consumer society; the more individuals consume, the happier they are.

thought to be only interested in having the company of souls in hell. Therefore, different frameworks are used for explaining the problems faced by the Third World. These range from analyses that stress the responsibility of rich or poor individuals for the state of the world to those that stress the economic, political and cultural forces that hold hapless individuals in their grasp. The work of satanic forces in perpetuating the problems is hardly ever used as a framework of explanation.

But the situation is changing. The impact of supernatural forces of evil on social transformation is becoming an accepted component of many Christian explanations for the social, economic, political and cultural state of the world. For example, Peter Wagner, the leading exponent of the concept of 'territorial spirits', believes that the forces of evil not only blind people to the gospel but also hold millions captive within unjust social structures. Roger Forster argues that the traditional division between discussion of the realm of the social/political and that of the angelic and demonic powers is a mistake. He is convinced that the two subjects belong together.[10] Nigel Wright writes in similar vein of a mistake that has dominated some evangelical thinking in the past:

> It is that of pursuing evil at one level, that is to say of demons, while quite ignoring other dimensions in which the spiritual conflict rages . . . it suits the power of darkness very well if the attention of Christians is diverted towards occult and demonic concerns and fully absorbed in them, while the wider stage of devilish activity in the political, cultural, national and international spheres is all but ignored . . . In recent years there has been a major shift in evangelical thinking away from an isolationist attitude towards the world towards social action and engagement . . . In the charismatic movement it can be currently perceived that the focus in spiritual warfare is shifting away from the needs of individuals to the needs of society.

---

[10] From an unpublished lecture delivered at the 'Word, Kingdom and Spirit Consultation', Malaysia 1994.

> There is a much greater sense of the need to engage the 'powers' that rule in our society.[11]

Part of the explanation for this growing recourse to a different level of explanation has been the growing sense of powerlessness that evangelical Christians working among the poor have felt in the face of seemingly intractable social problems. It is often so obvious to those involved with the poor that their best efforts can fall short of expectations because of economic, cultural, political or even natural forces beyond their control. These forces seem so powerful that they require a further level of explanation – that of the workings of the powers of darkness. As Charles Elliot puts it, 'To continue to act as though the poverty of nearly a billion people can be eliminated by aided projects, is to fail to take seriously both the nature of the problem and the nature of the world . . . it ignores the structures within which mass poverty is set . . . It ignores the Powers that hold the world in thrall.'[12]

We will examine two particular expressions of this growth of interest in the way Satan and his forces are at work in the world today, both in disrupting the proclamation of God's truth and in keeping people in poverty and powerlessness. They reflect a concern to move away from a mere theoretical acceptance of the existence of evil supernatural beings, to an understanding of how those evil forces are at work in the world. This understanding is intended to highlight how they should be resisted.

1. Power encounter and territorial spirits

There is a growing movement, particularly among charismatic and pentecostal evangelicals, that is developing a detailed and

---

[11] Wright, N., *The Fair Face of Evil* (London, Marshall Pickering 1989), pp. 132, 136. Cf. Samuel, Vinay, 'A theological perspective' in Yamamori, T., Myers, B.L. and Conner, D. (eds.), *Serving with the Poor in Asia* (Monrovia, MARC 1995), pp. 148–9.

[12] Elliot, C., *Comfortable Compassion? Poverty, Power and the Church* (London, Hodder & Stoughton 1987), pp. 179–180.

wide-ranging demonology to fill in the lack of explanatory framework for phenomena that missionaries and development workers in particular face. The key theorist of this movement is Peter Wagner.[13]

Fundamental to this approach is the belief that the earth is 'populated' by a host of evil spirits, the foot soldiers of Satan. These spirits possess a range of powers particularly over people and places. Some indwell human beings while others exercise authority over territory ranging from a copse or well to large, powerful nations. These spirits seek to keep people from faith in Christ. They may also lie behind the social, legal, political or economic problems affecting particular situations. In order to bring blessing into people's lives it is believed that these spirits must be defeated and banished first of all. The first step to dealing with them is their identification. In the case of possession of an individual, getting the spirit to identify itself is essential before exorcism can be performed. In the case of a territory it is essential to make a study of the religion of an area in order to discover what spirits are being worshipped, placated or contacted. In some cases this information is not easy to come by and has to be supernaturally revealed. The end of this process is the making of a spirit map of an area which will show what area or building is dominated by which spirit. Once this is done warfare prayer can then be targeted precisely at the various spirits in their locations. This is done by addressing the spirit and commanding it to depart in the name of Jesus. Such purging of land and buildings is a necessary preparation for successfully proclaiming the gospel.

This approach to evil powers is increasingly moulding the attitudes of development workers, particularly when they are faced with religious beliefs that hinder the alleviation of poverty. The following example is representative of a common experience among development workers:

> Mengo Hospital, near Kampala, have recently identified three wells in nearby villages, that they would like to

---

[13] See Wagner, P., *Territorial Spirits*'.

protect ... They provide the only source of water for many local people, but are constantly being polluted by animals and humans. By covering the wells, the water could be kept free of pollution and clean water could be obtained by a pipe. This would immediately help to improve the health of those who use the water. However the local people believe that the wells are haunted! A creature apparently half man and half fish, comes at night and has indicated that any interference with the wells will lead to them drying up.[14]

Development workers who are convinced by the power encounter/territorial spirits approach would take the well to be a place of demonic activity. They would expect demonic resistance if the development workers went in to work on the well without a prior binding of the demons involved. They are not simply taking the animist opinions of the indigenous population at face value and therefore concluding that certain places naturally serve as habitations for spirits. Rather it is only through the idolatry and disobedience of humans in a particular area that demons in that area are given a stronghold. Nevertheless, the animist views of the people enable the missionary or development worker to accurately map the configurations of the evil spiritual forces in the area. With reference to the problem of the haunted well therefore, the views of local people concerning the spirit beings associated with the well should be listened to with utmost seriousness. Indeed, if it is possible to determine some information from the locals as to the nature of the spirits, such as their names or the precise extent of their influence, it may be easier to bind the demonic forces.

So, the power encounter/territorial spirits model teaches that certain areas and objects can become demonically dominated through the idolatry of those practising local religions. To ignore these forces by failing to confront them in prayer puts the whole development process in jeopardy.

---

[14] *Footsteps*, no. 12 (Sept. 1992), p. 7.

Evaluation

The power encounter and territorial spirits approach has one major strength: it has highlighted that Christians must address spiritual realities wherever they are, thereby mobilizing many Christians all over the world to engage in serious intercession for their localities and for the world. This provides a healthy challenge to the many Western Christians who have absorbed so much Western scientific thinking that God and the spiritual world have been almost completely banished from life on earth. The power encounter approach returns to the biblical emphasis that people can be in bondage to demons and that the power of the demons must be broken. Jesus has proved that he is able to do this.

The New Testament testifies very clearly to the reality of demonic possession. The Synoptic Gospels contain four detailed and four brief accounts of exorcism. In three of the four detailed accounts the exorcism itself is not centre stage but is the backdrop to making a point about the ministry of Jesus. The possessed man in the synagogue was released on the Sabbath; the release of the daughter of the Syro-Phoenician woman proved that the blessings of the kingdom were available to Gentiles; the healing of the boy at the foot of the Mount of Transfiguration was an occasion for teaching about faith, prayer and fasting.[15] The one case where the individual possessed is centre stage is that of the man of Gerasa who was possessed by Legion. This is the only case where Jesus identified the demons before casting them out. It is also interesting that the man lived among the tombs, which suggests some link between his condition and a belief in the spirits of the dead.[16] Two of the detailed and two of the short accounts give information about the symptoms of possession. The man of Gerasa manifested violence with superhuman strength, which made it impossible for him to remain in any human society; the boy at the foot of the Mount of Transfiguration was subject to fits similar to epilepsy; in two of the shorter references one man was dumb while the other was blind and dumb.[17] In many cases the demon identified itself

---

[15] Mk. 1:21–8; 7:24–30; 9:14–29.
[16] Mk. 5:1–20.
[17] Mk. 9:32–4; 12:22.

by confessing to know Jesus and Jesus commanded the spirit to be silent.[18]

On one occasion at least Jesus explains the significance of his exorcisms in the language of conflict and struggle that is picked up by the adherents of the power encounter/territorial spirits approach.[19] He argues that the truth of his exorcisms was that he had first defeated Satan and removed his armour.[20] Because Satan had been rendered defenceless Jesus, and his servants, were able to free the demonized from his power. Jesus had vanquished Satan at the end of the 40 days of temptation in the wilderness but the final victory was won on the cross.[21] It is because of the Lord's victory on the cross that we are able to win people from his power whether they are demon possessed or not. Luke 11:22 also states that as a result of the victory over Satan there are spoils to be divided up. What has been selfishly amassed by Satan and his servants is now to be redistributed to the poor and needy.

Paul, like Jesus, is clear about the reality of demonic activity. He states that where idols are worshipped demons are present, 'the sacrifices of pagans are offered to demons, not to God'. Therefore those who take part in idol worship are 'participants with demons'.[22]

Paul is not saying the physical idol itself is supernatural since elsewhere he emphasizes that 'an idol is nothing at all in the world'.[23] Rather the physical idol becomes a location for demonic activity when it is worshipped. Therefore, Paul is clear that for wholehearted worshippers of the one true God there is nothing wrong in eating meat that has been offered to idols provided that an individual is not leading astray his weaker brother by such activity. Paul accepts the existence of demons

---

[18]   Mk. 1:24–5; 34; 3:11–12; 5:7.

[19]   It must be noted, however, that many of the conflict/warfare metaphors in the New Testament have nothing to do with casting out demons, but refer to other types of struggle against evil forces. See, for example, Jn. 16:33; Rom. 12:21; 2 Cor. 6:7; Heb. 12:4; 1 Pet. 4:1; 1 Jn. 4:4.

[20]   Lk. 11:21–2.

[21]   Col. 2:15.

[22]   1 Cor. 10:20.

[23]   1 Cor.8:4. See also 1 Cor. 10:19–20.

where there is idolatry, but where there is not an idolatrous attitude, demons have little power. Paul is realistic about the power of demons, but not superstitious. His key concern is to avoid idolatry, whether in the form of sacrifices to idols or greed.[24]

If demons were a reality with which Jesus and Paul had to deal there is no reason to doubt that they are a continuing reality with which Jesus' followers have to deal. This may be particularly true in cultures which believe in the existence of a multiplicity of spirits, and in particular the spirits of the dead. So, any attempt to move people to what may be considered a more enlightened view of the wells near Mengo Hospital, for example, will not be a blessing to them unless it happens in the context of dealing with the spiritual dimension. If this is not done then people are much more likely to move from a belief in spirits to secularism than to faith in Christ. It is not at all surprising that exorcisms and miraculous healings, as examples of power encounter, often accompany the preaching of the gospel in areas dominated by belief in spirits.

The power encounter/territorial spirits model has a significant weakness alongside its undoubted strength. This weakness involves the biblical foundations for its belief in territorial spirits. While exorcism is very clearly attested in the New Testament, evidence for the belief in territorial spirits and the type of spiritual warfare associated with that belief is very slim. Much of the biblical evidence that can be marshalled is questionable. Take, for example, the belief in the creation of heavenly/angelic beings called 'the sons of God' who were put in charge of the nations but who subsequently fell into sin and rebellion against their Maker. Their fall means that they need to be confronted and defeated through warfare prayer if people under their sway are to be saved.

The key references are Genesis 6:2, Deuteronomy 32:8, Psalm 82:6, read in conjunction with passages such as Job 1:6, Isaiah 14:12 and Daniel 10–12. Critical scholars believe that the reference to 'sons of God' in Genesis 6 is a reference to angelic beings while traditionally it has been seen as a reference to human

---

[24] 1 Cor.8:8–13; 10:28–30; Col. 3:5.

believers. 'Sons of God' in Deuteronomy 32 is an alternative reading from the LXX and Qumran to the 'sons of Israel' of the Masoretic text. Since 'sons of Israel' makes good sense there seems no good reason to reject it. The fact that Jesus refers to Psalm 82 to prove that it was not unbiblical for him as a man to claim to be a son of God is a strong argument for thinking that the psalm is about the behaviour of earthly and not heavenly rulers. None of these passages gives us incontrovertible evidence about the nature of the angelic/demonic realm.

Some believe that the reference to the fall of the 'morning star' in Isaiah 14:12 is a reference to the fall of Satan. Lucifer, which was the Latin Vulgate translation of 'morning star', came into popular Christian thinking from here. It is possible that Isaiah is alluding to a Canaanite myth of a fall in heaven, but he is writing about the fall of a very earthly Babylonian king. So we are left with Job and Daniel as clear witnesses to the reality of angelic beings, some of whom, such as Satan and the 'prince of Persia' are implacably opposed to all truth and goodness. But even in Daniel, which does teach that Persia was dominated by a territorial spirit opposed to God and his people, there is no suggestion that Daniel himself was directly engaged in conflict with this spirit. The impression given is of a spiritual conflict mysteriously linked to Daniel's prayer and fasting of which Daniel was totally unconscious. We are not told what the content of Daniel's prayer was on this occasion, but we can assume that it was similar to his prayer in the first year of Darius, which was all about repentance for the sins of Israel and God's glory.[25] The striking thing is that while Daniel was striving for forgiveness for God's people and the glory and honour of God, the angel, with Michael's help, prevailed against the 'prince of Persia'. This suggests that repentance and concern for the honour of God is the way to win the war in the heavenly realms.

In the New Testament, 2 Corinthians 10:4 is another important passage for those who advocate spiritual warfare against territorial spirits. The domination of a spirit over an area is often described as a 'stronghold'. 2 Corinthians 10:4 contains the one

---

[25] Dan. 9:4–19.

instance of this key term in the New Testament.[26] The context of this verse is the fact that some in Corinth were charging Paul with base motives with regard to the church there.[27] Paul accepts that he was indeed in the flesh, that is, a weak human being, but he was not striving against his enemies in Corinth in a fleshly way. To the contrary he fought with spiritual weapons which were able to pull down the strongholds put up by his enemies. These strongholds were the arguments and reasonings that his opponents put up to bolster their position against Paul. Paul says that the divine power given him will be able to demolish such arguments and 'every pretension that sets itself up against the knowledge of God'.[28] There is nothing in this passage about removing demonic strongholds from particular territories.

Not only is the biblical foundation for warfare against territorial spirits rather weak but sometimes the theological implications are also questionable. Satan and his demonic forces in some accounts are given far more credit than is their due. Satan and his followers are, after all, God's creation and what life they have continues to be sustained by God. In fact, neither good or bad angelic beings are centre stage in human life at any point as human life is portrayed in the Bible. There is not even clear biblical evidence that the angelic fall is primary. Demons, in particular, are very closely associated with human beings. They are never encountered as independent spirits. So, when people cease to believe in them the spirits lose their power. This is not to ignore the terrible things that Satan can do in the world. But his power is limited, and since he has negated all those glorious attributes which make God personal, it may be better to view him and his servants as ' "anti-persons", parasitic on human wickedness. The more attention human beings give to them and the more people believe in them, the greater their strength and dark glory'.[29]

---

[26] See, for example, Jacobs, C., 'Dealing with strongholds' in Wagner, *Breaking Strongholds*, pp. 73–95.

[27] 2 Cor. 10:2.

[28] 2 Cor. 10:5.

[29] Noble, T., 'The spirit world: a theological approach' in Lane, A.N.S. (ed.), *The Unseen World* (Carlisle, Paternoster/Michigan, Baker Book House 1996), p. 209.

2.　Walter Wink: evil and the structures of the world

Walter Wink in his trilogy of books, *Naming the Powers, Unmasking the Powers* and *Engaging the Powers*, provides an alternative model for understanding how satanic forces operate in the world today. Whilst they reject aspects of his approach, many evangelicals have been helped by Wink's analysis, particularly in its emphasis on the demonic influence over key systems and structures of the modern world.

Wink is worried that Christians influenced by the power encounter/territorial spirits approach will become so preoccupied with battling against 'demons in the air'[30] that they forget that Satan has an awesome grip over the social, cultural, political and economic world. Wink writes damningly of the popularization of spiritual warfare in Peretti's *This Present Darkness*: 'The view of evil is scary but finally trivial; his demons are simply imaginary bad people with wings, and the really mammoth and crushing evils of our day – racism, sexism, political oppression, ecological degradation, militarism, patriarchy, homelessness, economic greed – are not even mentioned.'[31]

To Wink much of the supernatural language of the Bible represents an attempt by first-century Christians to express the sometimes evil, sometimes good, power of the social, economic, cultural, political and religious institutions and systems all around them. The biblical authors recognized that there was a level of reality beyond the concrete manifestation of a particular institution's power. To describe this reality beyond natural appearances they had to use supernatural language. For example, in Wink's understanding 'Satan' is the name given to the 'real interiority of a society that idolatrously pursues its own enhancement as the highest good'.[32]

Wink seeks to preserve these divinely revealed insights of the first-century Christians in the twentieth century. Therefore, just as there was a deeper dimension to the institutions and systems

---

[30] Wink, W., *Engaging the Powers: Discernment and Resistance in a World of Domination* (Philadelphia, Fortress 1992), p. 314.

[31] Ibid. p. 9.

[32] Wink, W., *Unmasking the Powers: The Invisible Forces that Determine Human Existence* (Philadelphia, Fortress 1986), p. 25.

of the first century, so there is to those of the twentieth. Wink gives an example from the system of international economics: We are asked to imagine an individual in charge of a company, who seeks to improve the working arrangements of individuals under her care. She spends some company money on the improvement of conditions and increases the wages paid to her staff. As a result the workers' productivity improves. However, the company gradually realizes that despite increased productivity they can no longer compete in terms of the price of their product with the company in the neighbouring country which treats its workers like dirt, paying small salaries and spending nothing on working conditions. The economic system in which the woman is operating ultimately makes a demand: either obey its rules and focus on profits, not workers, or face exclusion from the system and therefore economic ruin, with the workers losing their jobs anyway. In a sense the system is greedy on the woman's behalf.

To Wink the system of international economics has a reality beyond standard economic descriptions and consequently it needs to be challenged at a deeper level than mere economic adjustment. Economic analysis and protest must therefore go hand in hand with prayer and spiritual confrontation. Social, economic and political action is essential, but ineffective, unless accompanied by engagement with the spiritual powers that drive the structures.

Evaluation

There are clearly problems with some of Wink's ideas from the perspective of evangelical biblical Christianity. In particular he is reluctant to accept that the supernatural beings of the first-century writers of the Bible are real supernatural beings. Instead he regards them as the projections of deep essences within the structures and systems of the world. The Bible, by contrast, clearly maintains the reality of supernatural beings. However, given this major criticism of Wink, we must acknowledge our debt to him. He has alerted Christians to the structures and systems that predominate in this world which harm the poor in particular. Furthermore, he has pointed Christians to the fact that there are powerful forces of good and evil at work within these structures that need to be addressed by prayer as well as by social, economic and political action.

The world, the flesh and the devil

While we recognize the contribution of the territorial spirits lobby and Wink to appreciating the spiritual dimension to any attempt to see justice done on earth, the traditional way of understanding what the Bible says about spiritual warfare may be more satisfactory. In seeing our warfare as being with the world, the flesh and the devil, justice is done to the structural, personal and supernatural aspects of the conflict.

World/Satan/Devil

The term 'world' is used in many different ways in the New Testament but in the context of spiritual warfare it is unquestionably a structural term. It is not just the earth (*gē*) or the inhabited world (*oikoumenē*) but the world as an ordered structure with human society at its heart (*kosmos*). Sadly, as a result of the fall, the ordered world has become '*this*' world. It has become a disordered and dysfunctional community under the domination of the Devil/Satan. This world, or this age (*aiōn*), has its wise men, scribes and disputers. They are the ones who claim to understand how human beings work and how best to order things so as to bring blessing into our lives. This world is full of their wisdom, which, in our age of electronic communication, dominates the ways in which people think. So, in the West, when social breakdown is manifested in senseless acts of violence, enlightenment is sought from secular sociologists, psychologists, politicians, economists, criminologists and the rest, but very rarely from those who see the ultimate answer to the human predicament in the cross of Christ.[33]

Human beings think about the earth and their place in it in relation to each other. How we behave flows, to a certain extent at least, from the theories that are formed as a result of this

---

[33] 1 Cor. 1:20–31.

process of thinking. Over centuries theories can become embedded in social structures that can have a powerful impact on the lives of many people. For example, in eighteenth-century Europe it was believed that the majority were born to hard labour so that the few could enjoy themselves. Even the institutional church sanctioned this unjust way of thinking. Such thinking meant misery for the many and the brutal suppression of any protest.

Paul sees this world as characterized by structures of thought which cannot but fail when applied to individual and social life since they originate from a profound rejection of God in the heart. Two of the dominant characteristics of this world's mind are pride and covetousness.[34] As individual sins these characteristics are typical of the flesh. When they infect the order of things they become structural. Political society comes to be organized in such a way that the position of certain families or class remains supreme irrespective of merit. Economic relations are so structured that the rich can become richer and richer while the noses of the poor are ground into the dust.

It is the responsibility of those who have the mind of Christ to expose the mind of the world for what it is. There is a crying need for godly politicians, economists, sociologists, psychologists and others to argue the case for justice and peace in the power of the Holy Spirit. Jesus has taken the literal sword from our hands and left us with the sword of his word of truth. It is a great tragedy when Christians are reluctant to wield it. Suffering may follow, but the truth spoken with the power of the Spirit is also able to bring down strongholds and release many from bondage.[35]

In taking up the challenge of this world we need to remember that it is very much under the dominion of Satan. Behind the structures that have been put in place to usurp the authority of God is the will and approval of the great usurper himself. He is the Prince of this world. He even believed that his authority over the kingdoms of this world was so complete that he could offer them as a prize to the Son of God himself, if only he bowed down

---

[34] 1 Jn. 2:16.
[35] 2 Cor. 10:4.

to him. As he is the great liar and deceiver, this claim could not be trusted but he certainly seems to have great power over the governments of the world. It is not surprising that Paul says that we need all the armour we can get if we are going to stand for truth and righteousness.[36] It is folly to begin to think that we can overturn this world's structures without the spiritual armour that comes from God.

Flesh/Satan/Devil

Like 'world', 'flesh' is used in a number of ways in the New Testament. It can mean physical life in its wholeness. To be 'in the flesh' in this sense is simply to be endowed with physical existence. When John declares that the Word became flesh he is saying that God's son became a human being. But because of the pervasive reality of sin our human desires pull us away from God rather than towards him. So Paul speaks of the lusts of the flesh. In this sense 'flesh' means the whole personality as directed away from God. The desire for God and the eternal is displaced by the desire for something or someone in the physical realm. It is the attempt to make an absolute out of the transient.

It is generally accepted that when Paul uses 'you' and 'we/us' in Ephesians that he is referring to the Gentiles and the Jews respectively. At the beginning of the second chapter, as already noted, he reminds the Gentile Christians that they used to be a part of this world which is under the dominion of Satan. He then goes on to say of the Jews that they lived among the Gentiles 'gratifying the cravings of our sinful nature[37] and following its desires and thoughts'.[38] What he is saying is that both Gentiles and Jews are just as much in need of salvation as each other. But it is significant that he does not include the Jews as belonging to this world that is under the dominion of Satan. Theoretically at least the Jews, as recipients of the law of God, did not belong fully to this world but because of the cravings of the sinful nature that is common to all human beings they were dragged back into it. As John puts it: 'For everything in the world

---

[36] Eph. 6:10–20.
[37] 'Sinful nature' is the NIV translation of '*sarx*' ('flesh').
[38] Eph. 2:3.

– the cravings of sinful man, the lust of his eyes and the boasting of what he has and does – comes not from the Father but from the world.'[39]

This text shows that there is a direct line of access from Satan through the world into our inner being. So, if we belong to God, the conflict with this world is mirrored within as the Spirit of God in our heart strives with the cravings of the flesh.[40] We dare not forget this internal conflict if we want to defeat the evils of this world. This is why the efforts of those who have risen up against social or economic injustice and neglected to attend to the problems within themselves end up in ruins. The oppressed soon become the oppressors. If the divine values which we long to see enthroned in society are not enthroned in our hearts we will never succeed. That is why the character of those who set out to serve the poor is as important as anything they may seek to do on their behalf. Those that are most intensely engaged in spiritual warfare at this level are the ones that will succeed in the conflict with this world or even in direct conflict with the Devil or his servants.

Conclusion

The King who has called us into his kingdom has shown us how to relate to one another in his law. Crucial to this is the way we are to be his people in the world and to handle the resources that he has graciously given us. He has called us out of the world not that we can wash our hands of it but be in it in order to win it to the side of the kingdom. He does not promise that we will have an easy ride. On the contrary it is a heated battle characterized by hand-to-hand fighting. No ground will be won without effort. The world of religion, politics, economics, the nations, women, population and the environment all need to be won for the King. All of life rightly belongs to him. In considering the various aspects of human life that have such a bearing on poverty in the rest of this

---

[39] 1 John. 2:16.
[40] Paul deals with this theme in Rom. 7–8.

volume we shall look at different areas of our human lives that need to be won for our King. The task is enormous: the forces arraigned against us seem so powerful. We are terribly lacking in the courage of the youthful David who asked, 'Who is this Philistine to defy the armies of the living God?' Yet we are encouraged to go in the knowledge that the God who saved us and who works in us to put to death the cravings of our sinful nature can also undo the evil in the world and defeat the works of the Devil.

Resources

Books

Green, Michael, *I Believe in Satan's downfall* (London, Hodder & Stoughton 1988), provides a useful introduction.

Arnold, Clinton E., *The Powers of Darkness* (Leicester, IVP 1992), covers most of the issues concisely, plausibly and biblically. It engages with different approaches to the subject from W. Wink to P. Wagner.

Wagner, Peter (ed.), *Territorial Spirits; Insights on Strategic-Level Spiritual Warfare from Nineteen Christian Leaders* (England, Sovereign World 1991). A useful introduction to the power encounter and territorial spirits approach.

Wink, Walter, trilogy published by Philadelphia, Fortress: *Naming The Powers* (1984), *Unmasking the Powers* (1986) and *Engaging the Powers* (1992). Stimulating, demanding non-evangelical treatment of the biblical material examining the relationship of the powers of evil to the structures of the world.

Page, Sydney H.T., *Powers of Evil, A Biblical Study of Satan And Demons* (Grand Rapids, Baker 1995). Scholarly biblical treatment.

Lane, Anthony N.S., *The Unseen World; Christian Reflections on Angels, Demons and the Heavenly Realm* (Carlisle, Paternoster/ Grand Rapids, Baker Book House 1996). Evangelical, academic and useful.

Articles

Urban Mission, vol. 13, no. 2 (Westminster Theological Seminary 1995) contains the following:

Conn, Harvie M., 'Spiritual warfare in the city'.

Rubingh, Eugene, 'Kingdom and power'.

Greenway, Roger S., 'Mission and Spiritual warfare: an historical sketch of recent thinking'.

Moreau, A. Scott, 'Evil spirits: biblical and practical issues'.

Polythress, Vern S., 'Territorial spirits: some biblical perspectives'.

The Intercession Working Group of the Lausanne Committee for World Evangelisation 'Statement on Spiritual Warfare' (1993).

Weerasingha, Tissa, 'Case study on spiritual warfare in Sri Lanka'.

Hiebert, Paul, 'The flaw of the excluded middle' in *Missiology*, vol. 10 (1982), pp. 35–47. A crucial article that has alerted evangelicals to their failure to engage with the question of whether and how evil forces are at work in the world today.

Hiebert, Paul, 'Anthropological and missiological perspectives', Samuel, Vinay, 'A theological perspective', Myers, B.L., 'Modernity and holistic ministry' in Yamamori, T., Myers, B.L. and Conner, D. (eds.), *Serving with the Poor in Asia* (Monrovia, MARC 1995).

SECTION 2

PRACTICAL APPLICATIONS

SIX

Religion, Poverty and the Kingdom

What's religion got to do with poverty?

An experienced missionary in East Africa once told a young Christian development worker who had just arrived that development is essentially a theological issue. The development worker strongly disagreed and insisted that development was simply about technique. He had not come to discuss theology or religion but to teach people more efficient and scientific ways of doing things which would enhance the quality of their physical existence. His task was simply to teach the people a new technology. Some years later, when he had come to the end of his period of service, the same young man was again taking tea with the experienced missionary. During tea he asserted with conviction that development is essentially a matter of theology!

This encounter highlights the development worker's realization that initiatives to help the poor cannot be introduced without taking religion into consideration. His initial view that what development workers and the recipients of their work thought about God/gods was of no consequence to addressing poverty, had proved to be wrong in three ways: Firstly, even if a community develops economically, politically and socially, unless it encounters God in Jesus, it will still be afflicted by the poverty of not knowing God. Furthermore, this spiritual poverty will sooner or later lead to other forms of poverty as forms of sin such as greed begin to dominate. Secondly, the religious perspective of development workers affects the way in which they help the poor. Thirdly, any development initiative whether economic, political, social or spiritual must take into account what the recipients of that initiative believe about the world in relation to supernatural forces. Otherwise the initiative will ultimately fail because what the people believe about the world and its relationship to the spiritual dimension, shapes the way they respond to everything, including poverty.

Religion, in combination with other factors such as socio-economic experience, determines the way in which people view their world. A world-view can be defined as 'the shared framework of ideas held by a particular society concerning how they see the world'.[1] This framework of ideas enables members of a society to identify their own roles and destinies. Their priorities, hopes, and fears are also determined by them. Above all a world-view enables people to explain the reality of their lives even if that explanation admits its inadequacies and limitations.

The experience of poverty is itself both defined and explained by a person's world-view. A simple example would be the contrast between a Christian and Marxist understanding of poverty. Some may be wondering what Marxism has to do with religion. From a Christian perspective Marxism is a 'religion' because it sets up the economic well-being of humanity as an ultimate goal. In religious terms it sets up an ideal humanity as an idol in God's place. This decision is not the result of scientific analysis but an act of faith that drives the whole system.

Christians and Marxists can agree about certain components of poverty. There might also be some agreement on the political and economic causes of poverty. However they would disagree as to whether someone who had never had the chance of responding to Christ was impoverished. A Christian would say yes, a Marxist, no. There would also be differences in their explanations of why the world contained impoverished people. A Christian would emphasize the effects of the human rejection

---

[1] Burnett, D., *Clash of Worlds* (Eastbourne, MARC 1990), p. 13. On the previous page Burnett underlines that 'world-view' is difficult to define and gives two possible definitions by other authors: ' "The central set of concepts and presuppositions that provide people with their basic assumptions about reality," Whiteman. "A world-view is a set of presuppositions (or assumptions) which we hold (consciously or subconsciously) about the basic make-up of our world," Sire'.

of God's authority, while the Marxist would restrict explanations to material factors. There would also be differences in their proposed solutions. The Marxist would emphasize economic and political change, while the Christian would point to the need for spiritual change in people's hearts.

Fundamental issues are at stake here. The way in which people think about who or what 'God' is, has a profound effect on the way in which all reality is viewed. The key difference between a Christian and a Marxist is the latter's denial of the existence of God. Marxism may be right in some aspects of its analysis of the way markets work, and certainly right in its solidarity with the poor, but its understanding of the ultimate meaning and purpose of human beings is wrong because God is left out of the equation. Christians are not surprised that the practical application of Marxist principles has always led to oppression and injustice.

Marxism has, by the late 1990s, largely been replaced by the religion of global, free market capitalism. It too usually defines, explains and combats poverty with no reference to the God who revealed himself in Christ. As they can agree with aspects of Marxist analysis in relation to poverty, so Christians can agree with certain of the definitions, explanations and prescriptions of free market capitalism. However, Christians resist the tendency of this new religion to reduce everything to economic realities and its tendency to treat economic success as the ultimate goal for humanity.[2]

Clearly therefore, the religious perspectives of the development worker and the poor are crucial to the objectives and methods of the struggle against poverty. We shall explore some facets of this interrelationship through this chapter. We begin with the biblical definition of religion.

'Religion' as opposed to 'godliness'

In the NIV the term 'religion' is found just five times and every occurrence is in the New Testament. It is used to translate three

---

[2] See ch. 8, 'Economics, Poverty and the Kingdom', for extensive development of this theme.

Greek terms: In Acts 26:5 and James 1:26–7 it corresponds to *thrēskeia*. In both these passages religion refers to what can be seen when one is looking at a religious person from the outside. Paul claims to have kept all the rules of the Jewish religion, and for James true religion is a matter of caring for the weak and marginalized and holy living. In Colossians 2:18 *thrēskeia* is translated 'worship', the reference being to 'the worship of angels'. It was a 'worship' very much taken up with externals, with what could or could not be eaten and drunk, festivals, New Moons and Sabbaths. The use of *thrēskeia* in Acts and Colossians is consistent with the bad sense that the term had generally. Religion is more often than not an empty form devoid of any substance. It is possible that this is also the case in James where it has been suggested that the apostle may be using the term ironically.

In Acts 25 the Roman governor, Festus, gives an account of his examination of the apostle Paul to the Jewish king, Agrippa. He says that as far as he can understand the charges brought against Paul by his accusers are to do with some 'points of dispute with him about their own religion'.[3] The word for religion here is *deisidaimonia*, which literally means 'fear of the gods'. It could have a good meaning such as 'reverence for the gods or piety' but it could also mean 'superstition'. Festus may have been deliberately ambiguous when he used this term to describe the Jewish religion. In the Christian context the bad meaning would have prevailed. *Daimōn* is the term used for 'demon' in the New Testament and Paul identified the worship of the Roman gods, in Corinth at least, directly with the worship of demons.[4]

In Acts 17:22, as he began his speech to the Areopagus, Paul says that the Athenians were *deisidaimonesterous*. This is translated 'very religious', but 'very superstitious' is also a possible translation. It is unlikely that Paul would begin his address on a negative and critical note, though what he says about God, if accepted by the Athenians, would lead to the inevitable conclusion that their polytheistic religion was indeed nothing but

---

[3] Acts 25:19.
[4] 1 Cor. 10:20–1.

superstition. So, the second term that can be translated 'religion' in the New Testament refers to a reverence for the gods which for sceptical Romans and Christians is nothing but superstition.

The third term, found in 1 Timothy 5:4, 'to put their religion into practice', here translates *eusebein*[5] which means 'to act reverently'. This could be towards God/gods, rulers, parents or anyone who deserves respect. Here Paul is focusing on showing the reverence that is due parents, so the reference to religion may not be appropriate. However, the noun, *eusebeia*, invariably means 'piety towards God' or 'godliness', a life which is consistent with the revelation of God in Jesus Christ.[6]

A brief look at terms which have been translated by 'religion' in the New Testament focuses very much on the externals of reverence for gods which is nothing more than futile superstition. 'Godliness', which is true reverence for God, is contrasted with this vain superstition. Godliness is seen as a response with the whole being to the one true God who has revealed himself in Jesus Christ. There is no real godliness without the engagement of the whole personality. In fact, Paul looks forward with horror to the time when many will accept the doctrines of Christianity but not live it out in their lives. He envisages a situation when even within the church it will be possible to have 'religion' in the sense of vain superstition.

Godliness, religion and the heart

In saying that godliness is a response to God with the whole being Paul was reflecting the Old Testament teaching that it is a *heart* response to God.[7] The heart is probably the nearest equivalent to 'person' in the Bible. It is the core of our being, the fundamental point at which we relate to or avoid our Maker.

---

[5] The only other example of the use of *eusebeō* in the NT is in Acts 17:23 where Paul says concerning the Athenians' worship of the Unknown God, 'Now what you worship/reverence [*eusebeite*] as something unknown I am going to proclaim to you.'

[6] Acts 3:12; 1 Tim. 4:7–8; 6:6; 2 Pet. 1:3.

[7] Gen. 42:28; Ex. 7:23; 9:14; 28:3; Deut. 4:9; 7:17; Judg. 18:20; 1 Sam. 2:35; 4:13; 16:7; 25:36. See article, 'Heart', in Douglas, J.D (ed.), *New Bible Dictionary* (London, IVP 1962), p. 509. Cf. Spier, J.M., *An Introduction to Christian Philosophy*, trans. D.H. Freeman (New Jersey, Craig 1966) fn. 1, pp. 16–17.

Jesus also makes this very clear in his controversy with some Pharisees over the matter of ritual washing of hands before meals.[8] The ritualism of the Pharisees was not able to deal with the profound problem at the core of our life as human beings. Ritual washing of hands, or eating prescribed foods prepared in a specific way has nothing to do with cleanness or uncleanness at the level of the heart. If there is uncleanness in the heart then it is bound to be expressed in external action and the external action, once performed, adds to the uncleanness of the heart. So, real cleansing or transformation must begin in the heart.

God is known universally at this most fundamental level of the heart. Even those who have not had the privilege of receiving the clear and unequivocal revelation of God recorded in the Bible have an innate knowledge of his demands.[9] Everything we are and do as human beings ultimately flows from what we do with this knowledge of God in our hearts. This is the fountainhead of our being both individually and corporately.

If a continual supply of poison is placed into the source of a river, despite the growing volume of water, traces of poison will be found in that river a very long way from the source. Even when the poison has been considerably diluted its presence will still be a significant factor in describing the quality of the water. Likewise a heart rejection of God has very far-reaching ramifications for world-views and culture in general.

Heart rejection of God and its consequences

Christians believe that the fountainhead of all human life has been poisoned by sin. That is the meaning of original sin. In a mysterious way Adam and Eve's rejection of God's authority had an impact on the whole human race. Sin and death became the universal experience of us all.[10] What is in view here is the most fundamental rejection of God which has had such dire consequences for the human race.

Within the overall framework of fallenness which characterizes all our lives there have been many other rejections of God

---

[8]   Mt. 15:10. The relevant passage as a whole is Mt. 15:1–20.
[9]   Rom. 2:14–15.
[10]   Rom. 5:12ff.

that have found corporate manifestation in a variety of beliefs about God and practices which flow out of those beliefs. Since response to God is crucial in defining the meaning of our existence it must be the most fundamental factor in defining worldviews. It may be necessary to distinguish between the heart response, which is known only to God, and the 'religion' that flows from it, but the heart response must drive one's worldview in the last analysis.

What Burnett says about understanding a world-view other than one's own confirms this. He suggests that a world-view will emerge when a number of questions are asked of a particular society or group: What beliefs are strongly held? What do people regard as major offences (sins)? Who are the trendsetters? These are just three of the ten questions that could be asked. The answers to these questions give the anthropologist an understanding of what a society thinks is ultimately important: its morality and its ideals. But on a more profound level the answers are conditioned by the fundamental heart response to God. If a society believes in a multiplicity of spirits that need to be placated with various rituals then that is because the heart knowledge of the one true God has been suppressed. A more relaxed attitude to adultery in some societies reflects a rejection of God's original intention for human beings which is known through our conscience. Many of the human ideals that we set up fall far short of the reality of our creation in God's image.

If world-views are driven by the heart orientation towards God, world-views, in turn, drive culture. Though the original meaning of culture is 'to till the ground' the term has come to mean everything that human beings have done with the raw materials of the natural world. That includes tilling the ground in order to produce food or beauty, that is, agriculture and horticulture. It also includes what human beings have done with their ability to produce and manipulate sound in order to communicate with each other and celebrate the world in which they live. Everyday language, poetry, drama, music and song belong to this sphere.

It would be possible to make a comprehensive list of the fruit of human endeavour under the heading of culture – painting and sculpture, politics, education, health care, a legal system and even religious institutions are cultural products. These various aspects of human life are held together by a world-view which is in turn controlled by a primal orientation towards God. We should, therefore, not be surprised to find aspects of culture which hold people in bondage because their source is ultimately in a heart rejection of the one true God.

Since the heart relationship to God lies at the root of world-views which drive culture, then the state of that relationship is crucial to human well-being. Because that relationship has been universally disrupted by sin, a heart conversion to God is crucial for the well-being of individuals and society. Conversion is a universal need, even for those brought up in a Christian context. Everything that has been said about the king and his kingdom, his laws, his wealth and his people becomes intensely relevant at this point. Proclaiming and displaying the reality of the kingdom is absolutely fundamental. But the kingdom is also the measuring rod by which we can assess all world-views and cultures. Christianity may have been the religion of the West for centuries but that is no reason for concluding that the West is best. The kingdom of God is a balance that can test the merits of Western world-views and culture as well as any other.

The Western world-view: pride and optimism

It is a general assumption of Western thought that people's relationships with each other and also, by now, with the environment are the primary relationships. Human well-being is founded on getting the economic, political, ecological or ethnic relationships right. There is a recognition that people's religion and world-view must be taken into consideration, but these aspects of human relationships are subservient to the Western secular view that human behaviour can be scientifically understood, predicted and then controlled for the common good. Human beings have taken back the reins of their destiny which they had in the past surrendered to a God who was little more than a figment of their imagination. Having banished God or gods the West worships material things. Acquiring possessions becomes the chief end of human beings. In gospel terms the West worships Mammon.

In a sense the dominant modern approach echoes the approach of the builders of the Tower of Babel. It is believed that humanity can build its own future independent of God. Coupled with this pride has been a basic optimism that with the application of the increasing store of knowledge about how nature and society operate, humanity will be able to build a Utopia on earth. Faith in God therefore has been replaced by faith in a scientific method which will ultimately deliver a heaven on earth.

Since the eighteenth century humanistic science and its technological application has become bolder and bolder in its claim to be able to solve all human problems. It may at times grudgingly recognize that many people immaturely need some divine prop to lean on. However, this religious activity is to be confined to people's private lives. In the public realm where the decisions which really affect people's lives are taken science must be the guide. Here human beings are in control and can discover by their own strength what principles need to be applied in order to create blessedness. The desire for control over the future, which is almost obsessive at times, is evidence of the fundamentally religious and apostate root of modern humanistic thinking and practice.

Inevitably the pride and optimism of Western science has affected the way in which richer countries have sought to help poor countries. Westerners have sought to understand, predict and control poverty, believing that its ultimate alleviation is within their grasp. They conveniently forget that poverty is still a significant reality in their own countries. The arrogance that lies at the heart of the Western endeavour in this context expresses itself both in the neglect of God's revelation concerning the problems of humanity and in the neglect of non-Western knowledge. The views of the poor themselves are rarely considered. Robert Chambers states:

> From rich-country professionals and urban-based professionals in Third World countries right down to the lowliest extension workers it is a common assumption that the

modern scientific knowledge of the centre is sophisticated, advanced and valid and conversely that whatever rural people may know will be unsystematic, imprecise, superficial and often plain wrong. Development then entails disseminating this modern, scientific and sophisticated knowledge to inform and uplift the rural masses. Knowledge flows in one direction only – downwards – from those who are strong, educated and enlightened, towards those who are weak, ignorant and in darkness.[11]

To critique Western models of explanation is not to devalue the tremendous achievements of Western science and technology, but to underline the need to distinguish technical ability and analysis from the humanistic philosophy that often accompanies it. Furthermore, it is important to remember that the scientific approach that is opposed to Christianity is only half the story. Western thinking may have produced the most severe challenge to any religious way of seeing the world but it is also heavily indebted to Christianity. The history of science witnesses to this as does the fact that a large proportion of scientists have always been Christians.

The story of the development of science in the West is very complex, but many scholars now argue that a clearer understanding of what the Bible teaches about the natural world was a crucial factor in its birth. There is agreement also that this clearer understanding happened during the period of the Reformation. Up to that time, despite centuries of Old Testament teaching, both Jewish and Christian, there was a tendency to deify nature. This is clearly the case in the ancient and sophisticated intellectual traditions of Egypt and the Middle East, India and China. But it was also true of Greek thought which, having been married to Christian thought, dominated Christendom throughout the Middle Ages. A nature that is ultimately identified with deity (pantheism) or that is at the mercy of a multiplicity of capricious spirits cannot become an object of scientific study and manipulation.

Even a superficial reading of the Bible makes it clear that the

---

[11] Chambers, R., *Rural Development: Putting the Last First* (Harlow, Longman Scientific and Technical 1994),' p. 76.

natural world is not divine. It is, rather, the creation of a sovereign and transcendent God. Nature is not God but something that has been brought into being by God. This natural world, which differs from God, is still sustained by him but his indwelling of it in this sense does not make it divine. When God came to make his will known to his people Israel at Mount Sinai there was a very explicit prohibition against attributing divinity to anything in the natural world. In fact at creation God gives the earth and all its potential to human beings to manage for his glory and their blessing.

When it was realized after the Reformation that God is transcendent over nature and is in no way limited by it, it became possible to think the thoughts of God after him by means of a study of the way in which the natural world works. Obviously, the transcendent God is not capricious – he is the one who brings order out of chaos. His creation is an ordered creation. So, thinking the thoughts of God after him also means discovering the order which he has imposed on the natural world. In philosophical or theological terms what is being referred to here is the conviction that the natural world is both *contingent* and rational. Many historians of science are convinced that science could not have emerged without the biblical teaching that the natural world is contingent, that is, dependent on God's will for its existence, and rational, that is, working in an ordered way so that, given the same conditions, a sequence of events can be predicted.[12]

The Reformation, particularly in its Calvinist form, was also responsible for creating a much more positive appreciation of the natural world than had prevailed in the Middle Ages. In the medieval church the Christian ideal was to forsake ordinary social life in order to seek the mystical vision of God. The really holy people were those who lived a secluded life of prayer and contemplation. Such a course, by definition, was only open to very few. The Reformation went a long way to democratizing knowledge of God. The reformers argued that a very real and

[12] For a treatment of this thesis see Russell, C.A., *Cross-Currents, Interactions Between Science and Faith* (Leicester, IVP 1985). Cf. Newbigin, L., *Foolishness to the Greeks* (London, SPCK 1986), pp. 65ff. and Kuiper, A., *Calvinism* (Amsterdam–Pretoria, Hoveker & Wormser, n.d. [c. 1899]), pp. 141ff.

meaningful knowledge of God was open to everyone. There was no need for withdrawal from the world either, because the world was God's world and the stage upon which every believer was called to live out their knowledge of God. Calvin in particular undermined the medieval distinction between secular and sacred vocation by insisting that to be a carpenter or a farmer or a ruler was just as sacred a vocation as any other. Science could not have flourished without this very positive attitude towards the natural world.

That biblical concepts and Reformation teaching about the nature of the earth and Christian vocation were important factors in the development of modern science does not tell the whole story by any means. While there is unquestionably a Christian thread running through the weave of modern science, another thread can be seen right from the beginning which pulls in the opposite direction. The cross-thread is the thread of Renaissance Humanism. While the Reformers of the sixteenth century restored the natural world to an honoured place in Christian theology and life, the Humanists of the same period exalted the natural world at the expense of the spiritual. Theirs was the secularizing emphasis in response to the medieval denigration of the natural as compared with the supernatural.

The Humanist thread in the development of modern science came into its own in the Enlightenment of the eighteenth century. Many of the leading intellectuals of that century rejected all ecclesiastical, dogmatic and biblical authority over their intellectual life. They claimed that truth about God and the world did not come through such authorities but by means of human reason alone. Man became the measure of all things.

This was a crucial step in the secularization of science. Not that the leading lights of the Enlightenment were atheists. Very few of them went that far in fact. What they did was to claim that human beings determine what is true about God and the world. Revelation is the key doctrine that is rejected by the Humanists. Christians believe that human beings cannot find out the ultimate truth about their origin and destiny in and of themselves. Our only hope is a Word from God. We believe that in many different ways God did in fact speak through the prophets of old and that what he said is recorded in the Old

Testament. We also believe that in the last days he spoke to us in his Son, the Lord Jesus Christ, and that the truth about him is recorded in the New Testament. It is our privilege and joy as weak human beings to accept this revelation and to build our lives and our understanding of the world and human community upon it. Humanists disagree. They deny that God has spoken and maintain that we ourselves are the source of all knowledge. From the point of view of revelation a science built on such a premise can become nothing but a demonic force working for the destruction of true and meaningful human life.

Those Christians who believe that Western expertise can play an important part in alleviating poverty need to make sure that their approach is not contaminated by a godless humanism. After all the society that such thinking has birthed in the West is nothing to be proud of. Western technology and know-how has produced immense luxury for millions, but blessedness is as elusive as ever. The Christian aim should be the blessing of the poor and not simply the meeting of their material needs.

Non-Western world-views

The Western world-view is spreading by means of global communications and increasing global trade. It always threatens local identities where it comes, with younger people particularly influenced. However, despite Western influence, many people, especially in rural areas, still live according to non-Western canons of understanding.

Many people in Third World countries still explain the complex realities of their lives by reference to spiritual realities. This contrasts with the Western framework of explanation which focuses almost exclusively on natural factors. In the non-Western framework of explanation disease can be the result of a spirit's curse, not viral activity, or one's station in life can be dictated by the spiritual law of karma rather than by the socio-economic or ecological realities to which a Westerner might point. Just as these non-Western explanations displace Western approaches, so the proud confidence that humans can better themselves is displaced by a fearful resignation to spiritual realities. Such resignation impacts the creation and maintenance of poverty in many ways. We shall illustrate this contention with reference to animist traditional religion and one aspect of the Hindu tradition.

Animist traditional religion

To understand the animistic world-view is difficult for those brought up in countries that have a long history of Christianity, that has been regularly renewed, and an Enlightenment legacy of confidence in science. Both these traditions have led to the banishment of spirits and the demonic from the natural world. For an animist, on the other hand, the natural world is throbbing with spirit beings that can exert a huge impact on the course of events in the natural world. These spiritual entities are of a different nature from purely earthly phenomena but they are very real. They are often described in anthropomorphic terms, 'The spirits live in this well', or 'walk along this path', or 'get piqued by people trespassing on their territory'. While in the main invisible, they are considered more real and influential than human beings. These spiritual entities are often considered to be the spirits of dead ancestors who look on to see what happens to their descendants and whether their memory is honoured. The ways in which humans interact with these beings are many and various. For example, the beings can be manipulated to some extent by magical techniques, offended by careless behaviour or appeased by rituals usually involving sacrifice.

Many animist cultures also believe in one transcendent, supreme God who created the universe. However, this God normally has little to do with daily living, whereas the intermediate spirits affect normal life in at least four ways:

Firstly, many illnesses are explained according to the activity of offended evil spirits who must be appeased. In such cases the local spiritual healer is more likely to be consulted than the Western health worker. Many people live in constant fear of becoming sick through offending a spirit or through an enemy manipulating spiritual forces against them. Significant resources of time and money are invested in keeping the spirits on one's side, even where such resources are scarce. In the event of illness, still more time and energy are invested in placating evil spirits.

Secondly, people's attitudes to nature become crippled by fear, as illustrated by the experience of David W. Shenk who grew up as the son of Mennonite missionaries among the Zanaki people of Tanzania. Shenk records:

> One day, Itini, the first Zanaki Christian, was confronted by tribal elders who accused him of not honouring the traditional nature gods. He had begun to fell a tree he needed for a rafter for his new house. The tree was part of a grove where the nature gods lived. The spirit experts threatened death by cursing if he did not desist.[13]

In this case the belief in spirits was strongly intertwined with social structure. It was the task of the tribal elders to make sure that the spirits were not offended. Their power over the community was preserved through the threat of cursing those who refused to toe the line. In this case Itini persevered. He was cursed but no harm befell him, which was a strong witness to the power of the gospel.

Thirdly, relationships between members of communities can become dominated by fear and suspicion. Peter Batchelor tells the story of a mother he once met in Africa:

> One mother's eyes still haunt me . . . They are the eyes of a human being who has given up hope. Her first child died of kwashiorkor (protein starvation). The second, a boy, became very ill . . . The mother went to a nutrition centre. In the weeks that she stayed there she learned what to feed her children and how to prepare it; the toddler recovered . . . Discharged, she went back to her hill community. The situation had not changed . . . Within days, the little boy's condition deteriorated . . .
>
> She was convinced that the reason for the death of her first baby, for the sickness of the second, and now for her own ill-health, was a curse that an enemy had placed on her. There was only one thing to do: taking the last of her

---

[13] Shenk, David, W., *Global Gods, Exploring the Role of Religions in Modern Societies* (Pennsylvania, Herald 1995), p. 181.

precious beans she went to the fetish leader with her gift. He agreed to cast a more powerful spell. To her dismay her sickness returned: the child got worse. She was left with no food, no money, no hope.[14]

This woman was caught in a cruel web of problems: the general economic depression of the area, domestic instability because her husband had left her with three small children, and so on. However, at the root of her situation was a fearful belief that an enemy had cast a spell on her, and the consequent sense of helplessness as the fetish leader failed to help.

Fourthly, in the context of African animist traditional religion, the chief of a clan is often imbued with divine power and esteem by virtue of his position as the representative of the ancestor spirits. In a sense he becomes such a spirit. This means that political power is sacralized and as a result the ruler has almost unlimited authority. To question the way in which a leader operates, therefore, is to question the sacred authority of the ancestors, which involves undermining the foundations of the identity and continuity of the state or community in question.

These examples illustrate the impossibility of addressing the issue of poverty in an animist society without taking religion into account. If there is no engagement with the religion any development work risks not only failing to address poverty, but also producing negative side effects of which the development worker may be tragically unaware.

An aspect of the Hindu tradition in India

Like most countries in the world India has been settled by different peoples over the ages. The most significant invasion from the point of view of the social structure was the Aryan which probably occurred as far back as the end of the second millennium BC. As is often the case with an invasion the Aryans did not exterminate the peoples they supplanted but used them as slaves/servants. This is the foundation stone of India's class

---

[14] Batchelor, P., *People in Rural Development* (Carlisle, Paternoster 1993) p. 81–2.

structure. It eventually developed into the four-class structure which then acquired scriptural sanction. The myth of the origin of man and society in the Rig Veda represents the primal Man being dismembered by the gods. 'His mouth became the Brahmin [Priest]; his arms were made into the Warrior [*Kshatriya*], his thighs the People [*Vaisya*], and from his feet the Servants [*Sudras*] were born.'[15] The first three classes are 'twice-born' and are given the sacred thread when initiated into society. Traditionally they are viewed as qualitatively superior human beings compared to the Sudras.

It is important to understand the relationship between these four classes and the thousands of castes (*jatis*) that still exist in India today. Caste has really more to do with group identity because of involvement in a specific occupation or even a religious sect. But there is a relationship between class and caste in that the castes are perceived to belong to a certain class. So, the launderers or leatherworkers' castes are always seen as fitting into the Sudra class and so on. The multiplicity of castes does not undermine the Brahmin conviction, for example, that they are superior human beings compared to the Sudras. At root, therefore, the explanation for the structure of Indian society according to Hinduism is a spiritual one.

The class/caste system has no legal validity in the Indian constitution, but in the villages, where most Indians still live, it is still very much in evidence. The low-caste area of the village is often clearly segregated from the rest and the higher-caste people avoid entering that sector and try to have as little direct contact with the low-caste people as possible. The low-caste people are allowed to enter the high-caste areas to serve but any fraternization is out of the question. Each caste is hedged in by rules of cleanness/uncleanness and since a low-caste person is considered unclean by a high-caste person they can never share the same food. Water supply can also be a problem in Indian villages because the high-caste people may object to low-caste people drawing water from the same well as themselves. There have been cases of low-caste people being persecuted and even

---

[15] *The Rig Veda*, trans. Wendy Doniger O'Flaherty (Harmondsworth, Penguin 1981), p. 31. The quotation is from the 'Purusha-Sukta', or 'The Hymn of Man'.

killed because they have claimed their constitutional rights to a share of the water from the village well.

In India a large proportion of its population is outcaste and treated very badly. The two main groups that belong in this category are what were traditionally known as the 'untouchables' and the 'tribals'. Untouchability, which involved a prohibition against holding property, among other disadvantages, was abolished in the constitution of independent India. But here again abolishing something on paper is different from abolishing something in reality. Gandhi called the untouchables *harijans* (children of god) in an attempt to affirm their equal status with other Indians. Untouchables themselves objected to this term because it smacked of patronage and condescension. They now prefer to call themselves *dalit* which means 'broken, trodden down, crushed'. This term highlights the fact that they see themselves as subjects of an unjust oppressive social system that is in urgent need of reform.[16]

The tribals have fared no better. Krickwin C. Marak, the Co-ordinator of the Centre for Mission Studies at Union Biblical Seminary, Pune, describes them thus:

> These tribals are not only obscure in their identity as 'Indians', they are also obscure in their very existence in their own lands in which they have lived freely for centuries. They are often called by fellow Indians such names as 'phaharia', 'backward', 'dirty', 'primitive', 'uncivilized', 'illiterate', 'chini', etc. Surely these names are not kind to them. But the irony is that these tribals are as they are called. They are the most undeveloped, most neglected people in our country.[17]

It is not surprising that excluded and despised people become what they are said to be. According to the 1981 census there were over 400 such groups numbering almost 52 million people in

---

[16] For a good discussion of the *dalit* issue see Prabhakar, M.E., 'Mission and the Dalit Issue' in *Doing Mission in Context*, Sumithra, S. and Hranghkhuma, F. (eds.), (Bangalore, Theological Book Trust 1995), pp. 83–115.

[17] Marak, K.C., 'The Brokenness of the Tribals in India and their Future' in Hrangkhuma, F. and Kim, S.C.H. (eds.), *The Church in India: Its Mission Tomorrow* (Delhi, ISPCK/Centre for Mission Studies 1996), p. 75.

total and making up almost 8 per cent of the total population of India.

Real change is impossible unless the profound conviction that people are unequal by nature is undermined and the only way to make progress on this front will be by religious conversion. This is the conviction of many Indian Christians at least. Vishal Mangalwadi, for example, in the context of comments on the practice of reserving jobs for scheduled castes, writes:

> Social engineering does not result in human dignity. One cannot take the benefit of being a 'low caste' through the reservation system, without also accepting the stigma of being a low caste . . .
>
> Education, free market economy and democracy can become antidotes to caste, provided they are undergirded by the Gospel. Conversion to truth will have to be the basic change. That is because caste is a darkness based, not only on vested interest, but also on a lie (or false idea) – that people are created unequal, some from Brahma's head, others from his arms, stomach and feet.
>
> The truth that can set India free from caste – its most important evil that pervades everything and corrupts everything – is the Good News; that all men are equal because we are made in God's image; we are all equal because we are all descendants of the same parents – Adam and Eve; all are equal because all have sinned and come short of the glory of God; all are equal because all are equally the objects of God's love revealed on the cross; and all can become equally God's children by becoming *dwijj* – twice born – through repentance and faith in Christ's work on the cross.[18]

The lot of the poor in India will not be substantially improved until the barriers of caste are broken down and to undermine caste means undermining the religious underpinning of Indian society.

---

[18] Mangalwadi, V., 'Mission in Rural India' in Hrangkhuma, F., Sumithra, S. and Kim, S.C.H. (eds.), op. cit. p. 133. Cf. Thampu, Valson, *Rediscovering Mission, Towards a Non-Western Missiological Paradigm* (New Delhi, TRACI 1995), p. 188.

Engaging with, not destroying, Third World cultures

To emphasize the link between Third World religion and poverty is not to condemn everything about Third World world-views and culture. The same is true for Western world-views and culture. Not everything that comes from the West is bad. There is a good biblical foundation for saying this.

The Bible is clear that God has revealed himself in creation. God has 'not left himself without testimony'.[19] As Paul says, 'since the creation of the world God's invisible qualities – his eternal power and divine nature – have been clearly seen, being understood from what has been made'.[20] One aspect of the creation which reflects God is humanity itself because we were made in God's image. Despite the fall we still bear the marks of that image. What we make or create as human beings must also bear marks of God's image. This continuity emerges particularly clearly in Paul's engagement with the philosophical and religious beliefs of the Greeks of Athens recorded in Acts 17:16ff. Paul takes up themes of Greek religious worship and shows how they find their true meaning only within a Christian revealed framework.

As already stated the reality of God's presence is universally apparent within the human heart. Even those who have not had the privilege of receiving the clear and unequivocal revelation of God recorded in the Bible have an innate knowledge of his demands. Paul had observed, as he visited various ethnic groups on his missionary journeys, that people everywhere had fashioned standards of behaviour and patterns of worship for themselves that, in some respects at least, were reminiscent of God's standard clearly revealed in the law.[21] In this observation Paul must also have been aware of Old Testament references to nations other than Israel who both know something of God's moral law and worship him, albeit in a limited way. Paul is not saying here that people everywhere do what God wants them to do, but that they know in their hearts something of what God

---

[19]   Acts 14:17.
[20]   Rom. 1:20.
[21]   Rom. 2:14–15.

demands. It is the 'requirements' of the law that are written on the heart and not the law itself, as in the case of the new covenant.[22] Part of this innate knowledge of God's law is the voice of conscience. Fundamentally, conscience is the inner awareness that we have as human beings of the character or quality of our actions. We know what we have done. When we know that we have contravened God's law which is written on our hearts then we feel the pain of inward accusation which we often try to avoid by defending or excusing ourselves.

Just as the early church, grasped by the truth of the kingdom of God, interacted with Jewish and then Greek teaching, so Christians today must interact with other belief systems highlighting fruitful continuities, while pointing to the supremacy of revelation in Christ. Kwame Bediako puts this powerfully in the context of his personal engagement as a Christian with his pre-Christian beliefs as a member of the Akan people of Ghana:

> We are to understand our creation as the original revelation of God to us . . . it was in the creation of the universe and especially of man, that God first revealed His Kingship to our ancestors, and called them and us to freely obey Him. Working from the perception of our creation as the original revelation to, and covenant with, us, we, from African primal tradition, are given a Biblical basis for theologising within the framework of the high doctrine of God as creator and sustainer, which is deeply rooted within our heritage.[23]

Consequently, to dismiss everything as evil in a religion, worldview or culture in a non-Christian community is not necessary because even a universally sinful world is still in the hands of a sovereign God. Sinners are still God's creation who, despite their sin, still image their Maker. We can still discover things about God's world which benefit us and create things of beauty that bring joy despite our sinfulness. Those things need not be jetti-

---

[22] Jer. 31:33.
[23] Bediako, K., 'Biblical christologies in the context of African traditional religions' in Samuel, V. and Sugden, C. (eds.), *Sharing Jesus in the Two-Thirds World* pp. 145–6.

soned when we are converted to Jesus. What needs to be jetti-
soned is what is opposed to God's revealed will. It may not
always be easy to distinguish between what is good and what is
bad in culture, so it is wise to err on the side of being positive,
unless it becomes very clear in the light of God's word that there
is a need to be negative.

Conclusion

Religion is unquestionably a live issue in the world today.
Western culture may have made a resolute attempt to marginal-
ize it but is having to recognize its importance in the life of the
majority of the world's population. The Bible says little about
religions but is in no doubt that people everywhere must be
called to bow the knee to Jesus who has been enthroned Lord of
all. Where the heart is concerned everyone everywhere responds
to the knowledge of the true God who is fully revealed in Jesus.
This is as true of the Western secularist as it is of a Tibetan
Buddhist. The universal tendency to turn away from God highlights the universal need for conversion.

Religion, in the sense of orientation of the heart, is the source
of individual and corporate life. It is the most fundamental level
of our existence and has a profound impact on world-views
and culture in general. That is why true conversion is not just
a case of adding some new ideas to the stock that was already
there. It must mean a radical transformation which permeates
the whole of life. There can be no significant social transformation without spiritual transformation. But the reverse is also
true: there can be no real spiritual transformation that does not
make itself visible in social transformation. Coming into a living
relationship with the Creator through Jesus must affect the
whole of our lives. One thing is certain: a human life that begins
to flow from the heart of God will not be content with the
injustice in the world which keeps millions in the bondage of
poverty. A godly world-view and culture cannot but be
inclusive.

Resources

Books

Shenk, David, *Global Gods, Exploring the Role of Religions in Modern Societies* (Scottdale, Herald 1995), is a very readable volume on a complex matter by a missionary statesman with wide experience of different religious traditions.

Burnett, D., *Clash of Worlds* (Eastbourne, MARC 1990), is a good introduction to a variety of world-views including the secular.

Newbigin, Lesslie, *Foolishness to the Greeks, The Gospel and Western Culture* (London, SPCK 1986), provides a superb analysis of Western 'scientific' culture.

Bavinck, J.H., *The Church Between Temple and Mosque* (Grand Rapids, Eerdmans n.d.) is a marvellous book on the relationship between the Christian faith and other religions.

Thampu, Valson, *Rediscovering Mission, Towards a Non-Western Missiological Paradigm* (New Delhi, TRACI 1995).

Bediako, Kwame, *Christianity in Africa, The Renewal of a Non-Western Religion* (Edinburgh University Press/New York, Orbis 1995).

Articles/Chapters

Mitchie, Sandra, 'Traditional beliefs and health problems' in *Footsteps*, no. 8 (1991), p. 10. The beliefs considered are cultural – their religious roots, if any, are not made explicit.

Transformation, vol. 2, no. 2 (Carlisle, Paternoster 1995). The whole issue is devoted to a 'Focus on caste and society'.

Chs. 3 and 6 of Hrangkhuma F. and Kim, S.C.H. (eds.), *The Church in India: Its Mission Tomorrow* (Delhi, CMS/ISPCK 1996), deal with mission to low-caste people.

Singh, David Emmanuel, 'The spiritual roots of Indian poverty with special reference to Sufism' in Kim, S.C.H. and Marak, K.C. (eds.), *Good News to the Poor, The Challenge to the Church* (Delhi, CMS/ISPCK 1997).

SEVEN

Economics, Poverty and the Kingdom

The source and purpose of economic activity

Before the Fall Adam was commanded to work the garden and take care of it, reflecting the mandate given Adam and Eve to 'fill the earth and subdue it'.[1] God intended from the beginning that the earth should yield its fruits as a result of human effort. Even in a state of perfection the earth was not meant to yield its fruit without effort on the part of Adam and Eve. This original intention of the Creator was not destroyed by the Fall. The major difference in the process of food production from the ground after the Fall was the cursing of the ground, which made the whole task so much harder.[2]

It was inevitable that families would produce more food from the ground or through domesticating animals than they needed. When this happened the question of what to do with the surplus arose. The moment the decision was taken to save it the root of all economic activity was present, because that decision implies a value for the surplus grain, fruit or animal that is other than its value to the producer. It is now seen as a means to an end rather than as an end in itself. Saving surplus produce also implies that there must be someone somewhere who does not have the produce, and who is likely to want it, or there would be no point in the producer saving it. Furthermore, the one who wants some of the surplus has something that its producer

---

[1] Gen. 2:15; 1:28.
[2] Gen. 3:17–19.

wants so that an exchange can be arranged. Initially this whole economic process was carried on by means of barter, but in due course money took over as a much more convenient way of measuring value. The root of all economic activity is the saving of calculated values.

The point of this very simplistic outline of the root of economic activity is to assert that it was as inevitable that this would happen as that human beings would learn to talk to each other or that they would form social institutions and so on. Granted that between us and God's original intention lies the horrible shadow of the Fall, we still retain something of the image of God, so we will inevitably continue to subdue the earth economically as in other ways. The issue is not whether we *should* engage in economic activity or not. That is part of our destiny. The issue is *how* we engage in it. The Bible has much to say on this issue.

The central thrust of biblical teaching on economic activity is that everyone should enjoy the benefits that accrue from it. In this sphere Old Testament law, prophetic pronouncements and the teaching of Jesus and his apostles are very much biased towards the poor.

The key note is struck in the law with its emphasis that the poor need a 'handup' out of poverty rather than a 'handout' which ultimately leaves them powerless. Consider, for example, the law of the gleanings. Leviticus 19:9–10 reads: 'When you reap the harvest of your land, do not reap to the very edges of your field or gather the gleanings of your harvest. Do not go over your vineyard a second time or pick up the grapes that have fallen. Leave them for the poor and the alien. I am the LORD your God.'[3] The gleanings that were left by the owner of a field or vineyard were not a handout but an opportunity for the poor. Like the owner the poor had to bring in the harvest if they were to benefit from the legislation. Ruth is a good example of a poor person who takes advantage of this provision. The law concerning the Sabbath of the land has the same thrust. Exodus 23:11 commands that land was to be left fallow every seventh year. One purpose of this law was that 'the poor among your people may get food from it'. In the seventh year the owners of the land

---

[3] Cf. Deut. 14:19–21.

took nothing from it but the poor were allowed to take as much as they needed of what grew of itself. However, here again the food had to be harvested.

In Deuteronomy God commands Israelites whose economic activity had produced a surplus to be open-handed towards the poor 'and freely lend him whatever he needs'.[4] This passage on its own would be evidence enough to confirm that God's desire with regard to the poor is that they should be helped to provide for themselves rather than depend on alms. A loan constitutes an opportunity for poor persons to use their strength and ingenuity to provide for themselves and in so doing to express their dignity as human beings created to be workers in God's world. This explains the strong repudiation of interest and usury in the Old Testament.[5] In the community of God's people Israel the rich were to supply freely the means for the poor to work themselves out of poverty.

It is when this Old Testament teaching is married with Jesus' teaching on wealth that we get the full picture of what biblical economic ethics looks like. His central emphasis is on sharing wealth with the poor while the Old Testament teaches us how it should be done. As we saw in chapter 4, 'The King's Wealth', Jesus is clear that we have to make a choice between living to enjoy our money or living to bless the poor with it.[6] This focus on using money to help others, particularly within the church community, continues in the apostles' practice and teaching.[7] This is not to deny that some of Jesus' actions had direct economic consequences. To give sight to the blind and wholeness to the lame made productive work possible for those that were healed. The raising of the widow of Nain's son gave back to the widow the provider that she had lost.

The teaching of the apostles, Paul in particular, seems to emphasize the giving of alms to relieve brothers and sisters in an emergency. But Paul also teaches that Christians should make every effort to earn their own living and not expect to be

---

[4] Deut. 15:8.
[5] Ex. 22:25; Lev. 25:35ff; Deut. 23:19f. See ch. 2, 'The Law of the King', for more detail and explanation.
[6] E.g. Lk. 12:33.
[7] See Eph. 4:28; Acts 20:34–5.

supported by alms. In his first letter to the Thessalonians he is particularly scathing about those who were not prepared to work for their living. 'For even when we were with you', he writes, 'we gave you this rule: "If a man will not work, he shall not eat." '[8] For Paul it is imperative that Christians work to support themselves, and not only themselves, but others also, as God blesses them. As he says in Ephesians 4:28, 'He who has been stealing must steal no longer, but must work, doing something useful with his own hands, that he may have something to share with those in need.' We are back with Jesus' motivation for creating wealth. But we now see how crucial it is that all human beings, and Christians in particular, should be able to work to produce the wealth to support themselves and others. Enabling the poor to earn, through the sweat of their brow, is a high Christian calling.

What William Booth, the founder of the Salvation Army, said about the poor in London at the end of the nineteenth century is still true of the poor in many countries at the end of the twentieth:

> Work, work! it is always work that they ask. The Divine curse is to them the most blessed of benedictions. 'In the sweat of thy brow thou shalt eat thy bread', but alas for these forlorn sons of Adam, they fail to find the bread to eat, for Society has no work for them to do. They have not even leave to sweat. As well as discussing how these poor wanderers should in the second Adam 'all be made alive', ought we not to put forth some effort to effect their restoration to that share in the heritage of labour that is theirs by right of descent from the first Adam?[9]

The biblical material on the purpose of economic production highlights God's perspective on economic matters. God does not view production and economic growth as a good in and of itself if it is not harnessed for his purposes. Economists tend to make the measure of economic growth the ultimate test of success or failure. If the Gross National Product (GNP), which

---

[8]   1 Thess. 3:10.
[9]   Booth, William, *In Darkest England* (London, The Salvation Army n.d. but Preface dated 1890), p. 31.

is the sum of everything produced by the citizens of a country, is rising, the country is declared a success. Such an approach is incompatible with our status as stewards of the earth on God's behalf because God is concerned that economic success stems from and leads to the fulfilment of all his purposes for the human and non-human creation. God is as concerned about the distribution and method of production as he is about the fact of production.

The currency of economic activity

In order to earn the money needed to sustain life, all of us, including the poor, must produce something. Economists are concerned with the various resources that are needed for production and particularly with the balance of the resources that is required in order to ensure the continuation of the process for everyone's benefit. The resources required are conventionally divided into the three categories of land, labour and capital.

Land includes the natural resources of the earth such as minerals, the properties of land and water that can be utilized to produce food and other raw materials, such as cotton or timber, and also simply the ground that may be needed to carry out a productive process.

Labour refers to all the different types of human service that are required for production which are often divided into manual and non-manual.

Capital refers to all the other services that are needed in order to produce anything such as tools, buildings, machinery and so on. Capital is goods that are used in order to enhance the production of other goods. The acquisition of these capital goods necessarily involves the postponement of consumption. To put it very simply, money is not used in this case to acquire goods for consumption but to purchase goods that improve the production of other goods with the aim of making a profit. The aim of saving money as capital is to end up with more than was originally invested. The cycle can then begin again with some of the money being saved as capital while the rest is spent on consumption.

A major debate in modern economic theory has been about who should own these resources. On the one hand some argue that the whole process should be in private hands. They are the advocates of the market economy, who believe that if left to operate freely on the foundation of private property the market will inevitably produce the greatest benefit for the greatest number. Ranged against them have been the socialists and Marxists who argue that the whole process needs to be brought into public control. They argue that a free market will inevitably lead to the exploitation of labour by those who own capital.

At present the tide is running very strongly in favour of the free market. This is not the point at which to discuss the relative merits and demerits of these two economic philosophies in the light of biblical revelation. They are referred to simply as background to the very practical matter of providing employment for the poor. With communist and socialist systems collapsing all over the world the reality of the present situation is that this whole exercise looks more and more as if it is going to have to be carried out in the context of the free market.

It is important to note, however, that both approaches can miss the ultimate dimension of God's ownership of the universe and our status as stewards before him. This is particularly true of Marxism which is an atheistic economic theory. It is not surprising that a system built on the denial of God fails to fulfil his purpose. But the free market theory is also capable of falling short of God's will. This is particularly apparent when profitability becomes the ultimate arbiter in economic affairs. In this case God's intentions for economic activity are simply replaced by greed. This is not a rare phenomenon in the free market! The many economic practices in the free market which are heavily biased against the poor and in favour of the rich are ample testimony to this fact. A pattern of exploitation has developed which the Old Testament prophets roundly condemned in their historical contexts. Their denunciation was based on God's law which sees economic activity as something which should enhance the life of all people, and even creation, not just the rich. It is vital, therefore, to identify contemporary patterns of bias against the poor in the dominant free market system. As Christians we can then denounce them on behalf of God with the same vigour as the prophets of old, and work towards a more just operation of the market.

The contemporary bias against the poor: the international dimension

The debt crisis

In 1994 the Third World owed various Western institutions the staggering sum of £1,297 billion. Africa's debt-servicing obligation for the same year was around £14,000 million though it only managed to pay £6,497 million. There are various reasons for this huge debt burden that hangs like a millstone around the neck of Third World countries. When the OPEC nations got together in the early 1970s and forced up the price of oil their success created an enormous inflow of funds into Western banks. Since the banks were expected to pay interest on these funds, they needed to invest them and it was believed at that time that Third World governments were excellent places to invest because it was believed that governments do not go bankrupt. So, vast amounts of money were in many cases pushed in the direction of Third World governments, often without much research to ascertain whether the investment was likely to be sound or not. Western governments and institutions like the World Bank also provided loans which were often for inappropriate and unproductive development. Then the world economy was hit by a severe recession in 1980–81 which led to a steep rise in interest rates. The result was that most Third World countries were left with a massive debt burden. Servicing this debt is now a huge drain on their economies and makes them substantial net contributors to the economy of the rich West.

Third World countries are dependent on their exports of primary commodities in order to get the foreign currency with which to repay their debt. When the bulk of the loans were made the price of primary commodities was high. However, since the mid-1970s, there has been a steady decline in the price paid for primary commodities due to a glut on the market. This glut resulted partly from increased production by Third World countries trying to raise funds to pay their debts. The situation has also been exacerbated by the flooding of markets with primary commodities from the West, where much of the farming is subsidized, enabling the goods to be sold at an artificially low price. Overall, therefore, the chief source of revenue available to meet Third World debt obligations has decreased steadily.

A possible solution would have been for Third World countries to reduce their dependence on primary commodities and move into the production of manufactured goods. But any such movement is often stifled by the tariffs raised by many Western countries against the import of manufactured goods from the Third World. Third World countries are still hindered by protectionist policies despite the rhetoric of free market economics that is preached in the West.

The result is that Third World countries find themselves in a 'no-win' situation where their debts are concerned. Whatever direction they go to improve the situation they seem to be blocked by the bias of the international economic system towards the rich West. This poses enormous problems to Third World governments as they seek to find money to meet their commitments to their own people as well as to foreign banks.

Zambia is representative of most Third World countries in relation to the debt crisis. Zambia's GNP per head is £253. This compares to a per head external debt of £479. The total external debt is £4.5 billion. Servicing the debt accounts for 31.5 per cent of export earnings. Zambia relies heavily on copper production which accounts for 85 per cent of export earnings. However, the collapse of international copper prices since the 1970s has left Zambia's economy crippled. The poor have paid the price. 86 per cent of the population cannot afford an adequate diet. 203 in every 1000 children die before their fifth birthday. Between 1990 and 1993, the government spent £22.5 million on primary school education compared to £790 million on debt repayments!

The International Monetary Fund (IMF) and the World Bank have stepped in with actions intended to alleviate the crisis. Loans from these two organizations can help directly to pay for debt servicing by providing loans at low or reasonable interest rates. But in return for these loans countries must agree to 'structural adjustment programmes' (SAPs). Third World countries have no option but to accept SAPs because if they try to become independent of the IMF and the World Bank they risk exclusion from the international financial community.

The following features and results of SAPs illustrates the subservience of the Third World economies to the needs of the West:

1. Steps are taken to increase the exports of Third World countries. Instead of an emphasis on food crops for internal consumption, land is used to grow cash crops for the international market. There may also be moves to develop manufacturing industries. However, it has become obvious that the international markets do not need many of the resources that the Third World has to offer. As countries undergoing structural adjustment expand their production of crops for export, such as cocoa or coffee, international markets, that were already oversupplied, become still more glutted. Prices fall still further and thus the hope of increased revenue from increased export earnings is disappointed. Ghana, for example, under the guidance of the IMF, doubled its production of cocoa only to see the price paid in the international markets dropping by 50 per cent. The net effect of their increased production was to provide cheaper cocoa for the rich!

2. Steps are taken to reduce imports. Among other steps, adjusting countries embark upon austerity measures designed to reduce consumer spending on imported goods. These austerity measures can include wage freezes and restrictions on the availability of credit. The local currency is devalued making imports more expensive and exports cheaper to foreign buyers. Wage freezes and price increases for essential foreign imports like fuel can hit the poor hard. In Rwanda, for example, after structural adjustment, people were forced to uproot coffee trees for fuel.

3. Steps are taken to improve revenue levels by reducing government spending, often on basic services such as health care and education. Poor people, therefore, who may have had free health care and education coupled with government subsidies

on their crops, now have to pay for services and survive in a free market usually weighted against them.

4. Countries are 'encouraged' to open up all their markets to foreign competition. Any tariffs erected against the import of goods must be removed. However, despite the rhetoric of free trade, richer countries continue to keep some protectionist measures to protect their own manufacturing industries and the agricultural activities of richer countries continue to be subsidized. This means that richer farmers can exploit the new markets in the Third World because they can afford to sell at artificially low prices. In Rwanda there is evidence that the influx of imported cheap grain into the Rwandan market led to the collapse of local agriculture.

The multinational corporations

The overwhelming majority of multinational corporations (MNCs) are based in the West. They are usually Western businesses that have expanded their operations internationally. They expand overseas in search of cheaper labour and resources as well as freedom from costly restrictions on their behaviour. Some have been concerned to access new markets by basing some company operations in particular countries, but many simply use the host country as a cheap place to make their goods which are sold elsewhere. Profitability is usually the bottom line. The trend at present is for multinational corporations to become transnational. While multinationals produce goods in many nations, transnationals franchise the production of parts of goods to many nations. This means that they have even less loyalty to nations where they operate than do multinationals. In fact they actively discourage national considerations in the interest of maximizing profit.[10]

MNCs have usually received a warm welcome from Third World countries. This is in part due to history. During the colonial era the colonial powers had established their systems of education in the colonies. The leaders of these colonies, when

---

[10] For a brief look at the distinction between multinationals and transnationals see Korten, David C., *When Corporations Rule the World* (London, Earthscan 1995), p. 125.

they became independent, had been through this educational system either in their own country or in the country of the colonial power. Therefore, the economic theories, whether capitalist or Marxist, which dominated their thinking when independence came, were Western theories. Those who embraced capitalist economics believed that the way forward was private investment in order to expand the modern industrial sector. They believed the Western idea that industrial growth by means of private capital investment leading to an improved GNP would bring the sort of universal prosperity enjoyed in the West. The way to attract private investment was to attract MNCs into their country. To do that incentives had to be offered. The lower cost of labour is an obvious incentive but host countries often add carrots such as cheap land for developing plant, and tax incentives.[11]

There is some truth in the belief that foreign-based multinationals benefit Third World countries. They do provide much-needed jobs and training but their profits still go elsewhere and they have little real loyalty to their adopted country. More serious is their tendency to pursue profit at the expense of the people or land of their host country. This can take many forms, as, for example, when an MNC uses prime agricultural land to grow luxury goods for the dinner tables of Western consumers while the indigenous poor of the host country struggle to find land on which to grow their basic needs. A well publicized example of exploitation is the destruction of areas of the Latin American rainforest by foreign-based multinationals seeking cheap land on which to rear cattle for beefburgers. Indigenous people are displaced and land is permanently damaged. The use of child labour is another complaint often made against MNCs. They are also often charged with polluting the environment and with having lower standards of safety for their employees than they do in the West. Overall they seem to be able to exploit their host countries with impunity and seem accountable to no one apart from their profit-seeking shareholders.

---

[11] This is true for Western and Third World countries. Taxpayers in the West now pay vast sums through government agencies to attract foreign corporations to different parts of their countries.

The contemporary bias against the poor: the national dimension

Within Third World countries themselves national structures and patterns are weighted against the poor. Within the overall inequalities of the international scene, the élite in Third World countries usually manage to secure significant wealth for themselves while the poor get poorer. There are many reasons for this. We shall focus on the introduction of inappropriate Western models of economic development.

In its early phase development economics was very committed to the growth of Western-style industries in the Third World as the answer to poverty. Much effort was put into understanding how the West had industrialized and grown economically so that successful models could be described and then applied to Third World situations. The emphasis was very much on the need for large-scale investment to establish mass production in technologically advanced plants. Such economically advanced production was largely dependent on MNCs moving in with money and expertise. Western governments also ploughed significant proportions of aid budgets into the development of industries. Much of the capital for this transition came from the West while land and labour could be found locally. There was often little sensitivity to the needs of local people displaced or affected by the new projects. The hope that the introduction of Western-style industry would cause economic growth that would benefit all the people in Third World countries has not been realized, except in rare cases such as South Korea or Taiwan. The more common pattern has been that minorities either through entrepreneurship or corruption have grown wealthy on the back of foreign investment while the poor, particularly in rural areas, have failed to benefit from the incoming resources.

Many thought that the development of wealthy minorities through industrialization would eventually trickle down into the development of a whole country. They argued that research on economic growth in the West had shown that the wealthy are better investors than the poor. So, if growth is the central aim, a greater inequality in income is not that important. What is important is the creation of capital and, in the Western context, research seemed to prove that the richer a person became the greater the supply of capital became. Since capital investment meant jobs, it was argued that inequality in wealth was really a good thing.

However, this theory makes at least two assumptions that are not necessarily true. The theory that the richer someone becomes the more they invest is not a pure economic equation. In the West the process of generating wealth went on within an ethical framework that emphasized the virtue of reinvestment. Unfortunately it seems that this framework is not there in many Third World settings because research is showing that the rich are not as good as the poor at investing their money. The Third World rich often use their money to buy luxury goods that are usually imported from the West, or place it in foreign banks where it can do no good whatsoever to their fellow countrymen.

The second false assumption is that investment in modern industry creates jobs. This may have been true at one time when productivity was dependent on labour. But the whole thrust of industrial development at the moment is in the direction of getting rid of labour and increasing productivity and profitability by means of mechanization. Investment in the modern industrial sector now means more often than not fewer rather than more jobs. If the modern industrial sector in Third World countries is to remain viable in the context of the world economy then there are going to be fewer jobs available than there are now. So, the rich will get richer and the poor will get poorer.

Hand in hand with the emphasis on industrialization came particular attitudes to agriculture and land. In the development economics formulated in the 1950s and 1960s the issue of who possessed agricultural land was not thought to be important. In fact the whole process of economic development was seen in terms of the transference of labour from the agricultural to the modern industrial sector. After all, this had been the experience of the Western industrialized nations who had succeeded in dramatically raising the living standards of a large proportion of their populations. That land for agricultural production should be left in few hands was seen as desirable because the answer to unemployment and poverty was to transfer labour from scratching a living on the land to the highly productive processes of modern industry. Poverty would be eliminated not through a more equitable division of land but through capital investment in mechanized industrial production. Land meanwhile could be turned over to large-scale, mechanized methods using new strains of crops and employing few workers.

However, in most Third World countries, despite the drift to the cities, the bulk of the population still lives in rural areas. Access to land is a crucial question for these people because most of them are dependent on it for their survival. Who owns the land is far from being an irrelevant question. In many countries a very large proportion of land that is available for agriculture is still owned by a very small number of people. This is particularly the case in many countries in Latin America. In some cases large tracts of land are owned by multinational companies which use it to produce cash crops for export to rich Western countries. Whether owned by multinationals or by wealthy locals the land that is used to grow cash crops is often cultivated by people who are treated very badly. Where there are tenant subsistence farmers the exploitation by landowners is often just as bad.

Restoring the balance: the international dimension

The debt crisis

In the light of what the Bible teaches about using wealth to encourage the poor by generous giving of interest-free loans, the high-interest loans which are crippling poor countries must be an abomination to God. They are a case of screwing the faces of the poor in the dirt so that the already rich can be richer still. Third World debt is a 'chain of injustice' that God wants his people to 'loose'.[12] So, Christians should redouble their efforts to campaign and lobby for the remission of debt as quickly as

---

[12] Isa. 58:6.

possible. The aim of Jubilee 2000 of substantial remission by the year 2000 is a perfectly reasonable one.[13] Such a step also makes pragmatic sense for the West, although that consideration falls far short of God's standard.[14] Achieving remission is a complex issue, but without it many Third World countries will remain bound in poverty.

Given the centrality of credit to the international economy it is also important to ensure that lending in the future is less reckless and government aid better directed. Perhaps most importantly, patterns of trade which cripple poor economies need to be examined. These issues are very complex and the role of Christians who do not work within business and economics is limited. However, all Christians can undertake, in the light of biblical standards, to raise the profile of issues of economic justice and to defend the cause of the poor.

Multinational corporations

One of the key problems with MNCs[15] is their lack of accountability. They can operate with impunity in countries whose governments are desperate to have them and hesitant to object to their actions even if they harm citizens and the environment. Consequently those who suffer from their policies have little opportunity to voice their grievances. However, MNCs are dependent on the continued consumption of their products. Their customers can demand certain standards which have to be met if an MNC is going to survive in an increasingly competitive market place. While they can ignore the concerns of poor people within their host countries, they cannot ignore the consumer. Obviously many consumers are only concerned with keeping the prices they pay low. This encourages MNCs to further exploitation of people and resources. There is a need for an increasing body of consumers who are concerned to ensure that

---

[13] See subsection 'Advocacy' in ch. 8, 'Politics, Poverty and the Kingdom', for more detailed examination of Jubilee 2000 in the light of advocacy on behalf of the poor.

[14] See George, Susan, *The Debt Boomerang* (London, Pluto 1992).

[15] A wide range of suggestions as to what ought to be done about MNCs can be found in Korten, *When Corporations Rule the World*, pp. 307–24.

the products they buy are produced in accordance with standards that protect workers, other inhabitants of host countries and the environment. Christians should be the first to join the ranks of 'ethical consumers' who are concerned to make MNCs act justly in the way they produce their goods.

Closely tied with ethical consumerism is 'ethical investment'. As Christians we neither want to purchase goods from exploitative or invest in abusive MNCs. Similarly, just as MNCs cannot ignore their customers, they cannot ignore their shareholders or prospective shareholders. The potential exists for people with money to invest to direct that money towards commercial ventures with high ethical standards and away from those without such standards. If all Christians in the West who contribute to a pension opted for an ethical pension fund they could make a significant contribution in this context.

Establishing 'fair trade' companies that seek to model the values that ethical consumers and investors want all companies to own is another option. Tearcraft, which is Tearfund's trading arm, is one example. It was established in 1974 to market crafts from the Third World in the UK. Tearcraft buys goods at a fair price so that the workers can earn a living rather than depend on charity. The working conditions of workers are good. Tearcraft seeks therefore to live out the biblical emphasis on giving the poor the opportunity to work themselves out of poverty. It also expresses the biblical concern that all are treated justly. Groups from which Tearcraft buys its products have to be run by evangelical Christians. In tying Tearcraft to this Christian criterion it makes the statement that the production of wealth needs to be accompanied by a love and respect for Jesus that provides the best context for its proper use. Without such a context wealth can soon become a destructive idol.

The groups that have produced goods for Tearcraft have utilized traditional crafts and also trained needy people specifically to produce goods for export. Lao Song Handicrafts from Thailand is an example of the former and Christian Missions Charitable Trust of Madras, India of the latter. The Lao Song people live in the central plains of Thailand but are considered a hill tribe people. They were brought to Thailand as prisoners of war from the hills of Laos over 150 years ago. In recent years their ancient methods of embroidery and patchwork, which were in danger of dying out completely, have been revived and put to use producing goods that can be sold in the West. The business, which is headed up by a daughter of Lao Song farmers, struggles with a lack of working capital and the lack of supply of raw materials, but the sales of crafts has enabled many people to remain in their villages. The alternative would have been the drift to Bangkok to look for work or even the selling of young girls into prostitution to stave off starvation.

Christian Missions Charitable Trust (CMCT), on the other hand, is an institution to help very poor women in Madras. There are 120 women involved in the Haven of Hope Handicraft Centre producing a range of towelling products that are sold both in local markets and through Tearcraft in the UK. In this case the women are trained in sewing and embroidery to the very high standard that is required for producing goods for a Western market. The products that they make are not traditional to the area they come from. So, this is a case of training very vulnerable women from scratch to make products primarily for an export market. This work is inspired by a missionary from New Zealand, Dr Colleen Redit, who became convinced that the gospel would not be good news to the very poor women with whom she was working unless it included an attempt to provide an honest way of earning a living as well as a message of eternal salvation.

Restoring the balance: the national dimension

Microenterprise

Microenterprise assumes many forms but it is essentially about enabling the poor, as individuals or in groups, to establish profitable commercial businesses. Access to capital is the biggest barrier to such enterprises. A revolving loan fund is one method that has been devised to get over this crucial initial hurdle. The initial capital may be raised in different ways such as through a credit union or by appeal to the charity of the rich. Loans are then made to the poor at a comparatively low rate of interest. Ideally the rate should cover administrative costs and slightly increase the capital stock. As repayments are made and the capital stock increases more poor people can benefit from the scheme. It is crucial that there should be a very high level of repayment for such a scheme to succeed. Encouragingly many such schemes are successful. Where capital is raised from the surplus of the rich they are an excellent example of using surplus wealth to fulfil the biblical mandate to give the poor a 'handup' rather than a 'handout'.

There are many different types of microenterprise schemes, but they all seek to foster productive, sustainable enterprise among the poor. Microenterprise has many advantages as a way of helping the poor in a world that is often set up against them. Whereas official aid packages, such as SAPs, focus on issues of national economic health, such as balance of payments and GNP, microenterprise schemes aim directly at very poor individuals and their families. Microenterprise starts with the poor instead of waiting for economic changes at a macroeconomic level to trickle down to them. In fact microenterprise often provides a lifeline for poor people in countries undergoing SAPs. As public services and imported essential goods become more expensive, while government jobs and subsidies disappear, microenterprise can offer a relatively insulated source of income to the struggling poor. Given that most microenterprise schemes use locally available resources, harness local technology and produce for a local market, they are also less vulnerable to international economic fluctuations.

Poor people, because of their lack of security, find it almost impossible to borrow money from banks, so they are often driven into the arms of exploitative moneylenders. The beauty of microenterprise schemes is that they can offer start-up capital at a reasonable rate. They are especially helpful for poor women who are often, in the increasing absence of fathers, the heads of households and who have to face societies that are structured to deal with men not women. Access to formal financial services is hard enough for a man but even harder for a woman. Women have gladly availed themselves of the opportunity where schemes have been set up and have proved themselves to be more reliable borrowers than men.

A key thrust of microenterprise is to encourage the poor to see themselves as people with God-given creativity, diligence and honesty. It seeks to empower people who have sometimes been reduced to passivity by the nature of previous aid. Aid, like welfare, often fosters a dependent mindset so that people passively wait for assistance rather than actively seeking to provide sustainable sources of livelihood for themselves.

While the strengths of microenterprise schemes should be recognized, they are obviously not the complete answer to the problem of poverty. Because they are small scale they tend not to contribute to the national economy. Microentrepreneurs usually do not pay tax which could support the government in provision of welfare services, education and health care. Also, while microenterprise does seek to reach the very poor, it often benefits certain sections of the poor, leaving others relatively untouched. The poorest of the poor may be so desperate that they have no inclination to invest some of the meagre available resources in any other project but their own survival. Their great need is love and hope which can come through the care of people inspired by the gospel. Hope is also a crucial ingredient in the success of any microenterprise.

A case study in microenterprise

The Kale Heywet Church (KHC) in Addis Ababa has set up a central fund from which the very poor can gain loans with which to start or perpetuate microenterprises. KHC realized after making surveys that many people were unable to access the necessary capital to start a small business. The Annual Report for 1992–93 states that in a needs survey, 'many people said that the lack of capital to start or expand small businesses was the main factor holding them in poverty'. The KHC was also conscious of the detrimental effect of SAPs on the poor. The devaluation of the Ethiopian currency had led to rises in the price of fuel, public and private transport and imported goods which was hitting the already vulnerable poor very hard. The Church's microenterprise scheme, operating within the informal economy, was designed to offer some income security amid these changes. Andy Meakins,[16] who was working with the KHC supported by Tear-

---

[16] Andy Meakins, who had served the Lord among the poor in Ethiopia for many years, was tragically killed in an air accident in 1996. He left an Ethiopian wife and three small children.

fund, in requesting support for the scheme in October 1992 noted that even 'the World Bank has recognized the importance of this informal sector of the economy to help cushion the poor from the effects of economic restructuring'.

In the KHC scheme, the poor save together, each contributing a set amount from their earnings to a central fund that was initially financed by Tearfund. The poor exercise ownership and control over this fund. At the moment 60 people benefit from access to the central fund which is not increasing at a sufficient rate to embrace new recipients. However, it is hoped that the scheme will develop into a revolving scheme that can help increasing numbers of people.

The KHC work among the poor is increasingly focusing on women because they are often the poorest and most powerless. In their July 1995 proposal to Tearfund they state that projects will 'focus on the poorest sectors of the communities living around the KHC local churches. The poorest and most under-privileged tend to be female-headed households. The opportunities for women to find regular employment in the formal sector of the economy are extremely limited. Therefore, the informal sector provides the means of survival for the majority of this group'. KHC calculate that 50–75 per cent of households in Addis Ababa are headed by women. While the microenterprise scheme offers a means of survival to some of the poor, the church recognizes that not all the poor have the confidence or ability to manage a small business.

Vocational training

In some cases the poor do not need to acquire skills that can be used to produce goods for sale since they already possess traditional skills that have been passed on from one generation to another. This is particularly true of traditional handicraft skills that have been perfected over many generations to satisfy the utilitarian and aesthetic needs of a particular locality or tribal group. Such skills can often be used to satisfy a much wider market. What is needed for this to happen is help with design and marketing. In this way such skills can be used not only to produce goods for a local but also for an export market.

In other cases the poor find themselves in situations where there is work available, in the formal or informal economy, but they do not have the necessary skills to take advantage of the opportunities. Where there is a shortage of necessary productive skills, there is plenty of scope for Christian involvement in equipping the poor for work. Evangelical Christians in many countries have set up training services to give young people skills that will enable them to set up small businesses or to get a job in the labour market.

These training services take two main forms: The first is apprenticeships. A church or organization puts individual young people in touch with people already established in a trade. The young are then 'mentored' by someone already established in a trade. The major advantage of this system is that it prepares people for the real working environment since they see an individual actually at work. The second form is vocational training within a school setting. Normally students will be unable to pay any or part of the fees for such training. The schools will often sell much of what the students produce to generate income, but they invariably remain heavily dependent on external funding. The funding of such schools is another excellent way for the rich to empower the poor.

Vocational training – an example

The Africa Inland Church training school in Limuru, Kenya, serves a community which was resettled on marginally productive land where there is a huge need for alternative sources of income. Most children are forced to leave school after the primary stage in order to help scratch out a subsistence from the poor land. The vocational school thus provides some of them with another chance to secure a long-term vocation. It provides vocational training in the areas of carpentry, masonry, metalwork, dressmaking, spinning and secretarial work. At any one time it will be training up to two hundred people. It does not provide accommodation for the students but, given the impoverished condition of many of them, it does provide a midday meal. The students do not have to pay fees because the school is externally funded.

The training itself is not a complete answer to the problem of unemployment in Limuru because even after training it can be very difficult to find work. Most will need to think in terms of being self-employed but the chronic shortage of capital with which to start up businesses makes this difficult. Therefore, if adequate post-course steps are not taken, such as the provision of capital, there is the real prospect that the training will prove pointless. The sort of capital injection needed could be tools, such as sewing machines, or a cash lump sum.

Access to land

In the area surrounding the remote village of Tuchin in northern Colombia, the inhabitants who belong to the indigenous Zenu tribe have been gradually deprived of their land rights by successive post-colonial powers. Now, virtually all of the land in the region is in the possession of a few wealthy non-indigenous landowners. That which is not has generally been seized illegally by militant indigenous peasants who often work in league either with drug barons or with militant communist groups.

Some individuals from the local churches in Tuchin decided in 1990 to do something about this situation. They were faced with, in their own words, 'the poor class and marginalized without work and without land on which to work'. They formed a 'Christian Social Foundation' (FUSCAL). Their initial plan was to secure funds to rent land which could then be lent to landless church members. However, it was eventually decided that it would be better to purchase 55 hectares of land. The circumstances of the purchase reveal much about the broader situation in Colombia. The rich owner of the land FUSCAL bought had previously been kidnapped and forced to pay a high ransom in relation to another plot of land. Fearing further action by militants he had decided that a quick sale on some of his other land was sensible; FUSCAL therefore got the land for at least 25 per cent less than its market value.

Months after making its purchase FUSCAL was also subject to pressure from militant peasants. 100 families occupied the land that FUSCAL had rented to other families. The traditional way of solving such disputes in Colombia is by protracted violence but FUSCAL sought a peaceful solution. It appealed to

the Zenu tribal chief who usually supported the violent acquisition of land. The chief was impressed by the peaceful way in
which FUSCAL operated, so, using his tribal authority, made
sure that the illegal settlers left.

Twenty-five Zenu families now farm the 55 hectares. Each
family has its own plot of land for its subsistence needs. Any
produce left over is sold. Some land is set aside to be farmed
collectively. The families have formed a co-operative which is in
the process of securing legal status. This co-operative in effect
mortgages the land from FUSCAL who, with money from Tearfund, purchased the land in the first place. The co-operative
collects repayments from the individual families who have had
to agree to certain conditions of repayment before joining the
co-operative. The co-operative will have to pay back the full cost
of the purchase of the land to FUSCAL before they are given the
title deeds for the land. However, they are paying back the initial
amount without any addition to cover inflation. FUSCAL will,
therefore, make some loss but what they receive in repayment
will be ploughed back into land purchase in other areas for the
benefit of the poor: the economic potential of the land was not
considered sufficient to make payment of the purchase price
plus inflation possible.

Summary and conclusion

As human beings we have no choice but to engage in economic
activity. Within God's plan for all humanity, we must work to
produce so that we can eat. Economics as a discipline has to do
with the various factors that are needed to ensure growth in the
level of production with the assumption that as many as possible
should benefit from such growth. The two poles of biblical
teaching focus on the great danger of acquiring wealth for our
own enjoyment, on the one hand, and on addressing the needs
of the poor on the other. These two main focuses are really the
two sides of the same coin. It is when the rich are free from the
domination of wealth that they are able to use what they have
to provide for the poor. That wealth is used in this way is no
light thing but a matter of eternal salvation.

The church needs to wake up to the implications of this biblical teaching particularly since it is surrounded by large-scale poverty. This is the responsibility of the leadership of the church to a great extent. Pastors and teachers, who must be free of the love of money themselves, must encourage the rich in particular to follow Jesus in the way of the cross and deny themselves for the sake of the poor. There is need to rediscover the diaconal function in the church and recognize those who have the special gift of channelling the wealth of the rich to benefit the poor.

We need to grasp the fact that the root of poverty is the lack of means to produce wealth. What the poor need more than anything, in the economic context, is work. Even the Old Testament law recognizes that a handup is more beneficial than a handout. Christians and others who are involved in development have been conscious of this for some time and much is being done already to provide work. Yet rich Christians have vast disposable incomes which could be used much more to provide capital and land, and to develop the skills of poor workers so that they can provide for themselves.

Meanwhile, big business through MNCs, international trade and debt continues to disadvantage the poor. Rich Christians everywhere need to understand that they are part of a system which is more often than not oppressive as far as the poor are concerned. This does not mean that they should all opt out of the system but they have a responsibility at least to use what they gain from the system to bless the needy. They also have a responsibility to use the power that they have to try and guide the system in the direction of justice. But that is as much a political as it is an economic issue and belongs to the next chapter.

Resources

Books

There seems to have been more interest in economics from a Christian perspective in the eighties than the nineties. Alan

Storkey's *Transforming Economics* (London, SPCK 1986) is a helpful introduction to economic issues for the layman. Klay, R.K., *Counting the Cost* (Grand Rapids, Eerdmans 1986), Kreider, Carl, *The Rich and the Poor* (Scottdale, Herald 1987) and Beisner, E. Calvin, *Prosperity and Poverty* (Westchester, Illinois, Crossway 1988), all focus on poverty. Beisner contains a lot of good biblical material which is combined with a very blinkered commitment to the free market as if there had never been a Fall.

Chester, Tim, *Paying the Price* (Teddington, Tearfund 1995) and *The Chains of Injustice* (Teddington, Tearfund 1996) are very helpful booklets, particularly on the issue of debt.

Not specifically Christian
In addition to the books by Todaro, George and Jackson already referred to, Schumacher, E.F., *Small is Beautiful, A Study of Economics as if People Mattered* (London, Abacus 1974), remains a classic.

George, Susan, *The Debt Boomerang, How Third World Debt Harms us All* (London, Pluto 1992).
Korten, David C., *When Corporations Rule the World* (London, Earthscan 1995), is a brilliant and disturbing study of globalized economics.
Holcombe, Susan, *Managing to Empower: The Grameen Bank's Experience of Poverty Alleviation* (London, Zed 1995) tells the story of a successful attempt to run a bank for the benefit of the poor in Bangladesh.

Articles

There is a lot of relevant material in *Transformation*, vol. 12, no. 2 (1995), which deals with 'The impact of the market economy on the poor'. Vol. 9, no. 1 (1992) is entitled 'Work, employment and economics'. The topic of vol. 7, no. 2 (1990) is 'Christian faith and economics', while vol. 4, nos. 3 and 4 (1987) is a double issue on 'Christian faith and economics'.

See also Donald Hay's 'Three statements on Christian faith and economic life' in *Transformation*, vol. 10, no. 1 (1993).

Mills, Paul, 'The ban on interest: dead letter or radical solution?', *Cambridge Papers*, vol. 2, no. 1 (1993).

EIGHT

Politics, Poverty and the Kingdom

Introduction

Every society needs a regulatory structure to preserve the possibility at least of communal life. No society on earth has been discovered that has no form of government at all. At present Western ideas about how society ought to be governed, like everything else Western, are becoming more and more pervasive all over the world. But where there are communities still relatively isolated from these influences they all have a select number of individuals who are the guardians of tradition, who define what it means to be a good member of society and who are responsible for punishing deviants. There is no such thing as a non-political society or community. The aim of this chapter is to look at politics in the light of the Bible with a particular focus on the plight of the poor.

The source of politics

Just as it was argued that economic activity is an inevitable development of the creativity implanted in human nature by the Creator, the same could be said for politics or government. Political activity would then be an inevitable unfolding of the potential of human nature created in the image of God. Some argue that the ultimate foundation of the human propensity to order society is found in the social concept of God implied in the doctrine of the Trinity.[1] Karl Barth, for example, argues that the image of God in people refers to the creation of human beings as man and woman. It is in the male–female, and by analogy, the human being–human being, capacity for relationship, that God's image is located. This understanding of Genesis 1:27 provides a strong motivation in Creation Theology for Christian political action. And if God in Trinity is the source and analogy of what human society should be, there is a strong foundation, not only for mutual respect and service, but also for equality in human relationships. The three persons of the Trinity are equal not only in essence or being but also in terms of resources and power.

There are some passages that support this social interpretation. Genesis 9:6 sees murder, the ultimate breakdown in relationships, as a capital offence because 'in the image of God has God made man'. James 3:9 implies that cursing other humans, again indicating interpersonal breakdown, is wrong because humans 'have been made in God's likeness'. Most clearly of all Colossians 3:9–11 emphasizes that one of the first effects of the restoration of the image of God in humans who have been born again is a restoration of social unity and harmony between Greeks and Jews, circumcised and uncircumcised, barbarians, Scythians, slaves and free.[2]

The human drive to form relationships and communities with organized structures of government has its roots in the creative purpose of God. The ultimate destiny of human beings in God's plan witnesses to this. Those who are remade in the image of God will not live eternally as isolated individuals but as members of an eternal city ruled over by the Lamb.[3] There is even a hint that some of the current political structures will continue in renewed form within the new heavens and the new earth; the 'nations' will walk by the light of the Lamb and the kings of the earth will bring their splendour into the New Jerusalem.[4]

---

[1] See Wright, C., *Living as the People of God* (Leicester, IVP 1983), pp. 104–5.

[2] For some arguments that question this social view of the image see Berkouwer, G.C., *Man: The Image of God* (Grand Rapids, Eerdmans 1962), pp. 72ff.

[3] Col. 3:9–11; 2 Cor. 3:12–18, Rev. 21:2ff.

[4] Rev. 21:24.

Politics in the context of sin

The breakdown in relationship with God described in Genesis 3 very quickly leads to a breakdown of the initial harmony in human relationships, first, between Adam and Eve and then between their sons Cain and Abel.[5] After the fall into sin the drive for relationship, co-operation and unity between God and humans, established at creation, is expressed alongside a more powerful drive towards independence as humans determine to conduct their lives without reference to their Creator. Similarly the drive to live in harmony with others is expressed in tension with the desire to live only for oneself and in consequence to exploit others for one's own ends. Individuals began to use their God-given abilities not to serve but to dominate one another.

The entrance of sin made the drive towards independence, self-gratification and the exploitation of others for selfish ends, the dominant drive in human behaviour. So, it is not surprising that political structures have often been the means to satisfy the lust for power and glory of certain individuals. On the other hand human beings cannot deny completely their creation in God's image. The drive for harmonious human relationships remains. Consequently political structures can also exist to control the human instinct to dominate and exploit others.

This is the focus of Paul's famous passage on what should be the Christian attitude towards government in Romans 13. Government exists, according to Paul, to ensure that those who do good are allowed to live in peace and to punish those who do evil. This theme is repeated by Peter who says that government is instituted by God 'to punish those who do wrong and to commend those who do right'.[6] Under God's sovereignty government should provide a context in which all human beings in a given area can live in unity and co-operation. This will involve the restraint of those who seek to disrupt such unity and the encouragement of those who seek to promote peace. Of course the universal human instinct for self-advancement at the ex-

---

[5] Gen. 3–4.
[6] 1 Pet. 2:13–14.

pense of God and other human beings will always limit the extent to which any political structure can facilitate unity.

In Romans 13 Paul points to the place of governments in the providence of God for the whole of humanity. In this emphasis he picks up a recurring Old Testament theme that God is sovereign over the government of all nations and expects certain standards from them as a result.[7] At times these authorities actually fulfil their divine mandate. Paul believed when he wrote Romans that Roman rule was just and deserved the respect of Christians.

However, there is an equally strong emphasis in the Bible on divinely instituted authorities turning their back on their mandate to serve in order that good may flourish, and instead, ruling for their own gain at the expense of others. This emphasis reaches a climax in Revelation 18 with its graphic portrayal of 'Babylon the Great'. Here we see a political power that has reached the height of arrogant independence from God with the terrible abuse of human beings that follows.[8] The image in Revelation represents the Roman Empire, but it has broader applications to any power that sets itself up in wilful independence from God's standards. The advice of God is not to respect such an empire as the righteous instrument of God, but to 'Come out of her, my people, so that you will not share in her sins'.[9]

Revelation reflects John's experience of the persecuting Roman Empire during the reign of Domitian (AD 81–96) which was very different to Paul's experience of Roman rule when he wrote his letter to the Romans sometime between AD 57–59. By the time John came to write Revelation the hands of the Roman authorities were covered in the innocent blood of Christian martyrs.

The Bible, therefore, holds two themes in a helpful tension: On the one hand, political authorities are instituted by God and are a part of his creative provision for all humanity. They have a high degree of responsibility before God to maintain his standards of justice within their jurisdictions. They should restrain and punish those bent on evil, while encouraging those who do

---

[7] E.g. Ps. 2.
[8] Rev. 18:13,20,24.
[9] Rev. 18:4.

good. In so doing they witness to the residual image of God left in all humans despite the Fall. However, on the other hand, as was seen so clearly in the life of Jesus and the early church, 'the kings of the earth take their stand and the rulers gather together against the Lord and against His anointed One'.[10] When rulers forget that their authority is delegated to them by God, it is inevitable that they lose their sense of responsibility to the people they rule. When this happens justice is sacrificed in the interest of self-gratification and self-glorification. As a result the dereliction of the duty to encourage those who do well reaches its zenith in the persecution of God's people.

God's people and the governing authorities

God's people in the Bible engage with the political authorities of their time in different ways. There are two main models of engagement in the Bible: a) Working within the political system, and b) Challenging the system from outside.

Working within the political system

There have been faithful followers of God throughout the ages who have been a part of the political process, but who have maintained their godly distinctiveness. Most of them have been servants of rulers who did not belong to the people of God.

In the Old Testament we have Joseph who became governor of Egypt and saved his family from famine. Interestingly, he was also responsible for a significant increase in the power of the Pharaohs which can be viewed as a judgment on the Egyptians. Daniel became a high official in the Babylonian court and was the means of leading Nebuchadnezzar into submission to God. There can be no doubt that, being humbled before God, he would take Daniel's advice as to how to govern his empire with justice. Esther was made queen to the Persian King Xerxes and was the means of stopping a massacre of the Jews. Nehemiah

---

[10] Ps. 2:2; cf. Acts 4:25–6.

was a cupbearer to Artaxerxes some years later and was given permission to return to Jerusalem as governor to rebuild the city walls. The generosity of the king towards him and his leadership in Jerusalem witness to his integrity as a ruler. These followers emphasized that their ultimate allegiance was to God and not to any political authority. Furthermore they alerted their political masters to the fact that their authority was delegated to them by God.[11]

Sometimes these faithful followers of God had to work within regimes set directly against the purposes of God. In so doing they expressed their obedience to God despite the nature of the regime. However their ultimate allegiance to God sometimes led them to disobey their rulers. The example of Obadiah, who was in charge of Ahab's palace, reveals this clearly.

Obadiah had been a 'devout believer in the Lord' from his 'youth' and held the prophet Elijah in high regard.[12] His ultimate allegiance to God led him to disobey Ahab's wife Jezebel by hiding and feeding a hundred of the prophets of the Lord whom she was intent on killing. Obadiah was not afraid of civil disobedience. However, when Elijah met him he was faithfully working for the corrupt regime of Ahab and Jezebel. Indeed in his job as ruler of the palace he was seeking to alleviate the effects of the punishment that God had brought on Ahab by finding fodder for his animals. Obadiah saw no essential conflict between his job and his faith. There were tensions at times but he was able to use his position to do what a just state ought to do and protect the Lord's prophets.

The pattern of God's people being used within regimes which can sometimes become corrupt is continued in the New Testament. There is reference to just a few individuals who were godly and who also belonged to the political establishment. Nicodemus and Joseph of Arimathea referred to in the gospels were both members of the Sanhedrin, the Jewish supreme court. Joseph is described by Mark as a 'prominent member of the council'. According to John he was a secret believer, because of

---

[11] E.g. Dan. 4:25.

[12] The story of Obadiah is found in 1 Kgs. 18:2b–16.

his fear, but he did provide a grave for Jesus.[13] Nicodemus, having had a private interview with Jesus, later defended his right to a fair hearing before being condemned and with Joseph was responsible for Jesus' burial.[14] Then there are a couple of godly centurions: the one who came asking Jesus for healing for his servant, and Cornelius, whose conversion marked a new step in the spread of the gospel.[15] Sergius Paulus, proconsul of Cyprus, became a believer during Paul's first missionary journey and by the time Paul came to write his letter to the Philippians there were believers in Caesar's household though nothing is said about their status. It is not impossible that some at least were in positions of responsibility.[16]

This brief summary of the biblical evidence suggests that it is possible to be godly and involved in the political process. It also suggests that godly rulers are able to do a lot of good. The emphasis in the biblical material considered above has been on godly politicians operating in an ungodly context because that is the political reality of the modern world. But there were a number of godly rulers in the history of Israel as well, with David as the supreme example. All this material put together makes it very clear that involvement in any of the various branches of the political realm can be a godly vocation. Paul reminds us that there will never be many of the great and powerful ones of the world among God's people. But there will be some, so he encourages Timothy to pray for the salvation of those in authority.[17]

In the modern world there are many ways in which Christians can be involved in politics, particularly with the spread of Western-style democracy all over the world. There is plenty of scope for exercising the spiritual gift of administration in the political realm. Church leaders should encourage the exercise of such gifts and make sure that the church supports with prayer and encouragement those who embark on a political career. It should also be very clear to the church that those who

---

[13] Mk. 15:43; Jn. 19:38.
[14] Jn. 3; 7:50; 19:39.
[15] Mt. 8:5–13; Acts 10.
[16] Acts 13:12; Phil. 4:22.
[17] 1 Cor. 1:26; 1 Tim. 2:2–3

aspire to authority in the state are not motivated by the desire for recognition or personal gain but by a desire to serve; in particular that they desire to be advocates of the weak and vulnerable in society and to see that the business of the state is run on just principles.

Challenging from outside the system: the prophetic tradition

The prophetic tradition emphasizes the distinction between the kingdom of God and the kingdom of this world. The great prophets of the Old Testament were almost of necessity outside the political process. The message of judgment and condemnation that they brought more often than not made it impossible for them to be anything but outsiders. In the previous section we saw how Obadiah could work out his obedience to God within the regime of Ahab and Jezebel. In this we examine how Elijah had to challenge the same regime from the outside.

Ahab's sin was idolatry after marrying a foreign wife who worshipped other gods.[18] Inevitably, such an attitude to God eventually expressed itself in abuse of power over one of his subjects, Naboth.[19] Ahab wanted to buy Naboth's vineyard but Naboth resolutely refused. In refusing he also invoked the divine command which had been given to protect individual families in Israel against the greedy intentions of those who wished to expand their territories. Ahab, under the influence of Jezebel, flouts this law by having Naboth killed and then claiming his land. Elijah is sent to challenge Ahab concerning his disobedience to God and abuse of others. Just as Ahab's idolatrous disobedience led to abuse, so Elijah's God-centredness leads to a passion for justice. The prophet of God stands outside the political regime, but observes its behaviour. This behaviour is then assessed in the light of God's standards for government.

Prophets also hold out an alternative vision of what government as God intended would look like. This alternative vision stands as a condemnation of much contemporary practice. Isaiah, Amos and others insist that justice and a concern for the poor must characterize those in authority, because their author-

---

[18] 1 Kgs. 16:31-2.
[19] 1 Kgs. 21.

ity is delegated to them by God and to be used in accordance with God's intentions for all people. The prophetic image of the ruler as a shepherd carefully tending his flock expresses this alternative vision powerfully. Ezekiel proclaims judgment on the 'shepherds of Israel' because they had exploited the flock when their mandate from God was to care for it. 'You eat the curds', he says, 'clothe yourselves with the wool and slaughter the choice animals, but you do not take care of the flock. You have not strengthened the weak or healed the sick or bound up the injured'. Having rejected the false shepherds God proclaims that he will take control himself and see to it that justice is done. This will mean acting on behalf of the weak. 'Because you shove with flank and shoulder, butting all the weak sheep with your horns until you have driven them away. I will save my flock, and they will no longer be plundered.' Then God 'will place over them one shepherd, my servant David, and he will tend them; he will tend them and be their shepherd. I the Lord will be their God, and my servant David will be prince among them'.[20] Significantly, Jesus fulfils this prophecy when he takes to himself the role of 'shepherd' over those who follow him.[21] His model of a shepherd is a powerful demonstration of the desire to serve, which should mould the actions of all with political power.

Overall, therefore, the prophetic tradition describes an alternative vision of government as God intended it. This government which is marked by a concern for justice and righteousness, puts a radical question mark against all existing forms of government.

The politics of Jesus

Jesus came as the fulfilment of a prophetic tradition that had looked forward to the coming anointed one who, as God's appointed ruler, would bring justice and righteousness to all nations.[22] Jesus, from the start of his ministry, was consciously

---

[20] Ezek. 34:3–4,21–4; cf. 37:2.
[21] Mt. 2:6; 26:31; Mk. 14:27; Jn. 10:1–18.
[22] Isa. 9:1–7; 11:1–9; Mic. 5:1–4; Jer. 23:5–6 and Ezek. 34:22–4.

fulfilling this tradition.[23] He had a clear conviction that all power was derived from God and, therefore, to be used in accordance with God's righteous purposes for all under that power. To understand the outworking of this conviction in the life of Jesus it is necessary to understand the political context in which Jesus lived.

Israel in the time of Jesus was under the overall control of Rome and had to pay the tribute that was due in taxes to the imperial authority. During Jesus' ministry Pontius Pilate was in charge in Judah. As a prefect he was a military governor in charge of a troublesome district of the empire. Galilee was ruled, on behalf of the Romans, by Herod Antipas. Despite the Roman hegemony Israel maintained significant freedoms in various areas. The Jews were not forced to adopt Roman religious beliefs. Neither were they subject to the Roman legal system. The legal system was still Jewish and, ostensibly at least, based on Old Testament law. This meant that though Israel was under Roman military control the authorities that ruled people's lives were the Sadducees who controlled the temple and the scribes and Pharisees who were the guardians of the legal tradition. So, there was no distinction between religious and secular law and the authorities that enforced the law were responsible by Roman permission, for all aspects of life. The only political authority that could be distinguished from a religious authority was Roman and that authority had little to do with the everyday lives of the people other than through the demands of the despised tax collectors.

If the power to punish wrongdoers, short of administering the death sentence, was vested in the Jewish judges, who administered a law that was based on the Old Testament, then they were unquestionably political authorities. They had power to govern. Any clash that Jesus had with them can, therefore, be legitimately described as a political clash. This combination of political and religious power is alien to most people who are used to living in countries where the political life of a country is separate from its religious life. Perhaps Muslim countries, where there is an insistent call for the strict imposition of sharia, would

---

[23] Lk. 4:17ff.

provide the closest parallel to the type of political regime that prevailed in the time of Jesus.

The political significance of Jesus' actions in the context of first-century Palestine emerges strongly in his cleansing of the temple, the repeated arguments about Sabbath observance and his challenge to the authorities concerning obligations to parents.[24]

The temple was the centre not just of the religious life of first-century Judaism, but of its political and economic life as well. To challenge it was to challenge every dimension of the authority of the Jewish leaders. The form of Jesus' challenge reveals at least two reasons for his righteous anger: First, the moneychanging business and the selling of doves in the temple had a detrimental effect on the poor in particular. The demand that the poor had to have temple currency in order to buy doves for the sacrifices provided an opportunity for the ruling authorities to make easy money from those who could ill afford it. Jesus was protesting about this prostitution of the worship of the temple to commercial ends. The temple was supposed to be a place of easy access to God's blessing, where tithes and offerings were brought in and distributed to the poor, and sacrifices were made to cleanse away sin. But it had become a place where the poor were exploited and used to buttress the power and authority of the ruling élite.

In this emphasis on social justice in the context of worship, Jesus echoes a constant Old Testament theme that religious observance without social justice is worthless.[25] It is not surprising, either, that the radical religious, political and economic threat in Jesus' challenge to the temple trade, was at the heart of the allegations against Jesus at his trial before the Jewish leaders.[26]

Second, the religious leaders had also forgotten that Israel and its unique form of worship had a universal mission. Jesus' justification for cleansing the temple was Isaiah's statement that the temple was to be 'a house of prayer for all nations'.[27] The Old Testament prophetic vision, with its roots in the covenant with

---

[24] Mt. 21:12–13; Mk. 11:15–17; Lk. 19:45–8; Jn. 2:13–25; Mk. 7:9–23.

[25] E.g. Isa. 58.

[26] Jn. 2:19; Mk. 14:53ff.

[27] Isa. 56:7.

Abraham, was of a day when people from all nations would come and find cleansing in Zion's temple. The Court of the Gentiles was symbolic of this expectation. However, it was the Court of the Gentiles that was being used for the temple market. So the subjection of temple worship to worldly ends was also a denial of the universal implications of what went on there. This was enough in itself to condemn the temple and to lead to its removal and replacement by Jesus who would become the new locus of God's forgiveness and justice.

Jesus challenged the priestly aristocracy when he cleansed the temple. He was also in constant conflict with the Pharisees and lawyers who represented the other half of Jewish political authority. The arguments over Sabbath observance is a case in point. Jesus consistently went out of his way to break the Sabbath regulations. He argued that the Sabbath law had not been intended as a burden but as a blessing to ordinary people and the poor in particular. Hungry people could pick some corn as they walked through a field on the Sabbath and sick people could be healed. The law was not about keeping regulations but about mercy and love.[28]

Futhermore, in a dispute over ritual cleanliness Jesus charges the Pharisees and lawyers with using the law to subvert the demands of justice in relation to obligations to parents.[29] Though the precise details are not absolutely clear the lawyers had devised a way whereby someone could will their property to the temple so that, though still owning the property, it could not be used except for the benefit of the temple. It seems that this law was used as a way of avoiding responsibility towards parents in a society where older parents were often dependent on their children. Jesus' point was that by clever legal manoeuvring the lawyers had made it possible to ignore the commandment to honour father and mother in order to enrich the temple establishment.

This protest against injustice is particularly instructive because it comes in the middle of a passage about ritual purity. The main point that Jesus makes is that purity is not something that is

---

[28] Mt. 12:1–14.
[29] Mk. 7:6–13.

achieved by means of ritual washings and other external obser-
vances but is a matter of the heart. Unclean actions flow from an
unclean heart and external rituals cannot clean hearts. This is
familiar territory for evangelicals who believe that the most fundamental change that is needed if society is to change for the better
is a change of heart. Such a change can only come through the
cleansing that is possible through the blood of Christ. But that
does not hinder our Lord from pointing out how the legal system
which had been devised by the lawyers was being used to justify
breaking the law. Here the need for justice in human relationships
and heart justification are closely related. Political change should
go hand in hand with spiritual conversion.

The disciples follow their master

The clash between Jesus and the Jewish authorities was part of
the process of converting the focus of God's rule on earth from
the nation of Israel to an international body of people drawn
from all nations sharing an allegiance to Jesus as king. It is to be
expected that this prophetic witness of Jesus should be replicated among his followers. This is precisely what happened in
the case of Peter and John.

They had gone up to the temple to pray one afternoon. As
they were going in a crippled man who was brought to the
temple gate every day to beg asked them for some money. They
had no money to give him so in the name of Jesus they commanded him to get up and walk. To the beggar's astonishment
he found that he had been healed and that his begging days were
over. The healed man's uncontrollable joy, and the fact that he
was well known to those who went to the temple, soon drew a
crowd and gave Peter and John an opportunity to proclaim
Jesus. They were hauled before the Sanhedrin and commanded
not to preach Jesus again. They refused to obey saying, 'Judge
for yourselves whether it is right in God's sight to obey you
rather than God. For we cannot help speaking about what we
have seen and heard.'[30]

---

[30] Acts 4:18–20.

On this occasion the apostles were not punished for preaching Jesus because the Sanhedrin was restrained by the presence of the poor beggar who unquestionably had been healed. They had enough understanding of God's law to appreciate that an act of such obvious goodness on the part of the apostles should not be punished. As with Jesus they were caught in the tension of wanting to hang on to power while being unable to deny that those who were challenging it were doing good. There is a key principle here for the prophetic role of the church with reference to the state. The church can only challenge the injustice of the state on the foundation of doing good to the poor and marginalized.

Principles of Christian political involvement

A number of principles have emerged from our examination of the biblical material which must inform a contemporary Christian response to politics. All political power is derived from God and therefore to be used according to his purposes for humanity. God's purpose in instituting political structures is that good people should be encouraged and that those who do evil should be restrained. Integral to this purpose is the prophetic mandate to 'seek justice, encourage the oppressed. Defend the cause of the fatherless, plead the case of the widow'.[31]

Some political regimes at certain times fulfil to some degree God's plan for them as the authorities Paul has in mind in Romans 13 seem to have done. Even such authorities are not perfect and have areas where improvement is needed. Other political authorities become thoroughly corrupt. Instead of encouraging the good they condone and commit injustices and exploit the poor. Their power is not harnessed to the needs of their whole jurisdiction, but to the whims of an élite. The apostle John seems to have had such a regime in mind in Revelation 13–18.

In these different situations Christians have to work out their response to the authorities prayerfully. The Bible gives a broad range of possible responses from obedience to separation.[32] Fol-

---

[31] Isa. 1:17.
[32] Obedience: Rom. 13:1. Separation: Rev. 18:4.

lowers of God can work within a system to transform it, as modelled perhaps most clearly by Daniel. Equally they can challenge it from outside, as expressed in the prophetic tradition. Often individuals and groups will find themselves at different stages operating both within and outside the system, as Elijah and Obadiah did. Whatever their method, their aim is to see human governments behaving in line with God's purposes.

Something of the breadth of these different Christian responses to complex political realities will be seen in the following three contemporary Christian initiatives which all seek to see government fulfilling its mandate before the God from whom it derives its authority.

Case studies of Christian involvement in politics

Democratization

A broad spectrum of Protestant churches in Ghana, through their representative body, the Christian Council of Ghana (CCG), has sought to develop a model of government appropriate for Ghana which best expresses God's aims for governments. The model seeks to promote structures that would restrain élites while providing a context in which everyone can seek the good of the country through representatives. It is a democratic model through which they hope that the concerns of all groups within Ghana can be heard and responded to.[33] The model has been

---

[33] The word 'democracy' comes from the Greek *demo* (the people as a whole) and *kratia* (rule, governance). It therefore means the exercise of political power by all the people of a given community. Democratization is simply a term for the movement towards democracy in a given situation. In small communities democracy may express itself in all members together making decisions. However, in larger contexts such as the government of countries, it is normally expressed by the whole people freely electing officers to rule over them and to make decisions in accordance with the needs of all sections of the community over which they have authority. The frameworks through which government for the people by the people are expressed, vary enormously from situation to situation. The bottom line of all such frameworks is that the leaders remain accountable to the people they represent. The word 'democracy' is also often used more generally to mark an attitude or culture that can shape any group of people, whether they be family, club or church. Here it refers to an equal treatment of all members with no arbitrary differences of status or privilege.

developed in a series of publications and has been promoted by the CCG among political leaders and church congregations throughout Ghana.[34] It has had a significant influence on the slow progress of Ghana towards multi-party democracy in the early 1990s. The emphasis is not just on change within the national institutions of government, but on the development of a democratic culture within Ghana that could permeate every aspect of society from family to church.

To understand this promotion of democracy as God's way forward, the experience of Ghana since independence in 1957 is significant.[35] Kwame Nkrumah led the newly independent country and within a year had turned the country into a one-party state. His government gave itself considerable powers to suppress any dissent. Nkrumah was deposed by an army led *coup* in 1966, but his reign had set the pattern for things to come. There followed a succession of military governments who did little to foster freedom of political opinion or the right of self-determination.

In 1981 Flt. Lt. J.J. Rawlings gained power in a *coup*. With considerable popular support he has led an economic recovery in Ghana. However, up until the early 1990s his military government, the Provisional National Defence Council (PNDC), had shown little interest in political change towards a multi-party democratic system. Indeed any dissent from his government policy was suppressed, critical newspapers were shut down and hostile individuals punished. Furthermore, recovery has been marked by a disparity in wealth distribution between southern Ghana and the poorer north. When Rawlings succumbed to the demand for a return to a more democratic form of government in 1990 the CCG was originally excluded from the debate but it insisted on being included and went on to make a significant contribution. The CCG was very conscious, as it became involved in the debate, of the need to avoid the mistake made during Nkrumah's time of becoming too identified with

---

[34] See resources section at end of chapter.

[35] It is very similar to the experience of other post-colonial states. See Cammack, P., Pool, D. and Tordoff, W., *Third World Politics, A Comparative Introduction* (London, Macmillan 1993[2]), ch. 1.

political authority. It has been determined, this time, to retain its independence and its prophetic mandate.

It is against this background that the CCG has pressed to ensure that all regions and groups in Ghana can have a forum in which to express their views. The CCG is concerned to avoid the common pattern in post-colonial states of one ethnic or regional élite securing control over the processes of government which they then seek to exploit for their own ends. Such a distribution of power usually leads to poverty for some alongside increasing prosperity for others.

If a representative and accountable system of government is to emerge, the CCG recognizes the need to work to transform the attitudes and expectations of all inhabitants. A culture must be developed in which all people, irrespective of ethnic identity, wealth or status, are seen to matter.[36] Those in any position of authority must use that authority in the interests of those they serve and remain accountable to those over whom they rule. The CCG believe that these values must infiltrate the dynamics of family and church life in particular before they can gain a firm grip on national political life. If an individual has been brought up fearing the absolute, sometimes violent, rule of their parents while worshipping in a church dominated by a leadership that ignores the concerns of its congregation, their chances of understanding representative and accountable government are minimal.

In its work towards the establishment of democratic culture in Ghana, the CCG insists that foundations of the basic elements of democracy lie deep in the gospel. They are also adamant that all systems of government, including those seeking to embody democratic values, remain subject to the judgment of God because they are devised by fallen human beings. Therefore, every system and party must be continually scrutinized against the values of the gospel. No system of government or political party, however enlightened, should be absolutized into the prescribed divine method of governance. The church must always preserve its critical distance from the parties and systems in power so that it can assess their performance against the values of the gospel.

---

[36] *Democratic culture, Constitution and Free and Fair Elections* (Accra, Christian Council of Ghana 1995), pp. 7–8.

Advocacy

Christians in many situations are members of, or are aware of, groups that are excluded from access to political power. This exclusion can often lead to poverty as groups are denied economic opportunity. In this situation it becomes necessary for other groups or individuals to speak up on behalf of the oppressed. This speaking up on behalf of others is what is meant by advocacy. When Christians undertake such action they stand in the tradition of biblical figures such as Elijah who challenged the authorities of his day to honour their God-given obligations to all their citizens.

We will examine three examples of advocacy at local, national and international levels. One important general point needs to be made about advocacy before looking at specific examples. Good advocacy does not leave the power relations that led to the injustice intact. It is not a matter of the powerful talking to the powerful about the powerless.[37] Advocacy should not be about leaving the powerless in exactly the same position as they were in the first place as powerless objects of charity. True advocacy must be combined with the empowerment of those on whose behalf the powerful speak, so that the poor can begin to speak up for themselves. True advocacy stands within the biblical prophetic tradition, also enshrined in Old Testament law, of strengthening the weak and powerless so that they can, with God's help, stand on their own feet.

1. Local

The work of ASHA (Action for Securing Health for All) in some of the slums of Delhi is a good example of what began with simply a desire to provide medical care for the poor leading to political advocacy. ASHA started in 1988 when Dr Kiran Martin responded to God's call to use her medical skills to serve the poor in a Delhi slum. Its work now reaches an estimated 180,000 slum-dwellers. Almost from the beginning Dr Kiran Martin became involved with representing the needs of the powerless slum-dwellers to the government authorities in the form of the

---

[37] See Elliot, C., *Comfortable Compassion? Poverty, Power and the Church* (London, Hodder & Stoughton 1987), for a useful exploration of this theme.

Slum wing of the Delhi Development Authority. She also acted on their behalf with some of the unofficial slum lords. However, increasingly Dr Martin works alongside the slum-dwellers and together they speak up for the needs of the slums. Out of the many examples of this type of work, three are highlighted below:[38]

a) ASHA trains women from the slums to work as health workers. It has become part of that training to teach the health workers how to approach local officials on issues such as housing, sanitation and water provision. Though at a very basic level, dealing with local officials who have the power to affect the way people live is unquestionably political activity.

b) ASHA organizes women's committees in the slums. The purpose of these committees is to develop means of income generation among the women and to give them strength from working together to improve the lot of their families and their environment. For example, when Dr Martin was pressing local government to employ sweepers for the slums some of the women accompanied her. They had been taught that shouting or fighting was not likely to help the cause and their peaceful corporate lobby was successful. A sweeper was appointed for every hundred homes and the women are now responsible for making sure that the work is done properly.

c) One of the most radical features of ASHA's work has been the mobilization of 475 slum-dwelling families into a co-operative housing authority. A dysfunctional slum was turned into an estate of houses with proper roads, drainage, clean water, electricity, health centre, school, park and a clean environment. At the heart of this mobilization was advocacy on behalf of the slum-dwellers. ASHA worked with the Slum wing of the Delhi Development Authority to organize housing loans at a low interest rate with the Oriental Bank of Commerce. Dr Martin in particular has had to defend the rights of the new community against the envious manoeuvrings of the slum landlords who are angry about their loss of influence in the area.

---

[38] See Batchelor, S., *ASHA*: 'Transforming slums by relationships' (Teddington, Tearfund 1997).

2. National

The National Evangelical Council of Peru (CONEP) has been involved at a national level with legal advocacy on behalf of those unjustly accused of terrorism.[39] In June 1994 CONEP was defending 35 individuals, some of whom were evangelicals, in this predicament. A number of cases CONEP has defended have come to national prominence. The case of Juan Mallea, suffering under the very obviously false charge of involvement with the Shining Path guerrilla movement, brought CONEP into direct conflict with President Fujimori. After Juan had been arrested on 10 July 1993 the President expressed his belief that Juan was guilty. CONEP refuted this charge on national television and ran a 'solidarity campaign' on Juan's behalf. This involved a national poster campaign. The same method has been used with other defendants as well. Juan Mallea was eventually acquitted and released in April 1994. R. Perez, the director of the Human Rights department of CONEP commented, 'Mallea's case is forcing within the church a greater sensibility to human rights. By embracing justice and speaking up for the rights of all and not just evangelicals, we can be a prophetic voice in this country.'[40]

3. International

In the chapter on economics we saw something of the impact of the debts owed by developing countries to commercial banks, national governments and international agencies such as the IMF and the World Bank. We also saw how these debts help keep people in poverty. In the United Kingdom Christians, in co-operation with others, have launched an initiative called Jubilee 2000 to address this issue. The overall aim of Jubilee 2000 is to press for the remission of a substantial amount of Third World

---

[39] Paredes, T., 'Peruvian Protestant missionaries and the struggle for human rights, 1980–1993' in *Transformation*, vol. 13, no. 1 (1996).

[40] For a comprehensive treatment of the work of CONEP see Rodriguez, D.L., 'A Critical Evaluation of the Theology of Mission of the National Evangelical Council of Peru (CONEP) from 1980 to 1992, with Special Reference to its Understanding and Practice of Human Rights' (Unpublished thesis submitted to the Open University in partial fulfilment of the requirements for the degree of PhD, 1997).

debt by the year 2000. It works by identifying the effects of the
debt burden at a grass-roots level. It also seeks to gain a thorough
understanding of the dynamics of world-debt relationships.
Armed with this dual perspective it seeks to mobilize an international lobbying response to the problem. To help achieve this
it hopes to organize the largest petition ever. Christians are
happy to be part of this effort because our God of grace is a God
who delights to remit debts and hates to see people crippled by
debts that they cannot pay.

Empowerment

The activities of the Christian Council of Ghana, ASHA, CONEP
and Jubilee 2000 could also have been included under the heading of empowerment. Indeed, unless advocates are concerned
to empower those on whose behalf they plead, the relationships
that keep the poor powerless remain intact. They are examples
of attempts to equip people to develop and use their access to
power and to play their part in the political process. They are a
fulfilment of the purpose of government, according to Ezekiel,
of strengthening the weak.[41] These activities assume that politics
is not something that is done by a select group in society over
which ordinary people have no control but is something that can
be influenced by their involvement.

In many countries central and local government structures
have little input into the lives of the poor. Consequently it is vital
that ordinary people are empowered to tackle their own needs
rather than passively waiting for government assistance.
Ordinary people, therefore, need to be given the power to influence their government both in terms of influencing the decisions
of governing authorities and in terms of taking up the reins of
their own development. We will focus on one initiative that
seeks to empower the poor in both these ways.

Whilst Cambodia is a country rich in resources, most of its
people since the 1970s have lived in poverty. Rural communities
have fragile food-production systems, inadequate water

---

[41]   Ezek. 34:4.

supplies and chronic health problems. The explanation for this poverty is not shortage of resources but a failure to access those resources. Cambodians view themselves as the helpless victims of circumstances rather than as a people whom God has equipped to be effective stewards of his creation.

There are at least two main sources for this self-perception: First is the people's experience under the brutal rule of the Khmer Rouge from 1975–78. During that awful time people were literally battered into passivity. One Cambodian has described it thus: 'My memories of that time are of the numbness and of trying to stay alive. Not even to think when people were taken from the road and killed right where I was. I couldn't help so I didn't think. Like drowning with no power at all.' After the Khmer Rouge, he continued, 'every institution of society had to be restarted but the people were still passive in the beginning. I felt no dignity at all . . . there was a habit of not being able to decide anything.' Second is the influence of Theravada Buddhism. While it can be argued that Buddhism can be a force for change in communities, the animistic, folk manifestations of it in rural Cambodia encourage people to live in fear of capricious spirits that stifle people's sense of control over their own circumstances.

This is the historical and religious context of the Agriculture, Business and Community Development Programme (ABCD) which was started by Christian Outreach (CO) in 1992 in the rural district of Prey Veng, Cambodia.[42] Cambodians themselves, and foreign development workers working with Christian Outreach, recognized from the start the need to tackle this legacy before any sustainable development could take place. The overall programme goal 'to increase people's ability to initiate change and make choices in an environment of loving relationships' reflects the concern to empower a people crippled by their history. It also highlights the fact that development

---

[42] For more detail see Batchelor, Simon, 'Transforming the mind by wearing hats' (Teddington, Tearfund 1997), a case study of the Agriculture, Business and Community Development (ABCD) work of Christian Outreach in Cambodia.

cannot be an individualistic process but must take place in the context of loving community relationships.

The emphasis of ABCD was on empowering people to think for themselves in order to develop their knowledge, skills and attitudes, but always in the context of the needs of communities. Community animators encourage people to be proactive towards change, setting their own agendas and solving their own problems. The emphasis is on communities making their own choices even if some of these end in failure. The priority, therefore, is not so much on concrete agricultural, water supply and health improvements as on people learning to own the future development of their communities. In the past much development work in Cambodia had focused on technical improvements imported from other countries, which only exacerbated the Khmers' sense of helplessness and powerlessness.

The results of ABCD have been impressive in two ways: Firstly, individuals within communities have been empowered to work together for their community's development, often in growing independence from any external input. The ABCD annual report for 1994–95 gives one example out of many. One particular community

> had had some discussion in the CO animated sessions about the health problems in the village and in particular the expense involved in getting good treatment. Without reference to CO, the Village Development committee called a village meeting. They suggested that the village form three associations. Membership would be voluntary. If a family was a member of the association and became sick (or died), everyone else in the association would give some money and a bowl of uncooked rice ... a sort of health insurance for everyone. The village agreed and over 90 per cent now belong to one of the three associations.[43]

Communities have also been empowered to stand against injustices that they passively accepted in the past. In Food for Work programmes, for example, they had been cheated out of some of the rice they rightfully earned through faulty weighing

---

[43] Ibid.

procedures. In the past they had simply accepted the unfairness. Now they sent back rice not of the correct weight demanding proper redress if they were to work again. The full quantity of rice returned. Ordinary Cambodians are learning to challenge corrupt practices.

Secondly, there has been a much better than normal improvement in the more standard 'development' activities of agriculture, water supply and health care as people have taken control over their own development. These advances are likely to be sustainable, in a way that much externally generated advances are not, because they are owned by the people themselves.

Significantly, empowerment at the political level has gone hand in hand with an increasing willingness to scrutinize critically, religious beliefs that were previously accepted automatically. Some have discovered their existing Buddhist and animist beliefs to be inadequate and have turned to Christianity. This discovery did not arise from specific evangelism initiatives, but from the combination of rediscovering critical faculties that had lain dormant for years and from the Christian attitude of CO staff.

The ABCD approach is consciously dependent on the work of Paulo Freire who is a key figure in the growing emphasis on empowerment among those involved in work among the poor.[44] Freire is a Brazilian Roman Catholic educationalist who worked for many years among poor peasants. As an educator he came to the conclusion that making illiterate poor peasants literate was not enough to lift them from the grip of poverty. Education for them had to include the fact that they were exploited and oppressed. Their need was not only to read and write but to understand the way their social and economic circumstances kept them in the grip of poverty. It is only when the poor come to see that their circumstances are no accident but the result of a system which operates in favour of the rich, and against them, that they can begin to move in the direction of freedom. This type of education empowers the poor.

Empowerment, for which Freire used the ugly term 'conscientization', must not be an individualistic process but a means of awakening a whole community so that when there is

---

[44] See Freire, P., *Pedagogy of the Oppressed* (Harmondsworth, Penguin 1972).

any move towards improvement, benefits will come to the whole community and not to some select individuals. It is this emphasis on the social which is at the root of the severe criticism of the advocates of conscientization of much Western development theory and practice. They see Western development as an individualistic process aimed at rescuing select individuals from poverty while leaving the majority where they are. It is perceived as a way of transferring a few from the impoverished to the comfortable class and thus perpetuating the division in society which ensures the comfort of the few and the impoverishment of the many. Some even go as far as to identify 'development' entirely with this process and, so, reject it entirely as unhelpful Western interference aimed at perpetuating poverty. Freire's approach is seen as a means of giving poor communities the confidence to believe that they can stand up for their rights and gain their freedom.

Since 'liberation theology' is a theology that sets out to understand the Christian faith from the perspective of poverty and oppression it is not surprising that a close link has developed between it and the insights of Freire. Empowerment is seen as an important aspect in the 'gospel' of liberation for the poor. This is seen very clearly in the formation of the Base Ecclesial Communities which are small groups of poor people meeting together to study the Bible, pray and work together to liberate their communities politically and economically. In this context liberation from poverty is seen as a process which begins in the hearts of the poor. The only hope is for the poor to appreciate their own value and to understand the forces that crush them. On this basis they can stand up together and demand, not only bread, but justice too. Demanding justice is a political activity. What the poor need most of all is to be empowered to engage in such activity.

There can be no doubt that the conscientization movement and liberation theology have introduced elements into development thinking that have tilted it in a more biblical direction. The focus on the dignity of the poor is obviously consistent with the biblical view of human beings and with the Old Testament legislation that specifically addresses the issue of poverty. The emphasis on justice to the poor is also consistent with the prophetic tradition of the Old Testament which teaches us that poverty cannot be divorced from economics and politics. These movements have also drawn attention to the fact that freedom from poverty begins in the hearts of poor persons. This emphasis is profoundly consistent with the gospel.

One problem flowing from the emphasis on conscientization is the inevitable potential for conflict. If the poor are taught to understand the reasons for their oppression, anger towards their oppressors is bound to be generated. So, how to channel and control this anger needs to be addressed. This is particularly relevant in a Christian context because anger can so easily become hatred of the oppressor. Added to this is the threat that the oppressors are bound to feel when the oppressed begin to question their behaviour. Violence and conflict is a very likely result. In these situations Christians need to consider the example of Jesus who, as we saw, challenged the political system, thereby arousing its wrath, but remained able to cry to God for the forgiveness of those who crucified him.[45]

In fact, without a strong emphasis on the cross and forgiveness, attempts at empowerment are in danger of leaving the poor in a worse state of powerlessness and victimization. Simply to convince the poor that they need to wrest power from the hands of their oppressors if they are to find economic freedom is to confirm the poor in their powerlessness. All that is achieved is the demonization of the rich, which breeds hatred and violent conflict, and a victim mentality, which breeds bitterness. Conscientization in the context of the cross creates a people who know their inestimable value to God and who are freed to love in the context of their family, community and society at large. Not that they ignore injustice, because injustice is a failure of love, but they recognize that the cross embraces oppressed and oppressor in its judgment and offer of forgiveness.[46]

---

[45] Lk. 23:34.
[46] See Perkins, J., *A Quiet Revolution* (Basingstoke, Marshalls 1976), especially ch. 19, 'Why I Can't Hate Anymore', and Sugden, C., 'Christ as Saviour from sin and death and as Liberator from socio-economic and political oppression' in *Evangelical Review of Theology*, vol. 18 (1994), pp. 128–36.

Resources

Books

Hatfield, Mark, *Between a Rock and a Hard Place* (Waco, Word 1976), is a powerful testimony of a respected Christian politician in the USA Senate.

Marshall, Paul, *Thine is the Kingdom: A Biblical Perspective on the Nature of Government and Politics Today* (London, Marshalls 1984).

Kirk, Andrew, *God's Word for a Complex World* (Basingstoke, Marshall Pickering 1987), focuses on politics as one major theme.

Bauckham, Richard, *The Bible in Politics: How to Read the Bible Politically* (London, SPCK 1987).

Wallis, Jim, *The Soul of Politics, A Practical and Prophetic Vision for Change* (London, Fount 1994), seeks to find a new political route that transcends the sterile conflict of Left and Right.

Schluter, Michael, and Lee, David, *The R Factor* (London, Hodder & Stoughton 1993), is a plea for a politics that is built around relationships.

Yoder, J. Howard, *The Politics of Jesus* (Grand Rapids, Eerdmans/ Carlisle, Paternoster 1994[2]), convincingly demolishes the belief that Jesus had nothing to do with politics.

Publications from the Christian Council of Ghana (CCG) include:

The Church and Ghana's Search for a New Democratic System: A Study Material for Christians (Accra, Christian Council of Ghana 1990).

Mensah, Robert, A. *The Church, Ethnicity and Democracy* (Accra, CCG 1994).

Democratic Culture, Constitution and Free and Fair Elections (Accra, Christian Council of Ghana 1995).

Not specifically Christian

This is probably the best place to mention Paulo Freire's *Pedagogy of the Oppressed* (Harmondsworth, Penguin 1996), which has had a very profound influence on work among the poor.

Articles

Here again there is a lot of material in *Transformation*. No less than nine whole issues have been devoted to political themes. The following are representative examples: 'Gospel to the nations: reflections on Christian political praxis' in vol. 14, no. 1 (1997); 'Sex, money and politics' in vol. 12, no. 1 (1995); 'Asian perspectives on church and state and nation building' in vol. 6, no. 3 (1989); 'Focus on human rights' in vol. 1, no. 3 (1984).

Batchelor, Simon, 'Transforming the mind by wearing hats' (Teddington, Tearfund 1997). A case study of the Agriculture, Business and Community Development (ABCD) work of Christian Outreach in Cambodia.

Batchelor, Simon, 'Transforming the slums by relationships' (Teddington, Tearfund 1996). A case study of the work of ASHA in the slums of Delhi.

NINE

Ethnic Identity, Poverty and the Kingdom

Including a chapter on ethnic identity in a book on God and the poor may be surprising to some readers. The reason for its inclusion should become obvious as its content unfolds but the following representative facts should be justification enough. According to the United Nations High Commission for Refugees (UNHCR) there were 27 million refugees at the beginning of 1996 and 50 million Internally Displaced People (IDPs) within different countries. A large proportion of this vast number of destitute people had been displaced as a result of conflicts with a significant ethnic as well as political component. In the USA the African-Americans are on average much poorer than Americans of European origin. In 1994 up to 800,000 people were murdered in Rwanda because of their ethnic identity despite the significant popularity and influence of the church in that country.

What is ethnic identity?

People's ethnic identity is their membership of a particular group of people who share combinations of the following: language, religion, territory, social organization, culture, race, common origin and common future. The group may comprise the majority of the inhabitants of a particular country, but more often it will be a minority of a country's inhabitants. People's ethnic identity may be more or less important to them depending on the way their ethnic group is treated. Awareness of ethnic identity is often intensified when a particular group experiences abuse or discrimination. In such cases the threat may be to one aspect of ethnic identity such as language, or, at its worst, it may be a genocidal threat to the continued physical existence of the group as a whole. A heightened awareness of ethnic identity can also be triggered by the propaganda of élites who seek to use it as a political weapon. This is what happened with terrible consequences in Bosnia and Rwanda in the 1990s.

The combination of shared characteristics will vary between different ethnic groups and over time within the same ethnic group. Many ethnic groups before the formation of modern nation states shared territory and social organization. Now they often share religion, culture and language while territory has to be shared with other ethnic groups. Ethnic distinctions can also be blurred by intermarriage, and language differences can be blurred by the language of a dominant ethnic group in a state. Thus 'ethnic identity changes in intensity over time'.[1] However, strong feelings of ethnic identity can exist even where many of the objective common bonds have been weakened. It can also be reconstructed by fear and clever propaganda.

Ethnic identity and national identity

'Ethnic' is derived from *ethnos* which is the Greek word for 'nation'. But what is a 'nation'? The definition in the Concise Oxford Dictionary is a 'large number of people of mainly common descent, language, history etc., usually inhabiting a territory bounded by defined limits and forming a society under one government'. The main problem with this definition is its identification of 'nation' and 'a society under one government'. Far from being the norm implied in this definition, nations in the sense of a 'large number of people of mainly common descent,

---

[1] Hettne, B., 'Ethnicity and Development: An Elusive Relationship' in Dwyer, D. and Drakakis-Smith, D. (eds.), *Ethnicity and Development: Geographical Perspectives* (Chichester, John Wiley 1996), p. 17.

language, history etc.', form a society under one government only in a small number of instances. There often seems to be very little correspondence between the administrative unit of the state and national identity in the sense of common descent, language and history.

This is particularly the case in the states that have gained their independence from colonial rule in the twentieth century. India is a good example at the most complex end of the spectrum. About three-quarters of the population is racially Indo-Aryan but divided linguistically into at least 16 groups. According to the 1971 census the total number of Indian languages was 1652 with 33 being spoken by more than 100,000 people. Hindi, English and 16 other languages have official status at some level of government. The Indo-Aryan racial group dominates in percentage terms but the numbers are so large in the Indian context that the three other racial groupings can hardly be considered insignificant. Then the racial groupings themselves are divided in terms of language and history, although the British Raj and post-independence India have created something of a common history. But on the whole there is very little in common between what defines a 'nation' and a 'state' in India's case.

Indeed, a comprehensive survey of all the 237 countries in the world in 1996 would confirm over and over again that 'nations' are *not* a 'large number of people of mainly common descent, language, history etc., *usually* inhabiting a territory bounded by defined limits and forming a society under one government'.

'Nation' in European thought and experience since the Enlightenment

To question the validity of a definition in a prestigious English dictionary is no light matter. In fact the definition could reflect correctly the way in which the word 'nation' is used in English so that what is being questioned is not the definition but the English understanding of 'nation'. This definition of nation, since it does not reflect the real situation, may be more of a reflection of Western European experience of nationhood since the period of the Enlightenment in the eighteenth century.

European nations have been organized and governed by their governments as if their populations were ethnically homogeneous. The ethnic majorities in the European nations have built national cultures, an understanding of history and governmental apparatus which ignores ethnic differences among their inhabitants. The active oppression of minority ethnic groups has been very commonplace.

The idea that people speaking the same language and with a common history and traditions should be united in one state became popular in Europe in the nineteenth century as a result of the French Revolution. Germany and Italy, for example, were divided into a large number of small independent states until Italy was united as recently as 1870 and Germany by 1871.

The thinking behind this European movement towards national unification had sinister consequences. The French believed that through the Revolution they had discovered their soul. They became united around an ideal which they believed would bring benefit to all mankind. In the wars that followed the Revolution the French saw themselves as crusaders in the cause of justice. This idea of uniting a people, not only because of the accidents of history and language, but around a superior ideal that was conceived as the soul of a nation, was used to justify the European imperialistic expansion of the nineteenth century. Its most terrible fruit was the horrible carnage of the Second World War.

The European nation-building process also describes the experience of Britain where the oppressive unification of different ethnic groups was never fully achieved, leaving festering problems. In 1800 Great Britain and Ireland were united under one government. This British state was predominantly English but it contained Irish, Scots and Welsh who were significant minorities with their own languages, history and traditions. The situation was further complicated in Ireland because the dominant religion was Roman Catholicism as opposed to the Protestantism of the rest of Britain. The dominant English administration deliberately set out to create uniformity which involved measures to discourage the use of minority languages.

In the case of Ireland it also involved the imposition of Anglicanism and the sequestration of land to English landlords. By the end of the nineteenth century there was a fully fledged nationalist movement in Ireland prepared to take up arms in the cause of political independence. This campaign led to independence for Southern Ireland in 1921. The cost was partition because the predominantly Scottish and Protestant north preferred to remain in union with Britain. The idea that nation, in this case the Irish Gaelic Catholic nation, and state must be united has been the root cause of the bitter conflict which persists in Northern Ireland. In so far as unification under one state remained elusive, the experience of Great Britain mirrored what would happen in the Third World.

'Nation' in the Third World experience

When the European colonial empires collapsed after the Second World War the new independent nations that emerged were a bewildering amalgam of different peoples, languages, history and traditions that had been thrown together for the convenience of colonial administration. The 'nations' were far from peoples of mainly common language, religion, territory, social organization, culture, race and common origin. Whilst 'in the pre-colonial world ethnicity was one of the principle foundations on which political entities were created' colonial powers had 'paid little heed to such fundamental local forces when recasting the political map of the world in the 19th and 20th centuries'.[2] Given their ethnic diversity, it is amazing that these new countries have remained as stable as they have done. In fact they have proved to be very resilient against the forces of disintegration in many cases. Nevertheless, beneath the appearance of unified nation states, ethnic divisions live on, as the example of India illustrates.

---

[2] Drakakis-Smith, D., 'Ethnicity, development and . . . geography' in Dwyer and Drakakis-Smith, *Ethnicity and Development*, p. 275.

Ethnicity, the nation state and poverty

The superimposing of nationhood on amalgams of different peoples not only masks the existence of ethnic groups, it often also masks their poverty. Traditional ways of measuring the relative wealth/poverty of countries are built on the assumption that the nation state is the unit to be assessed. Therefore economic indicators like GNP give some sense of the economic health of the nation state as a whole but ignore the distribution of wealth within the different ethnic groups comprising that nation state. In many nation states certain ethnic groups suffer even as the state as a whole gets richer. This is not reflected in national economic development statistics.

Statistics mask the common fact that 'development programs frequently are controlled and administered at the higher levels by members of the politically dominant ethnic group; and most of the fruits of development flow into the pockets of a tiny ethnic élite or at best are distributed in a limited manner within the same ethnic group'.[3] In short the ethnic interests of a particular section of a nation state become the interests of that nation state itself leading to the deprivation of other ethnic groups. Martin Luther King famously described the position of the Negro ethnic group within the USA as living 'on a lonely island of poverty, in the midst of a vast ocean of material prosperity'.[4]

Indeed the success of a country as a whole can sometimes be dependent on the exploitation of an ethnic minority within it. For example, when the demands of a nation state's economy for timber exports run contrary to the needs of indigenous forest-dwellers. An ethnic group suffers for the sake of a country run by different ethnic interests. Similarly when the need of an urban élite who monopolize power in a particular country for an electricity-generating plant leads to the building of a reservoir and dam that displaces indigenous ethnic groups. An

---

[3] Dwyer, D., 'Ethnodevelopment or ethnochaos?' in Dwyer and Drakakis-Smith, *Ethnicity and Development*, p. 5.

[4] From the famous 'I have a dream . . .' speech delivered on 28 August, 1963 in Washington, DC.

experience of poverty, therefore, is tied up with political powerlessness as the dominant ethnic groups push on with their
agendas.

The exclusion of certain ethnic groups from countrywide,
regional or community development can simply result in the
gradual decline of ethnic groups, sometimes into extinction.
However, some groups mobilize around their ethnic identity
and seek fairer access to resources and power. As a result various
forms of conflict arise producing yet more poverty.

Ethnicity and conflict

It is estimated that out 'of the 37 major armed conflicts in the
world in 1991, 25 were internal conflicts and that most of these
could plausibly be described as ethnic conflicts'.[5] Interpreting
such data observers increasingly agree that the world 'has been
moving during the course of this century from nation state
conflict to ideological conflict, to finally, cultural conflict . . .'[6]
Internal conflict along ethnic lines can create more poverty
within a country than international wars. It sends refugees to
neighbouring countries, displaces people within their own
country and those left in their own homes have to live with a
decimated infrastructure, a ruined economy and non-existent
public services. In particular, conflict within countries destroys
the social trust necessary for the healthy functioning of communities.

Internal conflicts along ethnic lines fall into two types: secession disputes and, more commonly, disputes over the distribution of power between different ethnic groups.

Secession disputes arise where one ethnic group resents the
control exercised by other ethnic groups over the political, economic and sociocultural structures of the nation state of which
they are a part. Consequently, they seek to set up their own
independent homeland. Unsuccessful attempts to break away
and form a national homeland include that of the Ibo in Nigeria,

---

[5] Dwyer, D., 'Ethnodevelopment' p. 3.
[6] Kaplan, R., 'The Coming Anarchy' in *Atlantic Monthly* (Feb 1994).

the Shaba in Zaire and the Punjab in India. Attempts still under way include the Tamils from the Sinhalese in Sri Lanka and the people of East Timor from Indonesia. Bangladesh is a rare example of a successful national breakaway from a nationally complex state. The Eritreans also fought a long war with Ethiopia which eventually led to independence.

What happened in Yugoslavia is a combination of a secession dispute and intense conflict over the distribution of power. However one tries to categorize what happened, it is a vivid example of the awful consequences of an ethnic conflict.

Yugoslavia was born during the Second World War as a complex amalgamation of different languages, religions and histories. Despite the very live memory of Croatian collaboration with the Nazis, which had led to the massacre of up to 500,000 Serbs, Tito was able to keep these two major groups together, as well as the Slovenes, Bosnians, Albanians, Macedonians and Montenegrins. These seven ethnic groups made up about 90 per cent of Yugoslavia's population. The remaining 10 per cent was made up of Gypsies, Hungarians, Turks, Slovaks, Bulgarians, Romanians, Arabs and Czechs. There had already been a lot of intermingling of these different groups before Tito came to power in 1945 because they had all been part of the Austro-Hungarian Empire. Under Tito, who ruled until his death in 1980, the intermingling continued, particularly in Bosnia.

After Tito's death the federation soon began to fall apart. Then with the collapse of communism in Eastern Europe the different nations were free to rediscover their distinctive religious and historical traditions. With this rediscovery traditional animosities were also rediscovered, particularly between the Serbs, Croats and Bosnians. The Slovenes to the north were able to break free and become an independent nation with very little conflict or bloodshed. Macedonia to the south has also become independent without conflict. The Montenegrins have remained bound with Serbia in what is left of the Yugoslav Republic. Croatia and Bosnia declared their independence but have been involved in a terrible territorial conflict with the Serbs who have laid claim to substantial portions of Croatia and Bosnia. Ironically these three nations speak a very similar language, although the Croatians and Serbs use a different script. Their differences are rooted more in a history of conflict linked to their religious traditions – the Croats are Roman Catholic, the Serbs Greek Orthodox and the Bosnians Muslims.

As they laid claim to parts of Bosnia and Croatia the Serbs cleared the territory they were claiming of all its non-Serbian population. The Croats also, in laying claim to parts of Croatia inhabited by Serbs, have driven out the Serb population. Serb, Croatian and Bosnian neighbours who had lived next to each other in peace for generations became enemies overnight and drove each other into exile. The chilling term 'ethnic cleansing' was coined to describe this process. Awful cruelty has been perpetrated by all sides. The Bosnians and Croats eventually came together to make a common cause against the Serbs but a terrible legacy of hatred and bitterness has been left for future generations.

Alongside struggles on the part of national groups to break away from a multi-ethnic state to form their own ethnically homogenous states, and inter-ethnic struggles after the break-up of federations, are struggles over the distribution of power within multi-nation states. In one sense this corresponds to the second stage in the development of the Western European ideal of the nation state. The first stage was the unification of the national grouping so that its 'soul' could be manifested in all its glory. The second stage was to assert the superiority of that 'soul' over the 'souls' of other nations. The normal expression of this superiority was military conquest but it could be expressed in cultural terms as well – as superior knowledge, athletic prowess, institutional forms, economic success, and so on. In multi-ethnic states a similar struggle occurs, but within the country itself, among different ethnic groups. This struggle for dominance has torn many countries apart in the past and continues to do so. In fact, there is room to fear that this type of struggle is on the increase. Among numerous examples, that of Rwanda will be focused on as a case study at the end of this chapter.

The evangelical contribution to the development of ethnic consciousness

From the beginning the modern Protestant missionary movement has laid a heavy emphasis on preaching the gospel in the language of unevangelized peoples. Central to this policy is the desire to give any unevangelized people at least a part of the Bible in their own language as soon as possible. It is now generally recognized that translating the Bible has played a significant part in strengthening ethnic consciousness. Many members of ethnic groups, whose language had not been written down before the missionaries came, witness to the ennobling effect of seeing the word of truth being clothed in their own tongue. The fact that God can speak their language gives them a sense of honour and dignity.

A second factor in the contribution of evangelicals to the growth in ethnic consciousness can be seen in the missionary policy that underlies contemporary church-planting movements. The 'AD 2000 and Beyond' movement is a good example. The battle-cry of this movement is, 'A church for every people and the gospel for every person by the year 2000.' To achieve this end it is attempting to define in detail what is meant by 'every nation, tribe, language and people'. The assumption is that if the task is clearly defined we can know when it will be completed. In view of their slogan the key term in the series of four in Revelation is 'people'. They speak of people *groups* as communities 'which perceive themselves as having an affinity with each other (e.g. a common culture, language, home or occupation)'.[7]

People groups are groups of people who can be distinguished from other groups irrespective of their original territorial location. For example, the Tamils, as an ethnic group, have been historically associated with the territory of Tamil Nad in South India. Some have migrated in such significant numbers that they

---

[7] *AD 2000 & Beyond Handbook* (Colorado Springs, AD 2000 and Beyond 1992), p. 73. Similarly, in *Mission Frontiers* (Jan–Feb 1993), p. 6, a bulletin of the U.S. Center for World Mission, A People Group/People is defined as 'a significantly large ethnic or sociological grouping of individuals who perceive themselves to have a common affinity for one another'.

can retain their identity in the place to which they have migrated. This is true of the large Tamil population of northern Sri Lanka but also of concentrations of Tamils in cities such as Delhi, Bombay and Bangalore. There are many such people groups, particularly in large cities, all over the world. The 'AD 2000 Movement' insists that these fragments of ethnic groups need to be touched by the gospel in the context of their own history and culture. What they are is to be affirmed. Assimilation of peoples is not on the mission agenda. The traditional evangelical missionary policy that people must be reached through their own language still prevails.

The outworking of this policy may have political repercussions for oppressed ethnic minorities. It is not impossible that some indigenous groups in South America, for example, having been empowered by the gospel, will eventually demand political independence for certain areas within countries that have been dominated by people of European origin.

The nations in the purpose of God

The origin of nations/ethnic groups

The origin of different ethnic groups can be found in the first command given by God to human beings: 'God blessed them and said to them, "Be fruitful and increase in number; fill the earth and subdue it." '[8] It was God's original intention that human beings should spread out over all the earth. This is re-emphasized in Deuteronomy 32:8: 'When the Most High gave the nations their inheritance, when he divided all mankind, he set up boundaries for the peoples . . .' This verse reflects the early history of humanity in which different ethnic groups were associated with different territories. As expansion, migration and conquest occurred this association of ethnic group with specific territories became more blurred. Genesis 10 shows how these nations inevitably came into being as families multiplied and spread out over the face of the earth, starting from the three sons of Noah.

---

[8] Gen. 1:28.

However, in Genesis 11 we find humanity trying to obstruct this creative process in the plain of Shinar: 'Then they said, "Come, let us build ourselves a city, with a tower that reaches to the heavens, so that we may make a name for ourselves and not be scattered over the face of the whole earth." '[9] Their reluctance to be scattered came from their desire to build their own security and reputation independent of obedience to God. Far from showing obedience, they sought to rival God. The serpent had promised Adam and Eve that they would be like God if they took of the forbidden tree and the reason given by God for expelling them from Eden and access to the tree of life was that they had 'become like one of us'.[10] The implication here is that fallen humans would be able to use the considerable powers given them by God to grasp at the throne of God itself. If they had continued to have access to the tree of life their ability to grasp at divine power would have been greatly enhanced. The same would have been the case if the situation of linguistic solidarity had prevailed beyond Babel. Confusing the language of the builders of Babel, therefore, was not a curse but a blessing. It was the means that God employed to bring about his original intention that human beings should fill the earth and not be able to unite in rebellion against him.[11]

This understanding of the purpose of God's action against the Tower of Babel should correct the view that the creation of many languages in Genesis 11 was a curse that was removed at Pentecost. It is very difficult to accept that a divine action directed towards fulfilling a divine intention for the blessing of human beings could ever be understood as a curse. What happened at Pentecost was that all the representatives of the many nations gathered together in Jerusalem heard the good news of the gospel *in their own languages.*[12] The wonder of Pentecost was not the denial of linguistic diversity but its affirmation. The message of Jesus was to be spoken in all the languages of the world.

---

[9] Gen. 11:4.

[10] Gen. 3:5, 22.

[11] See MacFhionnlaigh, Fearghas, 'Creative tensions: personal reflections of an evangelical Christian and Gaelic poet', in *Scottish Bulletin of Evangelical Theology*, vol. 4, no. 1, pp. 37–44.

[12] Acts 2:11.

God's sovereignty over the nations

To say that God is sovereign over the nations is but another way of saying that he is Lord of history. What this means is clearly spelt out by Paul in his address to the intellectuals of Athens: 'From one man', Paul states, '[God] made every nation of men, that they should inhabit the whole earth; and he determined the times set for them and the exact places where they should live.'[13] No nation is inherently superior to another nation because of its origin, according to Paul, because all nations have a common origin. Similarly, no human being is inherently superior to any other human being since they are all created in the image of God, although this image has been universally polluted by the Fall. Paul therefore challenges the Greek idea that they were superior to other humans because they had not come to Greece from somewhere else but had sprouted spontaneously from the soil of their beloved land.

It is significant that Paul sees the 'times' as well as the 'places' of the nations as under God's sovereign direction. This can mean, firstly, that in their interaction with each other the ascendancy of one or other of the nations has a fixed time. The domination of certain nations over vast tracts of the earth must have seemed very permanent at certain points in history. In the long view this is seen not to be the case. Every nation, every empire has had its 'time'. They have all risen, ruled and fallen into ruin.[14]

Secondly, it could mean that nations, in the context of human history at least, have a specific time allotted to them in absolute terms. Not only can nations flourish, but they can also disappear altogether. This happens when all its members die, as in the case of the Tasmanians, Mohicans and many other indigenous peoples, or when its members are assimilated into a more dominant nation, as is happening in many parts of the world at present. The fact that the number of tribal languages in Brazil has gone down from 1000 to 200, since the nineteenth century, witnesses to this process of assimilation. Since the disappearance of nations is the result of oppression and injustice it is unlikely that

---

[13] Acts 17:26.
[14] See, for example, Job 12:23.

Paul had this second possible meaning of 'times' in mind. The fact that nations can disappear reminds us that they are not absolute entities, and can never, therefore, command absolute allegiance. But just as the disappearance of flora or fauna off the face of the earth leaves everyone impoverished it may also be true that the disappearance of any nation or language has the same effect.

God's chosen nation

God's sovereignty over the nations is the vital backdrop to the central drama of the Bible which is God's dealings with his chosen nation or ethnic group, Israel. The chosen nation was created to play out a didactic drama for the benefit of all people groups. This was made clear to Abram, the father of the chosen nation, when God called him to leave the comfort of a sophisticated ancient civilization and become a wandering nomad in a land which would one day be possessed by his numerous descendants. God says to Abram that 'all peoples/nations on earth will be blessed through you'.[15]

The history of Israel in relation to other ethnic groups reveals how God views international/ethnic relations. In particular, the history of the Hebrew nation up to and including the life of Jesus can be seen as one of learning to live as an ethnic, religious and cultural minority often under the authority of aggressive empires.

The experience of the chosen people under the Pharaohs of Egypt provides the first experience of living as an ethnic minority under an alien and exploitative hegemony. Significantly, God has compassion on them as an alien minority suffering abuse.[16] Such compassion becomes enshrined in the laws given to Moses concerning the treatment of ethnic 'aliens' by Israel. Alongside compassion, God punishes Egypt for their failure to meet the standards of divine justice.

For some time after the conquest of Canaan God's chosen people enjoyed a period of self-governance. They ran their own ethnic state apparatus but they were expected to show compas-

---

[15] Gen. 12:3.
[16] Ex. 3:7.

sion to outsiders from other ethnic groups who sought to live in their midst. Some of those outsiders become key figures within Israelite history. Rahab the Canaanite and Ruth the Moabite are good examples. However, the experience of being a 'nationstate' was soon lost.

The northern Kingdom of Israel was conquered and dispersed by Assyria in 721 BC. Then Judah went into exile in Babylon in 586 BC. The exile was God's punishment on Judah, but the Babylonians who carried out the sentence were also guilty of injustice in relation to God's chosen people. After liberation from Babylon, the Hebrew nation lived on as an ethnic minority under the relatively peaceful rule of Persia. Then came the sometimes terrible period of Greek hegemony. By the time of Jesus, the Hebrew nation was in what has been described as a state of semi-exile under the ultimate jurisdiction of the Roman Empire.

The Old Testament, therefore, is full of information about living as an ethnic minority within an alien environment, as well as information as to what God demands from the behaviour of dominant powers. Christians within minorities throughout the world can learn from and identify with the experience of Israel, an experience which reaches its climax in the isolation and exclusion of the 'suffering servant' of Isaiah 53.

Ethnic identity transcended

As the story of God's chosen people unfolds, God's nation comes to be defined not so much in terms associated with ethnic groups such as territory, social structure and culture but in terms of faithfulness to God. This process reaches its climax in Isaiah's 'suffering servant'. God's servant is not the physical descendant of Abraham, but the 'suffering servant' who has 'not been rebellious' and has 'not drawn back'.[17] His qualification to serve God is not his ethnic origin from Abraham but his obedience. He will have no physical descendants but many children from all nations who, through him, will come to live in obedience to God.[18]

---

[17] Isa. 50:5.
[18] Isa. 42:1; 53:8–10; 56:6–7.

The story of God's chosen people, therefore, anticipates the New Testament concept of God's people/nation as those from every nation, Jew or Gentile, who make the Messiah their king. According to Paul the promise to Abraham that all nations would be blessed in his seed was fulfilled as the Gentiles were justified by faith in Jesus.[19] Christ's great achievement, according to Paul, was to open a pathway to God that transcended this fundamental national distinction. The gospel knows no privileged nation. Human beings from every nation can come to God in exactly the same way through Jesus Christ: 'Here [in Christ] there is no Greek or Jew, circumcised or uncircumcised, barbarian, Scythian, slave or free, but Christ is all, and is in all.'[20]

Peter picks up the same theme at the beginning of his first letter. He describes those to whom he was writing as 'God's elect . . . scattered throughout Pontus, Galatia, Cappadocia, Asia and Bithynia'.[21] He describes those that had become Christians from all these nations as 'a holy nation [*ethnos*], a people [*laos*] belonging to God . . . Once you were not a people [*laos*]', he goes on, 'but now you are the people [*laos*] of God'.[22] Peter is clearly saying here that Christians from a variety of nations have replaced the Jews as God's nation. He uses the Greek word *laos* that is used to translate *'am* in the Greek Old Testament. *'Am* is the word used to describe the special relationship between the Jews as a nation and God in the Old Testament. Allegiance to Christ, therefore, defines the most fundamental sense of community for the Christian. Being united in Christ with others from a whole variety of nations brings into being an alternative nation or people. This reconciliation of different ethnic groups within the church is integral to God's saving purpose. Ethnic identity, therefore, is made radically relative when a person becomes a member of God's new 'nation'.

---

[19] Rom. 4.
[20] Col. 3:11.
[21] 1 Pet. 1:1.
[22] 1 Pet. 2:9–10.

Ethnic identity not destroyed

Given God's original intention at creation to create human beings who would spread out all over the earth forming different nations, the book of Revelation re-emphasizes that the nations have a place in the eternal purpose of God. The key passage is Revelation 21:24–6, which is a part of the description of the heavenly city. There will be no need for sun and moon in that city because God will be its light and the Lamb its lamp. 'The nations will walk by its light, and the kings of the earth will bring their splendour into it . . . The glory and honour of the nations will be brought into it.' There is a strong echo of Isaiah 60:1–11 in these verses. Isaiah was looking beyond the judgment on the unfaithful nation of Israel to the time when the glory of Zion would be brighter than ever. At that time the nations will be drawn to Jerusalem to pay their homage and to bring their offerings. The wealth of the nations will be offered to the King of Kings. The 'glory and honour' of the nations to which John refers could include not only gold and silver and precious stones but also the craft and praise of the nations. Homage is not only expressed with material gifts but also with words and acts of praise. John could be referring to all that is best of a nation's material and aesthetic culture being offered to God in his glorious heavenly city.

Our calling, therefore, is not to deny our nationhood, but to sanctify it. Any contribution that any nation may have made in any sphere to the glory of the King is not going to be forgotten. As I. Howard Marshall expresses it in a comment on Revelation 21:12,26:

> Culture is inextricably bound up with people; it is people which form societies, and so if the people move over into the next world, to some extent their societies and thus some aspects of their culture go with them. It can be objected that this is not so, that in heaven they neither marry nor are given in marriage, and human society as we know it no longer exists and is replaced by a colossal individualism in which we are all joined to God in fellowship but not to one another, except perhaps in a holistic, undifferentiated way.

> But to argue this is to imply that the whole of human society-formation, blessed in this life by God, passes away, and the life of the world to come is infinitely poorer than the life of this world. Surely this is a ridiculous conclusion.[23]

The continued existence of nations prior to their presentation before God in the new Jerusalem, also serves a divine purpose that echoes the story of the Tower of Babel. It hinders us from uniting as a human race in our rebellion against God, which would unleash the most terrible evil on earth. The beast in Revelation 13 is presented as the head of a world empire with 'authority over every tribe, people, language and nation'.[24] His rule will be oppressive but the uniting of the nations under one ruler will make available tremendous resources which, because of human pride, will inevitably be used for evil purposes. The economic power of the West is taking us in the direction of such monocultural domination. The prospect that it might succeed is too awful to contemplate.

Paul's ethnic identity and his new identity in Christ

Paul's attitude towards his Jewishness is very instructive in treading a path between transcending and owning one's ethnic identity. On the one hand Paul, more than any other in the early Church, was responsible for demolishing the idea that there is any such thing as national superiority where relationship with God is concerned. In this most fundamental area of our being there is complete equality among human beings. Anything that distinguishes human beings from one another is irrelevant – sex social status and ethnic identity mean nothing where status before God is concerned.[25] All of humanity is under the universal curse of sin and the only way to salvation is by faith in Jesus who redeemed us by his death on the cross. Since this is the case there

---

[23] Marshall, I. Howard, 'Culture and the New Testament' in Stott, J. and Coote, R. (eds.), *Gospel and Culture* (William Carey Library 1979), p. 40.

[24] Rev. 13:7.

[25] Gal. 3:28.

is a profound unity between all who belong to the community of the redeemed. Consequently, Paul can hold his Jewish identity very lightly. Whilst 'to the Jews I became like a Jew, to win the Jews', to 'those not having the law I became like one not having the law'.[26]

On the other hand it seems that Paul saw no contradiction between his central conviction that relationship with Christ entailed a radically new identity, and what was essential to his Jewishness. He had a passionate and self-sacrificing love for his own people. 'I have a great sorrow and unceasing anguish in my heart', he says, 'For I could wish that I myself were cursed and cut off from Christ for the sake of my brothers, those of my own race, the people of Israel'.[27] This is seen clearly in the way he respected his own language and traditions. He was obviously a thoroughly Hellenized Jew in many ways. He was brought up in Cilicia in Asia Minor as a member of the Jewish diaspora. He was fluent in Greek and was a Roman citizen. But as a well-travelled missionary returning to visit Jerusalem he was very happy to observe some traditional Jewish rites that would show his fellow Jews that he had not forgotten his own roots. Having been attacked by a mob in the temple while performing these rites he was able to silence the crowd for some time so that he could speak to them. It is significant that he chose to make his defence in Aramaic which was the native language of Palestinian Jews. In fact it was when they realized that he was speaking Aramaic that the crowd went quiet and gave him a hearing. It may also be significant that Jesus, himself an Aramaic-speaking Jew, chose to address Paul in Aramaic on the road to Damascus. Jesus, like Paul loved his own people passionately despite his knowledge that his calling was to draw people from all nations to God.[28]

Case study: Rwanda

We end this chapter by looking at a situation where many who have claimed to be Christians have failed to live out the fact that

---

[26]   1 Cor. 9:20.
[27]   Rom. 9:3–4.
[28]   Acts. 21:26; 22:2; 26:14.

in Christ their new identity transcends, but does not destroy, their ethnic identity.

Ethnic identity in Rwanda

Rwanda's population is made up of three ethnic groups: the Twa (less than 1 per cent), the Hutu (85–90 per cent) and the Tutsi (10–15 per cent). The consensus among historians is that the three groups are the product of three movements of population into the Rwanda-Burundi area: The Twa from 2000 BC to AD 1000 the Hutu from AD 1000–1500 and the Tutsi from AD 1600–1900.[29] The Tutsi became the dominant military, economic and social force, despite comprising little more than 10 per cent of the population. Nevertheless, within this context of ethnic differentiation, Hutu and Tutsi intermarried, lived in close proximity, fought aggressors together, often belonged to common clans and shared a common language, religion and culture.

However, German and Belgian explorers and colonizers took the existing ethnic relations in Rwandan society and turned them into a full-blown ideology of racial supremacy. The Tutsi were portrayed as the intelligent, sensitive, and sophisticated ruler race while the Hutu became the simple, earthy people who needed to be governed by their racial superiors. This ideology was backed up by actions, particularly by the Belgian administration. Virtually all positions of government power went to Tutsis so that on the eve of independence in 1959, 43 chiefs out of 45 were Tutsi as well as 549 sub-chiefs out of 559.[30]

This ethnic mythology was radically inverted after Rwanda gained independence from colonial administration in 1962. The demands of democracy were now met and the Hutu majority took the reins of power.[31] The Tutsi became 'foreign invaders' who had conquered the Hutu and who could not really be considered as citizens of the new state. Instead they were threatening aliens. The

---

[29] For a brief introduction to the debate, see Waller, D., *Rwanda Which Way Now?* (Oxford, Oxfam 1996), p. 5.
[30] Prunier, G., *The Rwanda Crisis: History of a Genocide* (London, Hurst 1995), p. 27.
[31] *Joint Evaluation of Emergency Assistance to Rwanda Study 4* (Steering Committee of the Joint Evaluation of Emergency Assistance to Rwanda 1996), p. 28.

Hutu had been the native farmers enslaved by these aristocratic invaders but now they were the only legitimate inhabitants of the country. Even so Hutu and Tutsi continued to intermarry, live in close proximity and share a common language and culture. Most also shared at least a nominal Christian faith.

Rwanda became an example of a Western type of nation state in which government was run in the interest of the dominant ethnic group. But it soon developed into what became a typically post-colonial African state which excluded all but the dominant majority from the political process. Under President Habyarimana from 1973–90 Rwanda became a one-party state. During this time the President's family and close associates, called the *akazu*, became more and more powerful. As the economy was run for the benefit of one section of the Hutu population and poverty increased, tensions between Hutus also increased. Meanwhile the Tutsis continued to labour under grave disadvantages and some 600,000 remained outside the country as refugees having been exiled as a result of post-independence interethnic conflict.

The genocide

The tensions eventually exploded in the terrible genocide of 1994. However, the genocide was far from uncontrollable, tribal bloodlust. Rather it was a pre-planned attempt by the Hutu *akazu* to put an end to the threat to their monopoly of power from Tutsi and disgruntled Hutu. This élite manipulated the vast reserves of ethnic fear and hatred within Rwanda to secure their genocidal intent.

Consequently the target group in the genocide of 1994 were moderate Hutu, who had objected to the dominance of the *akazu*, and the entire Tutsi ethnic group. Estimates of the lives lost vary from 500,000 to 800,000. Some 10–30,000 of these were Hutu. The killing was organized systematically according to a meticulous plan prepared by 'higher officials in the local and national government, the army, the Presidential Guard' and President Habyarimana's MRND party.[32] Therefore, 'the killings were no

---

[32] *Joint Evaluation of Emergency Assistance to Rwanda Study 1* (Steering Committee of the Joint Evaluation of Emergency Assistance to Rwanda 1996), p. 51.

spontaneous outbursts, but followed instructions from the highest level'.[33] Orders ultimately came from members of the *akazu*. They worked through the administrative structures of government, the leadership structures of the *Interhamwe* (militias numbering c. 50,000), gendarmerie, Presidential Guards and the Rwandan army. Much of the killing was actually done by militia, police and soldiers, but much of it was also done by ordinary people often organized by government officials. One respected commentator has estimated that 80,000–100,000 people took part in the killing.[34]

Anti-Tutsi propaganda had been pumped into the uncritical masses of Rwanda. Habyarimana's wife had organized the radio station, Radio Television Libre Mille Collines (RTLMC). It broadcast messages designed to prey upon fears that in many cases had lain dormant for years. The basic message was that the Tutsi were about to overrun the country restoring centuries of oppression. The Tutsi were *inyenzi* (cockroaches) who should be stamped out, rats whose babies should be killed lest they return to trouble the Hutu again. It promised great riches to the increasingly impoverished Hutu if the Tutsi were cleansed from Rwanda.

The church and ethnicity in Rwanda

The church in Rwanda has not, in the main, shared God's understanding of ethnic identity. It has failed in three particular ways: First, it failed to address the basic issues of social justice in the country that stemmed from the history and manipulation of ethnic identity. The presence of many refugees from Rwanda in neighbouring countries was a destabilizing factor but also a denial of the human rights of those forced to flee on account of their ethnicity or political view. Yet church leaders did not speak out to urge their speedy repatriation. Indeed, one bishop had appropriated for himself the house of a Tutsi pastor who had fled as a refugee. Similarly the monopolization of political power often coupled with human rights abuses went largely unchallenged by the churches. Far from seeking fair political

---

[33] Ibid. p. 51.
[34] Prunier, The Rwanda Crisis, p. 342.

representation from an early stage, which may have averted the disaster, the institutional Roman Catholic and Anglican churches were closely identified with the dominant political faction. Any critical distance from the political powers was replaced by partisanship since 'if someone puts food in your mouth, then you are not free to speak out'.[35]

Second, the teaching of the church had been narrow in its focus.[36] Missionaries, similarly, preached a pietism that encouraged both 'the withdrawal from the public life of the nation into a spiritual ghetto' and 'a naive and uncritical support of whoever is in power'.[37] There was much repentance from personal sins such as lying, adultery or not paying a tithe, but little attention was paid to the societal evils of political corruption and ethnic discrimination. As long as the individual had their 'ticket to heaven', society could in a sense go to hell. Furthermore, there was a failure to apply the Bible to every area of the people's self-understanding. The result was a widespread syncretism in which converts held on to their ancient animist beliefs. These resurfaced during the conflict. For example, the belief that the spirit of a murdered ancestor would not rest until revenge was taken on the murderer by a living relative.

Beneath the surface of seemingly multi-ethnic churches, ethnic resentment festered on. Hutu could not forgive years of unjust subordination under the Tutsi. Tutsi could not forgive the persecution they had experienced from the Hutu since independence. In a country with so many professing Christians this must indicate a failure to teach the full implications of the believer's new identity in Christ. It is an identity which transcends, but does not obliterate, ethnic identity and enables people to forgive those who have injured them in the past. Instead the propaganda machines of politicians informed the people as to their identity and built on the prejudice born of historical injustice.

---

[35] According to Ian Wallace, Tearfund's International Services Group Leader, this is a refrain often heard in Rwanda concerning the church.
[36] Bowen, R., *Rwanda – Missionary Reflections on a Catastrophe* (An offprint from *Anvil* – An Anglican Evangelical Journal for Theology and Mission 1995), p. 39.
[37] Ibid. pp. 36–7.

Thirdly, influential individuals within the church in Rwanda had become intoxicated with status, power and material gain. Consequently severe tensions arose between church leaders of different denominations or even within the same denomination. Different denominations were in competition for resources from foreign development organizations. As a result different branches of the church were isolated from each other and thus in no position to stand together against the evil of ethnic tension.

Mercifully this is not the whole story of the Rwandan church and the genocide of 1994. Many of the Hutus who died were targeted because of their commitment to reconciliation with the Tutsi community. There are also many heroic stories of evangelical Hutus risking their lives to protect Tutsis. It is tragic that evangelical teaching had left believers with a very limited view of the implications of the gospel, but striking that so many of them were prepared to die rather than harm their Tutsi brothers and sisters. It is also significant that evangelicals are prominent in the task of reconciliation that is ongoing.

Conclusion

Rwanda is an extreme example of what can happen when Christians fail to take seriously the issue of ethnic identity. But ethnic tensions are very common all over the world, and likely to become more of a problem in the future. There is a great need to take on board what the Bible says on this issue. As evangelical Christians we need to continue to affirm ethnic identity. We must be careful to stand alongside those from ethnic minorities who are suffering injustice and oppression. On the other hand we affirm our identity in Christ which transcends our ethnic identity. It is in Christ that we can find the grace even to forgive our oppressors and to embrace them in his name. It is in Christ that we can become agents of reconciliation in a divided world. Reconciliation does not mean that we deny our identity. Like our Lord himself, or the apostle Paul, we can love our ethnic identity. Reconciliation means that we also love the stranger as much as ourselves. We love our own home and everyone else's home as well. A strong leavening of such people in the midst of the multi-ethnic countries and cities of the world can but hinder conflict which plunges so many into sorrow and destitution.

Resources

Books

Molebatsi, Caesar, and Virtue, David, *A Flame for Justice* (Oxford, Lion 1991), provides a challenging account of life for two black South Africans under apartheid; one chose violence and one chose Christianity.

Bilinda, Lesley, *The Colour of Darkness: A Personal Story of Tragedy and Hope in Rwanda* (London, Hodder & Stoughton 1996), provides a harrowing description of some of the effects of ethnic violence in Rwanda.

Mensah, Robert A., *The Church, Ethnicity and Democracy* (Accra, The Christian Council of Ghana 1994). A Ghanaian Christian sets out the necessity of overcoming ethnic division if countries are to develop.

Haslam, David, *Race for the Millennium, A challenge to Church and Society* (London, Church House 1996). Challenging and informative, non-evangelical examination of race issues in the UK.

Volf, Miroslav, *Exclusion and Embrace* (Nashville, Abingdon 1996). Evangelical treatment of ethnic issues by a leading Croat theologian.

Not specifically Christian

Dwyer, D, and Drakakis-Smith, D. (eds.) *Ethnicity and Development: Geographical Perspectives* (Chichester, John Wiley 1996), provides a fascinating, academic grounding to issues of poverty and ethnicity.

Hutchinson, J. and Smith, Anthony D., (eds.), *Ethnicity* (Oxford, OUP 1996), provides useful historical background as well as exploration of the major issues of ethnic identity from an academic perspective.

Prunier, G., *The Rwanda Crisis: History of a Genocide* (London, Hurst 1995). Brilliantly detailed and explanatory account of the Rwandan genocide of 1994 and its historical background.

Articles/Chapters

Transformation, vol. 12, no. 1 (1995). Articles focusing on Rwanda in relation to refugees, ethnicity and revival.

Kirk, J. A., 'Race, class, caste and the Bible' in *Themelios,* vol. 10, no. 2 (1985).

Ch. 4, 'The ideology of nation' in Goudzward, Bob, *Idols of our Time* (Downers Grove, IVP 1984).

Bowen, Roger, 'Rwanda – Missionary Reflections on a catastrophe', *Anvil,* vol. 13, no. 1 (1996), provides a movingly honest and perceptive confession of the failures of much international missionary intervention in Rwanda before 1994 by someone who was closely involved.

Themelios, vol. 21, no. 1 (1996). Whole edition devoted to issues such as nationhood, language and ethnic identity in the light of the Bible.

TEN

Women, Poverty and the Kingdom

It is impossible to deny the fact that a very large proportion of womankind throughout history have not been granted equality with men in the enjoyment of God's blessings to all. Women make up the majority of the world's poor. The following statistics witnesses to the truth of this statement today:

> While women work 67 per cent of the world's working hours, they earn only 10 per cent of the world's income, and own less than 1 per cent of the world's property.[1]
>
> Women still constitute 70 per cent of the world's poor and two-thirds of the world's illiterates. They occupy only 14 per cent of managerial and administrative jobs, 10 per cent of parliamentary seats and 6 per cent of cabinet positions.[2]

Statistical statements such as these point to the value attributed to women in the eyes of the bulk of the world's communities. This is not to deny there are many variations in the position of women between different continents, countries, regions and communities. The lot of women may be much better in some communities than in others. It is not the aim of this chapter to make a comprehensive survey of how women are treated everywhere but to focus on different types of ill-treatment which need to be addressed by those committed to biblical teaching.

---

[1] Eade, D. and Williams, S., *Oxfam Handbook of Development and Relief*, vol. 1 (Oxford, Oxfam 1995), p. 1.

[2] United Nations Development Programme *Human Development Report 1995* (New York and Oxford, OUP 1995), p. iii.

Women devalued

1. *Through traditions and customs*

There is evidence that women are considered of less value than men in many cultures. This is seen in the way females are discriminated against even before birth. 'According to a survey by a Bombay clinic, between 1978 and 1982, 78,000 female foetuses were aborted after sex-determination tests.'[3] ASHA, a Christian organization working in the slums of Delhi, has found that there is a high incidence of cot death syndrome affecting third or fourth female daughters, not sons. In a normal population the ratio of males to females remains constant at 50:50. The larger proportion of males in many Asian countries is firm evidence of a consistent, and for females fatal, bias in favour of male children.

Once born, male children will have priority, especially in rural areas, when it comes to the distribution of food and the provision of health care and education. Female children will from an early age be expected to shoulder some of the burden of housework. If the domestic demands become too pressing, they will be pulled out of education while their brothers carry on.

The inferior status of the woman in many cultures becomes very obvious in the context of marriage. It is at this point more than any other that a daughter is seen as a drain on a family's resources and not an asset. This is especially so since the wealth of a family in most cultures is passed on from one generation of males to the next. Many communities in Africa and Asia run on such patrilineal lines. Very often this social arrangement does not have the backing of a country's laws or religious leaders, but it dominates societies informally.

In this system property is inherited by the eldest son or divided between several sons on the death of the father. Prior to this death all the sons stay with the father in the family compound and bring their wives from other families to join them. The wife's family has to pay a dowry price to the husband's family. This dowry can take many different forms: it can be a

---

[3] Eade and Williams *Oxfam Handbook*, p. 2.

gift of some household equipment that will benefit the girl in her domestic duties, or perhaps it can be a gift to decorate the husband's home. Often there is no set requirement for a dowry. However, in some regions there is a more regulated system of cash payments that the family of the bride must pay. In Muslim communities especially the dowry can be considered as a way of giving a girl some share of her parents' inheritance. But this inheritance becomes the possession of the girl's husband. The family also lose a valuable domestic and economic asset when they lose a daughter. Overall, therefore, daughters cost money to their parents, but sons provide income and provision for their fathers. So, the birth of a daughter is not the cause of great joy but of regret and sorrow.

There is often a 'bride price' paid by the bridegroom's family to the bride's family as a form of compensation for the loss of their daughter. On the one hand such a payment can be said to recognize the fact that a woman is a productive asset. On the other the paying of a bride price can be seen as merely a way of purchasing authority over a female and thus emphasizing the fact that a girl is a movable possession (chattel) to be passed from the father to the groom on receipt of payment. Such contracts can lead to very serious abuse of women. For example, the murder of women in dowry-related disputes still goes on.[4]

Since in such a system boys are considered to be more valuable than girls, there is great pressure on a wife to produce a son. Failure to do so can have severe consequences. In an African context failure leads to loss of position in the family because the husband is very likely polygamously to take another wife,[5] while in Asia it often leads to divorce.[6]

---

[4] 'In India, five women are burned in dowry-related disputes every day. Women's groups claim the figure is nearer 25.' *The New Internationalist* (August 1995), p. 19. *The New Internationalist* is published by New Internationalist Publications Ltd.

[5] See, for example, Ogebe, Mary Dija, 'Social Injustice' in Mbugua, J. (ed.), *Our Time has Come: African Christian Women Address the Issues of Today* (Grand Rapids, Baker Book House/Carlisle, Paternoster 1994), pp. 61–2.

[6] D. Abecassis writes on Bangladesh, 'One in five of all marriages end in divorce, and nearly all are instituted by men against wives who have produced no sons or have lost their looks through a life of extreme poverty.' Abecassis, D., *Identity, Islam and Human Development in Rural Bangladesh* (Dhaka, University Press 1990), p. 55.

2. *Through violence*

When women are viewed as possessions by men it is not at all surprising that they are frequently subjected to violent treatment. The author was struck by the first question asked of him and a group of male pastors from the UK when talking to a women's group in Delhi: 'Do you beat your wives?' Being beaten was a common experience for the 30 or so women in that group. The author also remembers vividly the heart-rending sobs of a woman in Bombay who had lost her husband in the Muslim-Hindu riots that followed the destroying of the Ayodhya mosque. 'He used to beat me terribly', she said, 'but I had food for my family when he was alive.'

Violence against women is common worldwide. In the USA domestic violence is the leading cause of injury among women of reproductive age: between 22 per cent and 35 per cent of women who visit emergency rooms are there for that reason.[7] In the UK there has been a significant increase in the number of homes for 'battered wives' in the last few years. In Peru 70 per cent of all crimes reported to the police concern women beaten by their partners. Accompanying this violence is often a view of women as sexual objects to be used at men's pleasure. This can make it very difficult for women to protect themselves against HIV/Aids from a male partner. Violence towards wives is so ingrained in many cultures that it can continue after men's conversion to Christ.

3. *In work*

Women are considered inferior and often treated very badly by men. Then to add insult to injury they are often expected to do all the domestic duties whilst also producing much of what the family needs for survival. In rural India[8]

> they are the ones who work in the fields . . . make baskets
> . . . look after the whole family's cooking and washing and
> just about every practical aspect of home life or village life,

---

[7] *The New Internationalist* (August 1995), p. 19.
[8] Roughly 70 per cent of the Indian population lives in rural areas.

in terms of labour, is carried out by the womenfolk. Men usually do not work, unless they are hard pressed because the family has a very low income; only then would you find men going out and finding work for themselves.[9]

Furthermore, in many countries women are expected to give birth to a large number of children with little spacing in between. This puts massive strains on the mother's health. Consequently many women die during pregnancy or childbirth. Yet, despite this heavy workload, an Indian sociologist records, 'It is commonplace in India to receive a completely negative answer from men responding to the query: What do the women of your household do?'[10]

This is related to the commonly drawn distinction between public and private roles. The man has the public and the woman the private role. Men consider that it is only the public role that has any real significance. Within this distinction women's primary roles are seen as being in the reproductive and domestic sphere while the men take care of the productive sphere whilst also representing the family in the public domain. This does not mean that men do all the income-generating work; often it is the women who bear the brunt of the work. Rather, 'anything that is to do with dealing with the outside world, outside the family or outside the village, it's always the man's work'.[11] This will, for example, often involve the selling of produce that the woman has worked hard to produce. This role leaves the woman without any public voice. She has no freedom to protest even when treated violently by men.

4. *In decision making*

This lack of a public voice affects other aspects of a woman's life. Peter Batchelor records the experience of Elsie Ayah and her fellow-workers when they sought to work with women in the

---

[9]   Quotation from an interview (January 1996) with Prince David, Tearfund's regional adviser for Asia.

[10]   Mukhopadhyay, M., *Silver Shackles* (Oxford, Oxfam 1985), p. 2.

[11]   Quotation from an interview (January 1996) with Prince David, Tearfund's regional advisor for Asia.

Garu area of northern Ghana.[12] As they sought to find ways to improve the lot of women they encountered a serious problem. They found that the women would not co-operate with them without their husbands' permission which the husbands were reluctant to grant.[13] They needed the permission of the men even to talk to the women. When asked why they kept this barrier around their women the men explained, 'We think that it would be very bad for you to talk to the women. If you teach them anything, their eyes will be opened and they will feel very big and leave us and marry other men.'[14]

The enforced silence of women has often been accepted by the women as the 'way it should be'. David Abecassis writes concerning women in Bangladesh that 'some have completely internalized the inferior status of women so that their self-image is very low indeed and their creative spirit never flowers; they are the ones who believe that their inferiority is both real and inevitable'. The woman is conditioned from birth to believe that she is 'too foolish or ignorant to have any valid opinion on affairs outside the bari [household].'[15]

5. *In development work*

The voicelessness of women invariably means that their needs are not met by development workers. Peter Batchelor thus writes of the need to listen (once the women actually feel able to talk!) to the priority concerns of women in the rural context, because they are often not the priority concerns of men. He writes, 'it is women who do the grinding or walk long distances to motor mills. If men had to do it, perhaps they would be in a greater hurry to find alternatives.'[16] Similarly Janet Lim, chief of the UNHCR's Emergency Preparedness and Response section, highlights how easy it is to miss out on the real issues because of the silence of women, particularly in the presence of men: 'I

---

[12] Peter Batchelor is a consultant to Tearfund. This case study comes from Batchelor, P., *People in Rural Development* (Carlisle, Paternoster 1993), pp. 167 172.
[13] Batchelor, *People in Rural Development*, p. 167.
[14] Ibid. p. 168.
[15] Abecassis, *Identity, Islam*, p. 57.
[16] Ibid. p. 107.

once went on a high-powered inter-agency mission – five men
and me – to former Yugoslavia, and we went round and asked
if there were any problems, and everyone said no. And I said,
"Wait let me talk to the women", and the issues came up. No
sanitary towels. No proper, private bathing space to wash.
Gynaecological problems. No underwear. These were the things
they had never said.'[17]

Christians involved in development need to be alert to the
needs of women who may have little time or power to raise their
desperate needs to the attention of those who might be able to
help. For example, it is estimated that a quarter of all households
worldwide are now headed by women.[18] The causes include
'family disintegration, population movements between urban
and rural areas within countries, international migration, war
and internal displacements'.[19] In the overwhelming majority of
cases it is the woman who is abandoned for these various
reasons and left to care for a family as best as she can. Such
women have serious needs, but little opportunity to bring them
to the attention of others.

The presentation of a very bleak picture of the status of
women at the beginning of this chapter is deliberate. This book
has been written with those who have some leadership role in
the church in mind and they are overwhelmingly male. There is
a tremendous need for Christian leaders everywhere to appreciate the weight of female oppression and suffering in the world.
Such oppression and suffering is universal. But there are also
some signs of hope.

All over the world women are being liberated from the
traditional gender-role stereotypes and their consequent barriers to playing a full part in the life of a community: lack of access
to decision-making processes, limits on choice of occupation,
and so on. This is particularly obvious in many industrialized
countries where all visible barriers to women's participation in
all occupations, including government, have come down. There

---

[17] Marshall, R., 'Refugees, Feminine Plural' in *Refugees*, Edition II (Geneva,
UNHCR 1995), pp. 3–10.
[18] *The Beijing Declaration and Platform for Action* (New York, United Nations
1996), p. 25.
[19] Ibid.

are still cultural values and assumptions that need to be questioned, but women are at least on the path to equality of rights and responsibilities with men.

The proportion of women receiving education is increasing so that in some areas women outnumber men at the higher levels of education. Women are gaining the right to share with their husbands in deciding how many children they should have and when they should have them. They are entering political office increasingly, although there is a very long way to go before equality with men, in terms of political representation, is achieved. Women are speaking out about injustices which for centuries they were forced to endure.

Women in the Bible

The Old Testament

It can be argued that the affirmation of the value of women is one important theme in the history of God's relationship with humanity from the garden of Eden through to the coming of Jesus. This affirmation also cuts across the prevailing cultural context with regard to women in which the revelation was made. All evangelical Christians can agree with this statement, even though they may disagree with the precise way in which this history is counter-cultural. We shall examine these disagreements after a discussion of the common ground.

Hebrew society was undoubtedly patriarchal and this is reflected in the Old Testament. Some see this as a fulfilment of what God said to Eve as a result of the Fall: 'Your desire will be for your husband and he will rule over you.'[20] The subordination of women is a result of the Fall that disrupted the prior equality and harmony. Others would explain the patriarchal nature of Hebrew society as in part the outworking of a pre-Fall creation pattern in which Adam had ultimate authority over Eve. According to this view, there is a hierarchy of responsibility and authority before the Fall that makes the submission of women

---

[20] Gen. 3:16.

to men a creation ordinance. This authority is abused because of the Fall, it becomes a harsh, domineering exercise of authority.

Whichever view is taken on the origins of hierarchy, both approaches can share a common affirmation of women. Both women and men are equally made in the image of God[21] and both are given the same basic task by God: 'Be fruitful and increase in number; fill the earth and subdue it. Rule over the fish of the sea and the birds of the air and over every living creature that moves on the land.'[22]

In the more detailed description of the creation of woman in Genesis 2 she is described as Adam's help or helper who corresponds to or is like him.[23] It is quite obvious that Adam could not fulfil the mandate to be fruitful and increase in number without Eve! However, there is no justification to stop at this point. He also needed her to fulfil the mandate to manage the resources of the earth under God and for his glory. It was to be a joint subduing and ruling of the earth and its creatures. The fact that the woman is described as being *like* Adam, that is, the same as him, or not in any way inferior to him, suggests that the authority he was to wield over creation was to be a joint authority. This is corroborated by what happened after the Fall because both Adam and Eve were held to be morally responsible to God and thus both were punished for their disobedience.

Since women are made in the image of God it is not surprising that female imagery is sometimes used in the Old Testament to describe God.[24] A striking example is the description of God as Israel's father and mother in Deuteronomy: 'You deserted the Rock, who fathered you; you forgot the God who gave you birth.'[25] Of course to call God a father or a mother is to use earthly

---

[21] Gen. 1:27.

[22] Gen. 1:28. The force of this equality has been lost through the interpretation of a number of men in church history. Calvin for example saw woman as made in the image of God, but to a lesser degree than men. Calvin's interpretation sprang from a particular interpretation of the meaning of the expression: he saw it as meaning that because Adam and Eve exercised authority on behalf of God on earth, they were functioning as the image of God on earth. Calvin then worked out that man did more in terms of ruling the earth than woman and therefore was made more in the image of God.

[23] Gen. 2:18.

[24] Deut. 32:11–13,18; Isa. 42:14; 49:14–15; 66:9,13.

[25] Deut. 32:18.

imagery to convey a truth about a God who transcends any sexual distinctions. As Deuteronomy states: 'You saw no form of any kind the day the Lord spoke to you at Horeb out of the fire. Therefore watch yourselves very carefully, so that you do not become corrupt and make for yourselves an idol, an image of any shape, whether formed like a man or a woman.'[26]

The basic equality of men and women established at creation continues into the rest of the Old Testament. Women have parallel responsibilities to men in the covenant,[27] and can pray directly to God.[28] Whilst it is the stories of men that dominate the Old Testament there are women like Rahab, Deborah, Ruth and Esther who have important roles in modelling a right relationship with God. Then Proverbs 31 gives a fascinating description of the archetypal 'wife of noble character'. She is living within a patriarchal society. It is her 'husband' who 'is respected at the city gate, where he takes his seat among the elders of the land' (v. 23). She, meanwhile, 'watches over the affairs of her household'. Nevertheless, she is also the woman who 'considers a field and buys it; out of her earnings she plants a vineyard' (v. 16). She is not to remain hidden behind the success of her husband. Rather, 'let her works bring her praise at the city gate' (v. 31). Equally there are women playing vital parts in the history of Israel who are easy to miss in the overwhelmingly male- dominated expositions of Scripture. For example, the women who disobey men in order to secure Moses' safe passage to adulthood.[29]

The God who reveals himself in the Old Testament values women particularly when they are most vulnerable to being degraded. He is the God who comes to the aid of the widows.[30] In a patriarchal society widows are extremely vulnerable. They have left the protection of their father's home and have lost the protection of their husband. Prostitution is their only resort in many cultures even today. God rejoices at being their protector and invites those who belong to his covenant to stand with him to give the widows the comfort and honour that they need.

---

[26] Deut. 4:15. See also Num. 23:19; 1 Sam. 25:29; Hos. 11:9.
[27] Deut. 31:12; 2 Chron. 15:12–13; Deut. 17:2–5; 29:18–21; Deut. 13:6–11.
[28] Gen. 25:22; Gen. 30:6,22; 1 Sam. 1:10.
[29] Ex. 2:1–10.
[30] See, for example, Deut. 10:18; Ps. 68:5.

Overall, therefore, it is necessary to bring two perspectives to the Old Testament in order to understand its attitude to women. On the one hand one must recognize that the society in which the drama of God's revelation is played out is patriarchal. On the other hand one must recognize that the underlying direction of Old Testament teaching is towards the recognition of the equality of women with men. The seeds for a radical affirmation of women are there.

The New Testament

The Jewish society that Jesus grew up in had not fed on the implicit radicalism of the Old Testament. Philo[31] suggests that 'women are best suited to the indoor life which never strays from the house'.[32] This prohibition stemmed partly from the view of women as sexually tempting to men. Women were generally seen as promiscuous seducers of innocent men. Furthermore, many Jews interpreted Sarah's lie in Genesis 18:15 as indicating that women were predisposed to dishonesty.[33] Their weakness made them unsuited to learning the Law of God. A ruling in the Talmud states, 'Let the words of the Torah rather be destroyed by fire than imparted to a woman.'[34] Similarly, 'The man came [to the synagogue] . . . to learn, the woman came to hear.'[35] There were exceptions to this view, but the bulk of male opinion supported it.

There is evidence in the New Testament that these views were prevalent in the circles in which Jesus moved. The disciples are surprised to find Jesus talking to a woman when they return with provisions from Sychar.[36] When women report to the 11 that they had seen two angels who told them that Jesus was

---

[31] Philo was a wealthy Jew living in Alexandria between c.20 BC and AD 45. We do not know his exact date of birth or death, but we know that in AD 39 he became a member of the embassy of the emperor Gaius (Caligula). He sought to synthesize the theories of Greek philosophy with the beliefs of Judaism.

[32] Quotation from Evans, M., *Women in the Bible* (Exeter, Paternoster 1983), p. 34.

[33] Ibid. p. 35.

[34] Ibid. p. 36.

[35] Ibid. p. 35.

[36] Jn. 4:27.

raised, the disciples 'did not believe the women, because their words seemed like nonsense'.[37] Obviously this disbelief sprang partly from the miraculous nature of the account. However, within the cultural background it is right to see a further hesitancy introduced by the assumptions concerning the unreliability of women. The disciples often seem to mirror the prevailing attitudes of their culture, in contrast to Jesus.[38]

The cultural restriction of women to domestic affairs, coupled with their exclusion from teaching, helps explain the tension in Jesus' encounter with Mary and Martha.[39] Martha's high christological statement in John 11 perhaps reveals that she learnt her lesson.

Moving with the underlying direction of the Old Testament, Jesus blows apart the contemporary attitudes to women. Jesus treats women as human beings, not dangerous objects who should be hidden away at all cost and avoided lest they seduce helpless men. Jesus permitted women to follow him with the disciples. They supported his mission with their money and moral support.[40] Clearly they developed a very close relationship with him as evidenced by the faithful presence of women witnessing Jesus' death and returning to the tomb as soon as possible after his death. It was to Mary Magdalene that Jesus first appeared after his resurrection, according to the longer ending of Mark's Gospel.[41]

In the accounts of Matthew, Mark and John women are the first to see Jesus risen from the dead. In Matthew and Mark the women are entrusted with the task of telling the 11 disciples that Jesus had risen, a reflection of the subversive value God put on them as witnesses. Having been told by the women that Jesus has risen Peter then goes to check their report and in doing so meets Jesus himself. Similarly in John it is through the report of Mary Magdalene that 'Simon Peter and the other disciple' first hear of the empty tomb. It is possible to see the prominence

---

[37] Lk. 24:11.
[38] See, for example, Mt. 15:21–8; Mk. 14:5; Mt. 19:13–15
[39] Lk. 10:38–42.
[40] Lk. 8:1–3.
[41] Mk. 16:9

accorded to women as evidence of the authenticity of the resurrection in so far as the early church would have been very unlikely to invent a story which had women as the primary witnesses! Interestingly, a pagan critique of Christianity written by Celsus in the second century AD is built on the premise that the witness of a hysterical woman cannot be credible. In a context in which the testimony of women was consistently doubted the New Testament account is truly revolutionary.

Paul wrote to people influenced by the values of the Jewish community and of the Graeco-Roman world as well. Women were generally considered inferior in both worlds. For example, in a Greek public meeting (*ekklēsia*) women were not allowed to speak. Paul, therefore, is radical when he assumes that women, under the influence of the Spirit, will pray and prophesy publicly in meetings of the Christian community.[42] Similarly, in Greek and Jewish ethical instructions it was normal simply to address men. This was particularly the case when marriage was being discussed. It was sufficient to address the husband because he represented the wife. Paul's instructions to married couples on how to manage their sexual relationship is dynamically different. Men and women are addressed equally, since 'The wife's body does not belong to her alone but also to her husband. In the same way, the husband's body does not belong to him alone but also to his wife.'[43]

Paul was also radical in giving a noble place to single women – widowed or unmarried – in the Christian community. For him it was a positive virtue to remain unmarried because of the opportunity that gave to be completely focused on the Lord

---

[42] 1 Cor. 11:5. Some have sought to argue that the prohibition in 1 Cor. 14 is absolute on all utterance including prayer and prophecy. Their argument revolves around the idea that Paul in 1 Cor. 11 is addressing small, informal gatherings and not the public meetings that he is concerned with in 1 Cor. 14. This argument should be dismissed for a number of reasons outlined in Carson, D., 'On the Role of Women in I Corinthians 14:33b–36' in Piper, J. and Grudem, W., *Recovering Biblical Manhood and Womanhood* (Wheaton, Illinois, Crossway 1991), pp. 140–154.

[43] 1 Cor. 7:4. This verse is perhaps better translated, 'The wife does not have authority [*exousia*] over her own body, but the husband does. Likewise the husband does not have authority [*exousia*] over his own body, but the wife does'.

Jesus and his affairs.[44] He assumes that, in Corinth at least, it would be possible for an unmarried woman either to support herself or be supported by the church in giving herself fully to serving the Lord and his people. By the time he came to write his first letter to Timothy he had concluded that it was generally wiser for young widows to remarry and only for the older widows to remain single and serve in the church.[45]

The contemporary debate among evangelicals about the status and role of women in church and society

The biblical material considered up to this point has focused primarily on teaching that gives women honour and dignity. This has been done because all over the world women are still oppressed and degraded. The biblical material presented also suggests here and there that women are able to make a very valuable contribution to the life of the church, and of society in general, when given the opportunity to expand their sphere of influence beyond the domestic realm. Most evangelicals would now accept that women have a contribution to make outside the domestic sphere. The debate centres on how they relate to men in making this contribution.

There are broadly two schools of thought. The arguments between them are getting more and more technical and any attempted resolution is beyond the scope of this chapter. We must be content with a sketch of the key arguments of each school.

1. Equal status, different function

The traditional evangelical view is that men and women are equal in status but different in function. This equality and difference are rooted both in the order of creation and in redemption. All are made in the image of God. All believers are also 'sons of God through faith in Jesus Christ'.[46] But within this equality there are

---

[44] 1 Cor. 7:8,34.
[45] 1 Tim. 5:3ff.
[46] Gal. 3:26.

functional differences which are established at creation and endorsed by redemption. A part of the woman's function is to be under the authority of her husband. This school of thought finds an order of authority within the garden of Eden before the Fall. Because the woman was created after the man, was taken from him and named by him she is secondary to him. Being a helper also implies subordination. Finally, the woman was the one deceived by the serpent, therefore she should not be trusted with positions of authority; Adam's sin was to subvert the proper authority structure by obeying the advice of Eve to eat the fruit. Many argue that Paul picks up these arguments and applies them to women in the churches of Ephesus and Corinth.[47]

It is argued that Paul finds a basis for a hierarchy of authority in marriage within the facts of redemption in his teaching on marriage in Ephesians.[48] The wife's submission is to be modelled on the church's submission to Jesus and the husband's exercise of authority must be modelled on the sacrificial love of Christ who always seeks to free captive human beings into fullness of life. Evidence for hierarchy between men and women, not just husbands and wives, within the structure of the story of redemption is found in 1 Corinthians: 'Now I want you to realize that the head of every man is Christ, and the head of the woman is man, and the head of Christ is God.'[49]

Some find a further difference of function in terms of a distinction between public and private roles in society. Women should be, if they are married, essentially concerned with domestic affairs. Men are made by contrast to go out and be their family's interface with the outside world. That this is how things should be in the creation order and is implicitly endorsed by the epistles which seem to assume that the proper place for women is in the home.[50]

2. *Equal status, different function, no hierarchy*

The other school of interpretation would agree that there is an equality of value between men and women and a difference of

---

[47] 1 Tim. 2:11–14; 1 Cor. 11:3–16.
[48] Eph. 5:22–4.
[49] 1 Cor. 11:3.
[50] See, for example, 1 Tim. 5:14; Tit. 2:1–6.

function. However, they would disagree as to the nature of this difference in function. The difference is not to be thought of in terms of authority.

The account of Genesis 1–2 reveals, it is argued, that there is no hierarchical order in Adam and Eve's relationship before the Fall. The first hint of hierarchy comes as a result of the Fall which disrupted the prior equality.[51] Much of the exegesis is concerned with showing the faults of the reasons traditionally given for hierarchy in Genesis 1–2. If temporal priority implies authority then, according to Genesis 1, animals must be in authority over men. The fact that woman was taken from man implies her sameness with man not her subordination. The naming of the woman does not use the naming formula[52] that is used of the animals and which implies 'authority over'. The word 'helper' does not imply subordination because it is most commonly used of God in the Old Testament. While Paul does say that 'Eve was the one deceived',[53] he also uses the deception of Eve as a salutary warning to both men and women, thereby indicating that both are prone to being misled by Satan.[54] To argue that Adam's sin was to subvert the proper authority structure by following Eve's advice, is to read too much into the text. There is little indication of this structure prior to the Fall.

However, there is still a need to understand the way Paul uses the account of creation. Does he find hierarchy within the pre-Fall relationship of Adam and Eve? It can be argued, for example, that in 1 Corinthians 11:2–10 Paul is not seeking to establish hierarchy via Genesis, but a recognition of the differences

---

[51] Gen. 3:16.

[52] M. Evans writes 'in the standard naming formula we find both the verb "to call" and the noun "name"; as for example in Gen. 4:25 . . . It will be noted that in Genesis 2 these words are found together only in v. 19, when the animals are brought to Adam to be named. In v. 23 the noun 'name' does not occur'. Evans, *Women in the Bible*, p. 16.

It must be noted though that not all commentators agree with this analysis. Gordon Wenham for example writes that the naming in v. 23 is a 'typical example of Hebrew naming . . . Though they are equal in nature, that man names woman indicates that she is expected to be subordinate to him'. Wenham, G., *Genesis 1–15: Word Biblical Commentary* (Waco, Word 1987), p. 70.

[53] 1 Tim. 2:14.

[54] 2 Cor. 11:3.

between women and men. It can be held that a) 'Head' should be interpreted as 'source' rather than 'authority',[55] and b) the phrase 'the woman ought to have a sign of authority on her head' (NIV) should be translated as 'a woman should have control over what she does with her head'.[56] F.F. Bruce favours this translation. The verse in its context, therefore, states that each woman has the freedom to decide whether to prophesy or not.

It is further argued that as there is no evidence of a hierarchy at creation, there is evidence that within the redeemed community all notion of hierarchy has gone. The submission of women to men takes place within the context of universal mutual submission.[57] The woman has as much authority over her husband's body as he has over hers.[58] Neither sex is exempt from taking the place of servant in relation to the other.[59] While Galatians 3:28 is often quoted, it is acknowledged that this verse, in context, has a primary reference to salvation. Men and women share equally in the salvation to be found in Jesus. However, the unity of Gentiles with Jews and that of slaves with their masters will have

---

[55] This is not a new dilemma in interpretation. Throughout church history there have been notable theologians holding both views. *Kephalē* (head) most commonly in the NT refers simply to the 'physical head'. However in several places it clearly has a metaphorical meaning. Most translations take this metaphorical meaning to be 'authority over'. However any lexicon of the Greek language will give a wide variety of possible metaphorical meanings, just as in English the word 'head' can be used in a number of different ways: compare, 'head teacher', 'head of the river', 'use your head', etc.

It is thus, in a sense, legitimate to translate *kephalē* in a number of different ways. Any decision must be based on context. Paul arguably wants to use the word in both ways. Col. 1:18; 2:19 and Eph. 4:15 are perhaps places where he is using the word in the sense of 'source'. However, perhaps in Eph. 1:20 'authority' fits best.

Scholars, though, disagree as to the metaphorical meaning that Paul is using in the passages concerned with the relationship of women to men (Eph. 5:22–33; 1 Cor. 11:3–16). This disagreement highlights the dangers of assuming that 'head' always has connotations of authority. The context must decide.

[56] This interpretation has been challenged. See for example, Schreiner, T., 'Head coverings, prophecies and the Trinity' in Piper and Grudem, *Recovering Biblical Manhood*, pp. 124–140.

[57] Eph. 5:21.

[58] 1 Cor. 7:4.

[59] Phil. 2:3.

social and interpersonal applications as the rest of the New Testament and history make clear. Might not the same be said of the unity between men and women?

So what can be concluded from these two different accounts of the counter-culture of Christ in this area of gender? Both sides claim to build their case on Scripture but neither side has the monopoly on correct exegesis. The arguments of both reveal the unchallenged assumptions of each other. One thing is clear: it is vitally important to place the issue of the status and role of women within the broader context of what the New Testament says about power and authority. The example of Jesus must ultimately inform the attitudes of men and women to each other. If we are serious about following him, both the position of women and the tone of the debate about their status and role will be revoluntionized. It is the Jesus who 'being in very nature God' nevertheless 'did not consider equality with God something to be grasped, but made himself nothing taking the very nature of a servant' that we follow.[60] Given the current pride and preoccupation with power of many men, the example of Jesus presents a stark challenge to men in particular.

There is also agreement that women and men are equally created in God's image and that the stewardship of the earth was placed in both their hands. This is true even for those who hold that the man was to take the lead in fulfilling this mandate. That authority is placed in the man's hand does not undermine the equal ability of the woman to understand the way in which the creation works and so to contribute fully in the intellectual processes required in subduing, ruling and caring for it. Given the opportunity, women have proved over and over again that they are just as capable as men at any subject or profession they turn their hand to. It is amazing that even some Christians should be reluctant to recognize this fact, given the belief that women are created, like men, in God's image.

---

[60] Phil. 3:6–7.

Women, poverty and the church

The potential of women

If women created in God's image constitute the majority of the world's poor, it would be ridiculous to begin to tackle the issue of poverty without consulting them or understanding why this half of the world's population should be so disadvantaged. Furthermore, those intimately involved in the care of the poor have discovered that listening to women and empowering them is a very effective way of impacting whole families, communities and societies for the better.

Empowering women can have dramatic significance because many of the tasks done by women are directly linked to initiatives commonly undertaken by people involved in improving the lot of the poor. Many of these initiatives are in the fields of sanitation, health, water supply, nutrition, child care, food production. These areas are in the main the responsibility of women. It has been proved beyond any doubt, for example, that the education of women is the most effective way of reducing infant mortality. A woman who can read is able much more effectively to learn how to care for her children. She can better understand the need for cleanliness, for nutritious food, for a clean water supply, and so on. It is not at all surprising that a UNICEF report on the state of the world's children published in 1991 states that 'the education of girls is probably the world's best investment'.

There is also broad agreement among those who work with the poor that men are less likely than women to transfer the benefits of a particular development project to their families. For example, in a microenterprise development project run by EFICOR[61] in Delhi, 99 per cent of the participants in the scheme, by deliberate choice, are women. This is because the first thought of the women is for their family and so any additional income gained is ploughed back into the welfare of the family. The women do not spend scarce resources on alcohol as the men do. They are also more reliable in their attendance at

---

[61]   Evangelical Fellowship of India Commission on Relief

meetings and more prepared to think of the good of the community as a whole.

Women can also have a key role in reconciling a community that has been destroyed by ethnic conflict. MOUCECORE in Rwanda recognizes this.[62] MOUCECORE is an agency concerned to build unity in Rwanda through working with the churches, many of whom were split along ethnic lines prior to and during the genocide of 1994. There is now much peacemaking to be done particularly since many have lost family and friends in murders carried out by people they may have known, indeed may have sat next to, in church.

MOUCECORE has decided that women are the key to this process for the following three reasons: Firstly, the cultural history of Rwanda. Women have been undervalued within the church and society, and have a low sense of self-esteem as a result. Yet, women do most of the work in the home and for the family. Secondly, following the recent ethnic tension and conflict, women comprise the majority of the adult population of the country and are therefore an important factor in any change. The heart of the Rwandan woman has been wounded by loss and the effects of the war. They carry added family responsibilities and need to learn new organizational skills and methods to facilitate their tasks. Thirdly, in a balanced Rwandan household, the woman is considered the heart of the family. She should have the same influence on the church and the country. As such she could be a vital instrument of reconciliation. These reasons, with modifications according to culture, could be repeated for the women of many communities in the world that have been torn apart by conflict.

The neglect of women's potential

Despite the role women can play in the transformation of families and communities, their voice is often unheard and their potential contribution ignored. Attention and resources are directed to men rather than women. In many poor communities men are the representatives of women and children; they are the

---

[62] See case study on Rwanda in Ch. 9, 'Ethnic Identity, Poverty and the Kingdom', pp. 228–33.

interface between families and the local community, between the community and the political authorities and between the national situation and the international community. At all levels they should voice the concerns of the family but in many cases only the concerns of the men are advocated. As the interface, men often receive resources which, if not squandered, are often directed into activities that do little to benefit their wives or their children. The misdirection of resources occurs at all levels of representation. Even well-intentioned men have less of an idea of what might benefit the family than women do, simply because they have less involvement in the family. Listening to the voice of the wife and mother is vital if any progress is to be made.

The neglect of women in society is sadly adopted by many contemporary churches. The church as an institution often lags behind in recognizing the God-given gifts of women. Its leadership structures continue to be heavily dominated by men. It may be granted that women are in no way inferior to men and that they are free to use their God-given gifts to acquire a whole range of skills that were once denied them. They can be honoured members of a whole range of respected professions, where they daily take crucial decisions affecting the lives of many people, but in the church they are only allowed to make tea and sweep the floor! Both men and women should be happy to sweep floors and make tea as unto the Lord, when such menial tasks need to be done, but it does seem strange that God should give gifts to women that can be used to bless society at large while denying their use in his own special community.

To make such statements about the abilities of women is not necessarily the same as advocating full equality between men and women in the leadership of the church, but it should lead to a serious review of church structures where decision making is completely dominated by men. If it means nothing else, the sort of mutual submission taught by Paul should lead to the opening up of all sorts of opportunities for women to make their voice heard.

The adoption by the church of many prejudices and practices of society has been described powerfully by African Christian women. In August 1989 Christian women leaders from 36 African countries came together in Nairobi for the Pan African

Christian Women Assembly (PACWA) sponsored by the Association of Evangelicals of Africa and Madagascar (AEAM). The report of their deliberations was edited by Judy Mbugua and published with support from the World Evangelical Fellowship in 1994.[63] Church leaders all over the world would do well to listen to the voice of the godly women of PACWA.

Mary Dija Ogebe, for example, makes a list of injustices faced by African women in society at large. Some of these injustices, such as the inferior value of a female in a patrilineal society, have been discussed already in this chapter. The crux of the injustices is that women are considered to be insignificant, so that their opinion on all the crucial decisions in life is neither sought or respected. When they try to escape from their shackles the legal system is often used to keep them enslaved. In Mary Dija Ogebe's experience husbands who have been guilty of beating their wives cruelly will use the law to get them back when they have escaped somewhere for sanctuary.

What of the church? On the positive side Mary Dija Ogebe observes that the 'gospel has delivered women from, a) the stigma of being a woman and therefore less than a man, b) polygamy, c) being only a piece of property, d) lack of inheritance'.[64] However, on the negative side she writes: 'What of the Church set-up? Are Christians freed from the problems of . . . prejudice? I wish I could give an emphatic "Yes" but I cannot.'[65] It is not surprising that the PACWA covenant states, 'We are appalled that in many African nations women are discriminated against in matters of social justice; barred from highest levels of leadership in church and society; and often denied access to economic sources of production'.[66]

If the church as a whole neglects the glorious potential of women, some of that potential is expressed throughout the world in different para-church organizations usually set up and run by women. Since there is no distinction between males and females in Christ, groups like this should be welcomed and

---

[63] Mbugua, *Our Time has Come.*

[64] Ibid. p. 63.

[65] Ibid. p. 61, p. 63.

[66] Ibid. p. 147.

supported by the church as a whole and seen as an integral part of its ministry. SUMUCAJ in Peru is one example of such groups and there are many others.

SUMUCAJ was set up by Sra. Juanna Cueva de Ortiz in 1989 with the help of a number of other Christian women from different denominations within the Cajamarca province. SU-MUCAJ describes its general objectives as, 'contributing to the re-evaluation of the woman as a person of worth and intelligence, capable of participating in solving problems in her home and community, developing her skills and raising her spirituality, culture and socio-economic level . . . [by promoting] self-determination and participation in decision making'. It is involved in literacy work among women and training in different handicrafts to provide sources of income. The focus of the literacy work is to enable the women to study written materials on particular craft techniques as well as to understand their own rights and to read the Bible for themselves. SUMUCAJ give the following reasons for setting up the work: a) In large sections of Peruvian society, women are discriminated against economically, politically, socially, culturally and educationally. The macho behaviour to which most women are subjected does not allow them to develop as people and to participate fully in life. b) Women have an important and far-reaching effect on society through the home and by earning an income. c) Therefore, women need help to see themselves as intelligent and having dignity and able to participate in solving their own problems both in the home and in the community, and to develop their God-given abilities and raise their standard of living.

The role of men

In focusing on women, particularly as the key to improving the lot of the poor, there is a need to be very careful not to ignore the men altogether – or worse to characterize them as completely useless to their families because all they do is demand that women should prove their virilty and waste the family's income on drink. In a wider context a more biblical view of woman demands that a man revises the traditional view of his role.[67] It means a considerable loss of power and authority. This is historically a very difficult thing to do. The fact that Christian leaders who are supposed to be very close to God find this very difficult to do is abundant testimony to this fact.

When women are empowered, at least three responses have been observed among men: a) Some men respond angrily because they can see that what is happening is a challenge to the traditional gender divides. Their role as the public face of the family is threatened. b) Some are not angry, but content to sit back and enjoy a life of ease while the work burden of their wives increases to include domestic duties and income generation. c) Finally, there are men who begin to respect their wives as they see their productive skills and ingenuity for the first time. The aim should be to make sure that the conditions exist to engender the third response. In Christian terms it is to generate love because love drives all sorts of fears away, including the fear of losing face.

Conclusion

If the counter-cultural affirmation of women that should characterize Christianity is to occur, a number of steps should be taken:

1. The role that women play in their churches and communities needs to be recognized. This involves a close examination of the tasks and responsibilities of men and women within a given church or community. Out of this will emerge a picture of the balance of duties within particular situations. The access of women and men to resources will also be gauged. Those with no power within the community can be identified. It is very likely that women will form the majority of the powerless and it is the genius of the gospel to raise up the weak.

2. The needs of women must be identified by giving them a voice with which to raise their concerns. Women need to be

---

[67] See, for example, McCloughry, R., *Men and Masculinity* (London, Hodder & Stoughton 1992).

consulted as to their perceived needs. This consultation will require great sensitivity. It may offend or worry other sections of the community or church, particularly the men. It may be difficult to get the women to voice their concerns. Some of the issues that women bring up may present complex ethical dilemmas to the Christians seeking to help them. For example, one of the biggest perceived needs of women in the developing world is for a measure of control over their own fertility.[68]

3. The potential of women within their churches and communities needs to be recognized. Women have massive potential to transform churches, communities and societies because they are made in the image of God and, if followers of Jesus, co-members with men of the kingdom of God. This chapter has attempted to set out some aspects of that potential.

4. A culture in which women are valued must be built. Christians should affirm the potential of women to transform their communities. Christian women must also be affirmed as co-workers for the kingdom. Churches and parachurches must communicate this message through words and by an active modelling of the values of the Bible within their own structures.

Resources

Books

Mbugua, Judy (ed.), *Our Time has Come: African Christian Women Address the Issues of Today* (Grand Rapids, Baker Book House/Carlisle, Paternoster 1994). An excellent introduction, written by African Christian women, about the problems and opportunities they face. Their situation has many similarities with that faced by women all over the world.

---

[68] See Ch. 11, 'Population, Poverty and the Kingdom'.

Storkey, Elaine, *What's Right with Feminism?* (London, SPCK 1989). An analysis of the merits and problems of feminism from an evangelical perspective.

Evans, Mary J., *Women in the Bible* (Carlisle, Paternoster 1984). A biblical defence of the 'Equal Status, Different Function, No Hierarchy' approach.

Piper, John, and Grudem, Wayne (eds.), *Recovering Biblical Manhood and Womanhood* (Wheaton, Crossway 1991). A biblical defence of the 'Equal Status, Different Function' approach.

McCloughry, R., *Men and Masculinity* (London, Hodder & Stoughton 1992), provides a perceptive analysis of how men should react to the changing roles of women in society.

Not specifically Christian

Mosse, Julia Cleves, *Half the World, Half a Chance* (Oxford, Oxfam 1993).

Wallace, Tina, and March, Candida (eds.), *Changing perceptions: Writings on Gender and Development* (Oxford, Oxfam 1991).

Articles

Tripp, Linda, 'A Voice for Women' in *Transformation*, vol. 6, no. 2 (1992), pp. 21–5. Concise, accurate introduction.

Footsteps, no. 24 (Teddington, Tearfund 1995). Articles by development workers on women's health issues in the Third World, with useful resources section.

Batchelor, Simon, 'Transforming the Slums by Relationships' (Teddington, Tearfund case study series 1996). A case study showing Christian and non-Christian women fighting poverty in hostile circumstances.

The New Internationalist, no. 270 (New Internationalist 1995). Introductory articles on situations facing contemporary women.

ELEVEN

Population Growth, Poverty and the Kingdom

It cannot be denied that the world's population has grown very rapidly in the twentieth century, or that it will continue to grow for the next 50 years at least, even if birth rates continue to fall. The current population of the world is 5.8 billion. The UN[1] projects that the world population in 2015 will be somewhere between 7.27 billion and 7.92 billion. For 2050 the UN low projection of population is 7.8 and the high projection is 12.5 billion people. Most of the growth will occur in the poorest regions of the world. 70 per cent of the increase is projected for the very poorest countries of Africa, Latin America and Asia.

The most common and influential attitude among the world's policymakers at present is that population growth is a key cause of poverty. The following two statements are representative. The first comes from a report by the World Commission on Environment and Development published in 1987 and the second from the UNICEF *Progress of Nations Report* for 1996:

> Present rates of population growth cannot continue. They already compromise many governments' abilities to provide education, health care and good security for people, much less their abilities to raise living standards. This gap between numbers and resources is all the more compelling

[1] Information in this section comes from *The State of the World Population 1994* (Geneva, UNFPA 1994) and from the final document of the United Nations International Conference on Population and Development, 1994.

because so much of the population growth is concentrated in low-income countries, ecologically disadvantaged regions, and poor households.[2]

Meeting only the existing demand for family planning would reduce pregnancies in the developing world by up to a fifth, bringing at least an equivalent reduction in maternal deaths and injuries. Add in the many other benefits of family planning for all – fewer abortions, better health and nutrition of women and children, faster progress towards gender equality, slower population growth, reduced environmental pressures – and the costs are almost derisory.[3]

The second quotation is particularly revealing since it assumes that high rates of population growth are to be avoided essentially because they lead to various manifestations of poverty. The large number of development organizations that now operate on this premise do not deny that much of the world's poverty is caused by injustice. However, they see high rates of population growth as a decisive factor in the maintenance of poverty. Therefore, it is seen as imperative to reduce it as soon as possible.

Despite the fact that various bodies attached to the UN and many other governmental and non-governmental organizations are committed to the thesis that increase in population will inevitably lead to an increase in poverty, the formula is still a matter of debate. In fact there is a whole range of views between the two poles of extreme pessimism and extreme optimism.

Pessimism

The pessimist view of the future of the world and its people is apocalyptic. They see rapid population growth leading to a situation where the number of people will outstrip the capacity

---

[2] World Commission on Environment and Development, *Our Common Future* (Oxford, OUP 1987), p. 95.
[3] UNICEF *Progress of Nations Report* 1996, p. 5.

of the earth and the ability of governments to provide adequately for them. Consequently, natural processes will take over and ensure that population size reduces by killing off large numbers of people. Starvation, epidemics and massive reductions in the general quality of life will become commonplace unless population growth rates are drastically reduced very soon. Even if the world were made to be a fairer place in which the poor were given equal access to resources, the population pressure would still lead to catastrophe. Ehrlich, the arch-pessimist, says that

> there is no reasonable way that the hunger problem can be called only one of distribution, even though redistribution of food resources would greatly alleviate hunger today. Unfortunately an important truth, that maldistribution is a cause of hunger now, has been used as a way to avoid a more important truth – that overpopulation is critical today and may well make the distribution question moot tomorrow.[4]

In short, there will soon be too many people for the earth to sustain and governmental structures will be totally incapable of providing for them.

Pessimists define overpopulation in reference to the 'carrying capacity' of the world. Carrying capacity is the 'capacity of the environment to sustain human activities'. An area is overpopulated if the 'long-term carrying capacity of an area is clearly being degraded by its current human occupants'. A distinction is often drawn between sustainable human uses of the worlds' resources and use which depletes the basic resources themselves. For example, sustainable use of the world's fish resources would mean that the fish are reproducing at the rate at which they are harvested. Non-sustainable use would be the exploitation of fish stocks at such a rate that the fish do not reproduce at the same rate. It is argued that if current rates of population growth continue, humanity will be forced into more and more non-sustainable use of the worlds'

---

[4] Ehrlich, P. and Ehrlich, A., *The Population Explosion* (London, Arrow 1990), pp. 20–1.

resources.[5] Indeed, they claim that 'the demands of our generation now exceed the income, the sustainable yield of the earth's ecological endowment'.[6]

Optimism

The optimists claim that people produce more than they consume, therefore, steady population growth is to be welcomed not feared. Very rapid population growth does strain resources in the short term but in the long term all the young consumers will become net producers. Humans are not the passive consumers of a static supply of resources. Rather they interact with the earth to maximize the potential of the earth to supply what humanity needs. Humans therefore will develop new technologies with which to maximize the earth's resources as well as discovering new resources to be harnessed.

The free market will also help to ensure that we never run out of anything, by acting as an impetus to increased efficiency and the use of different resources. The evangelical economist Calvin Beisner points to oil as an example:

> Some of us would like to know when the earth itself really will run out of oil. From an economist's standpoint the answer is 'probably never'. Why? Because if recoverable oil ever begins to dwindle sufficiently, its price will rise enough that people will conserve more, find more efficient uses for it and substitute other energy sources more. Long before it's all gone, it will be so little used that hardly anyone will think about it.[7]

The way in which the market has operated in the past has shown that human ingenuity can maximize the benefit of the earth's resources and provide for a much larger population than would

---

[5]   Lester Brown draws an analogy from economics, 'the distinction is between consuming interest and spending the capital stock itself'. Brown, L., *State of the World 1996* (London, Earthscan 1996), p. 4.

[6]   Brown, *State of the World*, p. 4. Brown has in mind the following resources: topsoil, fish stocks, water supply, wood.

[7]   Beisner, E.C., *Prospects for Growth* (Westchester, Crossway 1990), p. 120.

have been thought possible at an earlier stage. The optimists see no reason to doubt the ability of people to do the same in future.

They recognize the injustice of a world in which 20 per cent of the population own 80 per cent of the worlds' resources. It is this disparity that makes population growth a potential problem in some regions. Prosperous countries can support large populations because they are well organized and have access to significant resources. Poor countries and regions often have lower population densities but greater poverty because of the unfair distribution of the world's resources. The urgent task facing the world, therefore, is not to reduce birth rates, but to enable poorer countries to support their own populations. If this redistribution takes place, population growth rates will inevitably level off as they have done in the more industrialized countries. There is an optimism, therefore, that good government and good economic practices will be able to cope with existing numbers and some steady growth in population. To ask people to restrict their families is an inadequate response to poverty. What is needed is higher economic production. Without that even small families can still suffer.

Three basic issues: resources, services, the environment

The shape of the debate between the pessimists and optimists on the relationship between population growth and poverty becomes clearer when focused on three basic issues: 1) the limits of the world's resources, 2) the provision of basic services for people, and 3) the state of the world's environment.

1) *Limits of the earth's resources*

Humans harness many different resources offered by the earth, but we will focus on the fundamental question of food supply as illustrative of the principles governing the debate about all the earth's resources.

John Guillebaud, who is an evangelical pessimist, is clear about the relationship of population growth to food supply:

> To take the example of Africa where many of the people
> are already starving: it is said that with proper manage-

ment of agriculture and land use it could feed four times its population. However from my experience many Africans do not find this convincing and want to reduce the numbers drawing on its resources. They understand that Africa is a finite land area and that many African countries are doubling their population in about twenty years. Despite the 'green revolution'[8] it is rash to bank on continuing to produce enough for populations which grow exponentially ad infinitum.[9]

Optimists, on the other hand, point to falling commodity prices as an indication that the world is becoming saturated by primary commodities which include basic foodstuffs. The reason why people starve is not a question of production but of distribution. 'Starvation is the characteristic of some people not having enough to eat. It is not the characteristic of there not being enough food to eat.'[10] Furthermore, incredible claims are made as to the potential that the earth has, in co-operation with humanity, to produce food for future generations. Max Singer claims that the earth could produce more than enough food for 100 billion people if required.[11] The logic behind these predictions is that the strain put on the earth's resources by population growth acts as a catalyst to technological innovation to improve efficiency and/or the discovery of new resources to replace the existing ones.

The pessimists respond to this hopeful analysis with examples of where gains in food production have been made at the expense of the environment. Evidence of the erosion of topsoil

---

[8] A movement in Asia that dominated the 1960s and 1970s, to improve agricultural production through the use of a cocktail of high-yielding varieties of crops, fertilizers, pesticides and improved irrigation. It did lead to huge increases in production although there are increasing signs that now soil erosion is reducing yields.

[9] Guillebaud, J., 'Human needs and human numbers' in *Transformation*, vol. 13, no. 2 (1996), p. 3.

[10] Jackson, B., *Poverty and the Planet* (Harmondsworth, Penguin 1994), p. 37. He is quoting from Sen, A., *Poverty and Famines* (New York, OUP 1982).

[11] Singer, M., *Passage to a Human World: The Dynamics of Creating Global Wealth* (Indianapolis, Hudson Institute 1987), p. 118.

[12] Ehrlich and Ehrlich, *The Population Explosion*, p. 28.

because of overproduction is one example.[12] They also argue that global warming will lead to climate changes that will decimate the earth's ability to produce sufficient food.

2) *Provision of basic services*

Basic services include the provision of health care, housing, education, adequate sanitation, efficient transport systems and a reasonable level of welfare services such as care for the elderly or mentally ill when families do not take responsibility for that care. Such basic services are not available in many rural and urban areas at present. Here the question is whether there is any link between population growth and the ability or inability of governments and private enterprises to provide these basic services.

In the urban context it is not possible to make any direct link between population levels and provision of services since equally densely populated cities can have vastly different levels of service for their inhabitants. However, it is clear that rapid population growth does put a great strain on the provision of services in much the same way as an ageing population does. In both cases there is an increase in the number of people needing services, but due to their age (young or old) contributing little to the city government's income. Many of the young people will eventually become contributors to the system, but in the mean time they require education and health care in particular. The extent to which the old and young are an economic burden on the rest of society must of course be qualified by the role they often play in the informal economy.

Meanwhile cities, in the Third World in particular, struggle to cope with growing populations. In cities some 600 million people are estimated to have no proper home; a billion lack sanitation and 250 million have no easy access to safe water. The prospect of unchecked population growth in the urban context, therefore, seems to lend weight to the pessimist argument that population growth leads to poverty.

However, some counter-arguments can be made to this pessimistic analysis. First, some cities, notably in the industrialized world, do regularly cope with periods of rapid population growth. It puts an immediate strain on the capacity of the city, but in the long term children become producers who pay back what they owe to the system. Reducing family sizes may mean that short-term strains are avoided, but it is storing up problems for later when there may be an ageing population with few economically active people to support them.

Second, many of the problems faced by cities are caused not by population growth, but by large-scale migration from rural to urban contexts. Since many migrants are of childbearing age there will be a rapid increase in population, despite the tendency in cities to have smaller families. This growth due to migration puts an enormous strain on the infrastructures of cities throughout the world. The problem, therefore, is not so much one of family size as the distribution of people. The answer is to improve the economy of rural areas so that migration to the city becomes less desirable.

3) *The state of the environment*

Most agree that the world's environment is facing problems that will increasingly lead to poverty and suffering among parts of the population: global warming, ozone depletion, acid rain, topsoil erosion, desertification, ground water supply losses and reductions in ecological diversity.[13] But there is disagreement about the relationship between population growth and environmental destruction.

Ehrlich, the arch-pessimist expresses his doomsday model in the formula:

Environmental Impact I = Population P × Affluence A × Technology T [I = PAT]

He accepts that the affluent West consumes far more than the Third World. Therefore, in this area the West contributes more to the process of environmental destruction. It is this consumption that drives world technology. Slowing down consumption and making technology more sustainable, therefore, is vital for the preservation of the environment. But, Ehrlich goes on to argue that if population growth is not curbed all the effort

---

[13] For more detail see ch. 12, 'Environment, Poverty and the Kingdom'.

made to reduce consumption and to make technology more sustainable would soon be eroded by the inevitable consumption of more people.[14] Population growth threatens to deplete the resources of the world even if the affluence of some is reduced and technology is made more environmentally friendly.

There are at least two counter-arguments to Ehrlich's position. Firstly, his model seems to assume that all additions to world population will consume at the expense of the environment. But the problems are really caused by the very high consumption levels of the Western lifestyle.[15] The relatively low levels of consumption in poorer countries, where populations are growing, does not contribute as significantly to environmental degradation. There might be more danger for the environment from people in the Third World adopting a greedy Western lifestyle with its attendant reduction in population growth. Secondly, people can be extremely innovative, in the most unlikely circumstances, in improving the quality of their environment.[16] A mixture of technological advance and greater conservation could drastically reduce pollution levels.

The possible impacts of pessimism on government policy

The fact that most policymakers have favoured the pessimistic view for more than a generation has sometimes had a profound impact on people's lives. This is particularly the case in countries that have set official targets for the reduction of population growth.

China is probably the best-known example with its imposed one-child policy. Another example is the policy of female sterilization implemented by the Puerto Rican government as early as 1950. As a result large numbers of women who were

---

[14] Ehrlich and Ehrlich, *The Population Explosion*, p. 59.

[15] For example, kgs of oil used per person in 1991: USA, 7662; UK, 3743; Korea, 2569; Mexico, 1525; Zambia, 158; Bangladesh, 59.

[16] Cf. Chambers, R., *Whose Reality Counts? Putting the First Last* (Intermediate Technology 1997), pp. 23ff., where evidence is marshalled against the belief that more people are bad for the environment.

dependent on the public health system because of poverty were sterilized without their knowledge. Between 1950 and 1977 the fertility rate in Puerto Rico fell from 5.2 to 2.7. As a result of the economic crisis of 1966 India also adopted a policy of setting targets for reducing population. In the beginning this led to the coercive sterilization of men, which caused a very strong backlash. The government was forced to temper the policy primarily by moving the focus of attention to women but health professionals still have target levels of fertility to achieve.

There has been for some time a consensus of opinion on all sides of the population debate that governments have no right to impose limits on family size. Even the Chinese have been forced to abandon the one-child policy as unworkable in the rural areas. But the policy still applies to the urban population of the most populous country in the world. The Puerto Rican government was forced to abandon its policy of sterilization in 1978 as a result of international pressure. But giving health professionals targets still provides a strong incentive to use coercive methods to achieve them in India. The same is true in Indonesia which is often held up as a model of government involvement in population control. The very detailed and ambitious targets set by health professionals lead to undue pressure being put on individuals and couples. It is somewhat worrying to find that the Council of Churches in Indonesia is fully involved in implementing this government policy.[17]

There is a danger that the 'doom scenarios' presented by some could lead to a greater sympathy with coercive policies again. The following sentiments are found in a recent volume on the state of the world:

> As other countries realize that continuing on their current population trajectory will prevent them from achieving a similar food/population balance more and more may decide to do what China has done – launch an all-out

---

[17] See Corrêa, S., *Population and Reproductive Rights* (London and New Jersey, Zed/New Delhi, Kali 1994), pp. 25ff. This volume is strongly feminist and pro-abortion but contains a lot of helpful information. See also Mesach, O., 'The role of the Christian community in the family planning movement in Indonesia: a case study', *Transformation*, vol. 13, no. 2 (1996), pp. 31ff.

campaign to stabilize population. Like China, other countries will have to carefully balance the reproductive rights
of the current generation with the survival rights of the
next generation. [We may be forced to consider a] trade-off
between the reproductive rights of the current generation
and the survival rights of the next . . . The time may have
come to limit tax deductions for children to two per couple:
it may not make sense to subsidize childbearing beyond
replacement level when the most pressing need facing
humanity is to stabilize population.[18]

Another factor to be taken into consideration is that much of the
debate is simply concerned with the relationship between economic growth and rates of population growth. Essentially economic well-being is the key goal to be reached and this
well-being is measured in terms of certain measurable resources
per head such as land and capital. In the language of Western
economics, people can become, in effect, a nuisance, a drain on
a country's resources. An extra child is a drain on a family's
resources and by extension a country's resources, until that child
begins to earn for itself. It is a debate dominated by Western
economists. It is a debate, furthermore, that could be predicted
to emerge from the materialistic Western nations that seem to
understand everything primarily in terms of acquiring more
wealth.

   We need to realize that much of what is said and done in the
area of population control is an expression of Western culture
with its emphasis on each individual's right to enjoy all the
benefits that life in this world can offer. Many in the West
already enjoy such a lifestyle. At best, the desire of Western
academics to see the populations of the Third World controlled
can be seen as a desire for the Third World to enjoy the same
material benefits. At worst it is a case of diminishing the threat
to a Western lifestyle posed by population growth. But one thing
is clear – there is a crying need for Christians to speak with a
clear biblical voice on this issue.

---

[18]   Brown, *State of the World*, pp. 12–13,17,20.

Christian perspective on population

A Christian perspective on population must provide principles that will enable policymakers to address national, regional and global concerns in a way that will honour the Creator and bring blessing to people. It must also give some guidance to wives and husbands as to how many children they would like and when they would like to have them. Since as Christians we have the Maker's manual for humanity we have much that is vital and transforming to bring to the secular debates that rage around the population issue.

The Christian perspective as it encompasses the global and local must deal with two distinct questions: 1) What is the optimum population size as defined by God in the Bible? This will include both optimum family size as well as optimum global population. 2) How does God intend us to get to this optimum population size?

1. *The biblical optimum*

Secular thinkers approaching the population issue normally have a particular view of what the optimum world population would be. How they define this optimum depends on their judgment of what is important. At the moment the most popular emphasis is that the optimum level of population would be that at which the environment is preserved rather than plundered. Population, therefore, is at its optimum point when a sustainable relationship with nature can be maintained. Others still tied to economic categories think of the optimum population as being the level of population that produces the conditions most conducive to economic growth whether that be the growth of family income or GNP. Underlying both these approaches is a utilitarian value system which believes people exist to maximize their happiness and minimize their pain. So, it is necessary that they both have a sustainable relationship with the natural world on which they depend and that they maximize economic production. The ultimate value is human happiness and everything must be subordinated to this goal.[19] Admittedly, some urge respect for nature as an absolute value. They do not see respect for the environment as merely a way of securing long-term human happiness. However, most secular thinkers concerned with the environment have an essentially utilitarian approach to it.

On this utilitarian basis the values of economic productivity or environmental sustainability often dominate the debate. As a result population growth can be seen merely as a factor in the equation. Often it is considered an unhelpful factor. Therefore, writers can resort to the language of disease to describe population growth. P. Ehrlich is not alone when he describes population growth as a 'cancer-like disease'.[20] Population growth is a 'bomb' that has 'exploded' and is threatening to wreck the environment, economic growth and the happiness of the world. Population growth is not a good in itself. Because it threatens other values it is a disease, a curse. In the language of ethics, population growth is not an absolute but a relative value. If growth in population accompanies growth in productivity and is environmentally sustainable then it is considered good. But relative to environmental destruction, or loss of economic well-being, it is considered a bad thing.

A similar pattern of ethical reasoning can emerge at the level of family decision making. Children are valued relative to their ability to satisfy certain requirements. At its most obscene the value of children is measured in terms of the fulfilment they will or will not bring to their parents. For example, a young couple

---

[19] Wogaman's criticism of this utilitarian view highlights a weakness at the heart of the utilitarian system: 'if the objectives of individuals in approaching questions of population policy should be their own private happiness, the goal would be quite understandable, though selfish and of doubtful ethical standing in the long run. If on the other hand, the goal should be the happiness of the greatest number of people, some ethical principle broader than happiness itself would be required for the obligation to make *other* people happy.' Wogaman, J. (ed.), *The Population Crisis and Moral Responsibility* (Washington, DC, Public Affairs Press 1973), p. 9.

[20] Ehrlich and Ehrlich, *The Population Explosion*, p. 23.

discover that the woman is pregnant. In view of their career plans it is not a good time to conceive, so the baby is aborted. Another obscene relativization of the value of individuals can be seen in societies which place a premium on male babies for religious or socio-economic reasons. Relative to the need for a male heir a girl child is deemed superfluous. If not aborted she will be treated with less care than her brothers. These are extreme examples of what happens when socio-economic well-being, social status or religious requirements are substituted as the currency of ultimate value in deciding the relative value of a human being.

In opposition to this utilitarian approach the Bible teaches that: a) each individual added to the world's population is a blessing from God that is more valuable than anything else on earth, and b) God desires that each individual experiences life on earth as a blessing.

a)   The Bible makes it clear that population growth is a blessing at a global, national and family level. Globally, because God blessed human beings at their creation and 'said to them, "Be fruitful and increase in number; fill the earth and subdue it." '[21] Some theologians have attempted to read as much as possible into the word 'fill' and argue that the earth is as yet nowhere near as full of human beings as it could and should be.[22] It cannot be denied that some parts of the inhabitable earth are nowhere near as densely populated as others and that more often than not it is the richest parts that are more densely populated. Nationally, because God's promise to Abraham to make his 'descendants as numerous as the stars in the sky and as the sand on the seashore'[23] underlines the fact that increasing in numbers is a blessing to a nation. To be great in numbers is an important part of what it means to be a great nation. Within the family, one

---

[21]   Gen. 1:28; 9:1–2 for the almost identical blessing given to Noah.

[22]   C. Beisner, for example, understands it to mean 'to fill completely so that nothing is left over'. He then asks, 'Is the earth "filled" to this extent? Certainly not, and it appears unlikely that it will become so in the foreseeable future . . .' Beisner, *Prospects for Growth*, p. 50.

[23]   Gen. 22:17. See also Gen. 12:2; 13:16; 15:5.

of the great blessings of fearing the Lord is a wife who produces a quiverful of sons and children are seen as a reward from God.[24]

Population growth is essentially a blessing because of the identity of each individual who makes up that growth. This is how David describes his identity in relation to God from his conception onwards:

> I praise you because I am fearfully and wonderfully made; your works are wonderful, I know that full well. My frame was not hidden from you when I was made in the secret place. When I was woven together in the depths of the earth, your eyes saw my unformed body.[25]

Each individual, both male and female, are made in the image of God.[26] The constant refrain in the Old Testament that God is on the side of the widow, the orphan and the alien witnesses to the value he puts on human beings. In the context of society these categories were the least valuable in terms of their productivity or their contribution to the life of the community, yet God protects them. The same could be said for the poor. Jesus confirmed this teaching by his life, his death and his words. He gave sight to blind beggars, he raised the widow's son, he forgave prostitutes and tax collectors their sins. He reassured his followers that when they became the rejected of the earth and devalued by society at large that he would continue to value them. 'Are not five sparrows sold for two pennies?' he said, 'Yet not one of them is forgotten by God. Indeed the very hairs of your head are all numbered. Don't be afraid; you are worth more than many sparrows.'[27]

The biblical emphasis on the absolute value of each individual must make us very wary of all analyses of population problems that in subtle ways suggest that some population increase is a nuisance. All population increase has irreducible value because God has poured his creative power into each individual born. The glory of each individual must never be subsumed within

---

[24] Ps. 128:3; 127:3–5.
[25] Ps. 139:14–15.
[26] Gen. 1:27.
[27] Lk. 12:6–7.

impersonal categories of progress. A child is not an economic asset or an economic liability, but a gift of God.[28]

b) God's intention for humanity is not simply that they fill the earth. He wants the inhabitants of the earth to experience life as a blessing. Isaiah foresees the fulfilment of this intention in the glorious vision of the new heaven and *new earth*:

> Never again will there be in it [the earth] an infant who lives but a few days, or an old man who does not live out his years . . . They will build houses and dwell in them; they will plant vineyards and eat their fruit. No longer will they build houses and others dwell in them, or plant and others eat. For as the days of a tree, so will be the days of my people; my chosen ones will long enjoy the works of their hands. They will not toil in vain or bear children doomed to misfortune; for they will be a people blessed by the Lord, they and their descendants with them.[29]

It is true that this picture of longevity, prosperity and peace can only become a complete reality in heaven but it is a picture firmly rooted in the earth. The full revelation of God's kingdom is yet to come but the kingdom is also present now in Jesus and in the power of the Spirit manifested through his people. Humility, sorrow for sin, meekness, a passion for righteousness, mercy and peacemaking are possible now. Wherever these virtues are manifested they bring blessing and show what the future glorious kingdom will be like. To be true disciples of Christ is to be something of the kingdom now.

However, it is not always easy to be caught between the 'now' and 'not yet' of the kingdom. I will never forget my visit to a family in a remote village in northern Colombia. Both parents lived with their 11 children in a small and very rudimentary

---

[28] There is increased deliberate childlessness in the West. The reasons are complex but research from the Joseph Rowntree Foundation in Britain suggests that the primary reason is an increased individualism amongst adults. They see children as a threat to their independence and their fulfilment. A secondary reason is the opinion that children are an economic burden both in terms of their consumption and in terms of the pressure their existence puts on adults to suspend their careers during the early years of their upbringing.

[29] Isa. 65:20–3.

shack with no water supply or sewerage system. The whole family were suffering from TB. I was visiting this family because there were disciples of Christ in their village who cared for them and who wanted to bring blessing into their lives. They obviously wanted them to hear about Jesus and his love for lost sinners but they were not content, simply, with getting them to trust in Jesus and leaving them to die of TB so that they could go to be with him in heaven as soon as possible. The 'not yet' of the kingdom as portrayed in Isaiah and other places has impacted their 'now'.

The 'now' for the villagers is a situation of political and economic oppression. They belong to a once-noble indigenous people who have been reduced to poverty by European invaders, and subsequent post-colonial forces, who came and took their land from them. They live in a sparsely populated area where most of the land is owned by a few landowners who use the fertile land very inefficiently to raise cattle. Any work that most of the men in the villages can get is dependent on the landowners' seasonal needs for labour. Since they have no access to any means to produce wealth they are forced to live in abject poverty. The pattern of land distribution laid down for Israel and the picture of the glorious new earth say that justice would be done if the land were taken away from its greedy owners and distributed equitably among the people so that all should have enough to live on. With good food, a good house, clean water, sanitation and medical care it is not impossible for 11 children to be born to a family without destroying the life of the mother, and live a life of contentment and joy.

Sadly such radical economic and political change is very difficult to achieve. In the village in northern Colombia the Christians were trying to move in the direction of justice by buying some land from a landowner so that a number of very poor labouring families – including the family I met – could farm the land as a co-operative to raise their standard of living. They were also seeking to address the problem of TB in the family. Being from a Western context, where family planning has become such an accepted part of life, I asked whether large families in the area were the result of lack of access or ideological resistance to such practice. I was told that men were rather resistant to family planning because they thought that their virility was proved by producing many children. Women, on the other hand, want to have fewer children and to have longer spaces between those they have. In the desperately imperfect 'now' of their situation it seems harsh to deny these women the freedom to use methods that human beings have devised in God's providence to control the size and spacing of their families. To give them access to land, medical care to deal with the TB and family planning advice to make their family complete could all qualify as bringing this large family nearer to the peace of the kingdom in Jesus' name.

The key to God's vision for humanity, is for people to live in peace with each other, with God and with his creation.[30] This peace is more than the absence of conflict. It is rather the establishment of healthy, nourishing relationships. Clearly in the Bible this peace requires certain material conditions to flourish. This is inevitable given that God chose to demonstrate his love for humanity through creation. One of the prominent biblical images for peace in the Bible is that 'of a man sitting in the shade of his own fig tree with security of land, freedom from fear of his enemies and enough to live on'.[31] It is this concern for the material conditions necessary for life in all its fullness that drives the Old Testament prophets in their denunciation of the exploitation of the poor. It is the injustice perpetrated by the rich that prevents people having the physical and emotional elements necessary for flourishing.

---

[30] The Hebrews thought in terms of *shalom* which is commonly translated as peace, health or wholeness. It conveys the fullness of a life that is lived according to God's guidelines and within God's creation as it is meant to be. *The New Dictionary of Christian Ethics and Pastoral Theology* defines it as follows, 'To experience *shalom* is to flourish in all one's relationships – with God, with one's fellow human beings, with the non-human creation, with oneself' Atkinson, D. and Field, D. (eds.), (Leicester, IVP 1995) pp. 19–20. See Gen. 26:29 for peace between humans; see Isa. 54:10 for peace with God; see Isa. 32:18 for peace between humans and the non-human creation. There are also close links between *shalom* and health, 'The punishment that brought us peace [Hebrew word translated "peace" is derivative of *shalom*] was upon him, and by his wounds we are healed' (Isa. 53:5).

[31] McCloughry, R., *Population Growth and Christian Ethics* (Cambridge, Grove 1995), p. 16. See also Mic. 4:4.

It is also important to emphasize that God's vision for human life encompasses the health and well-being of mothers. Virtually all people involved in health care in the Third World identify the health of mothers as a particular problem area. There are many interlocking reasons for this situation, but many health workers see childbirth rates as a key factor since it puts repeated strain on women's bodies. This general exhaustion is a contributory factor to the high rate of mothers who die during pregnancy and childbirth.[32] The Bible is clear that problems in childbirth are not in God's original intention for women. Rather, they are the terrible effects of the Fall, which Christians should struggle against.[33]

2) *How does God intend us to get to the optimum population size?*

While agreeing that each individual added to the world's population is a blessing from God, and that God desires that everyone experiences life as a blessing, there is less agreement among Evangelicals on the role of family planning in achieving this. There are at least three different positions held by evangelicals:

a) Population growth is a sign of God's providential blessing. To worry about the rate of world population growth is symptomatic of a lack of faith in God's providential love.[34] Consequently individual Christian families should reproduce with the abandon that comes from a belief in the providence of God. As Beisner says, 'By choosing to have fewer children, we not only turn down what Scripture calls a blessed gift and reward from God (Ps. 127:3), but also reduce the number of most likely

---

[32] It was estimated that in 1996 585,000 women worldwide would die in pregnancy or childbirth. There are huge country-by-country and region-by-region differences. Maternal deaths per 100,000 live births expressed in regional averages: Sub-Saharan Africa, 980; Middle East and North Africa, 300; Central Asia, 560; Asia and Pacific, 390; Americas, 140; Europe, 36. (Statistics from UNICEF's *The Progress of Nations 1996*, pp. 8–9).

[33] Gen. 3:16.

[34] Beisner, *Prospects for Growth*, p. 153.

candidates for service in obeying the Great Commission.'[35] Christians should encourage non-Christians similarly to embrace this position since God's providence extends to them as well.[36]

This type of thinking can be linked into the secular model described earlier which puts its faith in the free market and human resourcefulness.[37] Because people are producers first, and then consumers, more people results in more prosperity and, therefore, fewer people in need. Beisner claims that, 'we get more land, food, and other resources, and less pollution *per person*, as the world's population grows. This view indicates not an idealistic faith in man (something entirely contrary to my belief in original sin and total depravity), but faith in the marvellous providence of God working through His creatures despite their moral corruption'.[38]

This position is not necessarily against contraception, but its confidence for the future is definitely not in contraception, but in the providence of God.[39] The Christian's task is not to make family planning available but to rejoice in God's providence. This type of approach has no fears concerning the distribution of population either. It sees cities essentially as places of opportunity and economic efficiency. They are also a part of the gracious plan of God for humanity.

b) Family planning is a part of God's providential gift, giving people the ability and responsibility to plan the size of their families. This is currently the dominant model among evangelicals. As Tim Stafford puts it: 'Nowhere does God guarantee that He will divert disaster no matter how we behave. Just the reverse: human ingenuity, planning and creativity are part

---

[35] Ibid. p. 175.

[36] See, for example, Mt. 5:45.

[37] Beisner, *Prospects for Growth*, p. 103.

[38] Ibid. p. 65.

[39] Beisner for example has no particular problem with contraception, although he does urge people not to worry about the resources/mouths to feed problem. On contraception he states, 'Liberty should extend to people's choices about their lives (including the choice to have or not to have children, but not the right to kill children once conceived) and their property'. Beisner, *Prospects for Growth*, p. 186.

of God's providence. They are a way in which He characteristically provides for our needs.'[40] Similarly, 'we are not under a divine call to produce as great a quantity of offspring as possible, but to bear children who can be nurtured and given appropriate attention, instruction, love and material resources'.[41]

Much of the argument for this position is concerned with the realities of people's lives. Access to family planning will drastically improve the health of the overburdened mother. It will enable a family to put all its children through education as opposed to only a few. In short it will lead to a fulfilment of God's vision for the quality of human life. The basic thrust of this argument is that we have a responsibility before God to ensure the possibility of a good quality of life for present and future generations. This will involve a reduction in population growth rates. Since this reduction will not happen inevitably, family planning services need to be provided.

Many Christians holding this second position acknowledge the problems associated with contraception. They agree that the sexual act has lost the weight it used to have when conception was at stake. As a result promiscuity has crept in. However, they have sought to acknowledge the truth of this argument whilst also endorsing the proper use of contraceptives. It is possible to use contraception in the context of righteous decisions within the context of the family. A key distinction is also drawn between contraception and abortion on the grounds that human life begins at conception.[42]

Part of the impetus for the Protestant change in attitude towards contraception has been a change in thinking about the purpose of sexual union. At the beginning of the twentieth century the primary purpose was procreation. At the end the primary focus is relational.[43]

---

[40] Stafford, T., 'Are people the problem?' in *Christianity Today* (3 October 1994), pp. 45–60.

[41] Atkinson and Field *New Dictionary of Christian Ethics*, p. 195.

[42] See, for example, O'Donovan, O., *The Christian and The Unborn Child* (Cambridge, Grove Books 1986). It contains a brilliant defence of the view that human life begins at conception.

[43] Compare the 1662 Book of Common Prayer description of the purposes of married union with the Alternative Service Book description of 1980.

c) The issue is not population growth but the equitable distribution of the earth's resources. The destiny of current and future generations is tied up with whether we resolve this basic issue of justice. Rather than criticizing the Third World for its high birth rate, we should be criticizing the West for its high consumption rate. The Bible has much to say on justice and rather less on population issues, so we should get on with striving after fairness in the distribution of the world's resources.

Those who advocate this view object to the use of aid to encourage birth control in the Third World. They deplore the fact that the outcome of the UN Cairo Conference on Population and Development in 1994 will be the investment of $15.5 billion in population control and $1.5 billion in Aids research by the year 2000 to the neglect of basic health care, the provision of clean water and so on.[44]

This view balances a belief in the providence of God with a recognition of the effects of the fall upon human relations. From Cain and Abel onwards human beings have abused and exploited each other. Therefore Christians should be concerned to work for the redistribution of resources. If the experience of the West and of wealthy Christians in the Third World is typical, to have a fair share of the earth's resources will inevitably lead to a lower birth rate. Focusing on birth control is, therefore, putting the cart before the horse. At worst it is an attempt to maintain existing inequalities of distribution while minimizing the potential for unrest.[45]

---

[44] Smeaton, J., 'A personal interpretation of Roman Catholic teaching on population', *Transformation*, vol. 13, no. 3 (1996), p. 4.

[45] Pope John Paul II, 'The Pharaoh of old, haunted by the presence of and increase of the children of Israel, submitted them to every kind of oppression and ordered that every male child born of the Hebrew women was to be killed (cf. Ex. 1:7–22). Today not a few of the powerful of the earth act in the same way. They too are haunted by the current demographic growth and fear that the most prolific and poorest peoples represent a threat for the well-being and peace of their own countries. Consequently, rather than wishing to face and solve these serious problems with respect for the dignity of individuals and families and for every person's inviolable right to life, they prefer to promote and impose by whatever means a massive programme of birth control. Even the economic help which they would be ready to give is unjustly made conditional on the

Conclusion

Not one of these positions has a monopoly on biblical truth. There are emphases in all of them which seem consistent with God's will:

i) *Providence*. Secular analyses often come close to panic when considering the future.[46] Christians must counter this pessimism with an assertion of God's control over every aspect of human activity, even those which stem from fallen and irresponsible attitudes. God is in control of history. It is he, ultimately, who secures provision for the world's population.[47] However, this confidence must not descend into fatalism. Within his providence God gives humans responsibilities in relation to their fellow humans and the rest of creation. Human abilities are a part of God's provision for humanity.

ii) *Responsibility before God*. We have a responsibility before God to ensure that children grow up in situations that convey the gracious provision of God for them. This may mean a responsible decision to limit family size. It also means that Christians should recognize some truth in global analyses that point to the strains on the worlds' resources that further rapid population growth could produce. However, this must not lead to coercive policies that threaten the right of individual families to decide their own family size according to their own situation.

Whilst recognizing the place of family planning within responsible parenthood, Christians must ensure that family planning never threatens the esteem in which children are held. In the West family planning has been a contributory factor in the rise of the 'fear of the child'.[48] Children are always and everywhere a supreme blessing of God. The only place for family planning

---

Footnote 45 (*continued*)   acceptance of an anti-birth policy'. Quoted by Smeaton, J., 'A personal interpretation', *Transformation*, vol. 13, no. 3 (1996), p. 7.

[46] See for example Brown, L., *State of the World 1996* (London, Earthscan), pp. 3–21.

[47] Mt. 5:45.

[48] A phrase coined by Mother Theresa of Calcutta to describe some Western attitudes.

is within this broad assertion of the supreme value of each human being from the moment of conception.

Protecting the health and well-being of mothers should be vital to Christians. Women often suffer terrible guilt and stigmatization if they produce no children and in particular no male children. This reduces women to baby-producing machines. Instead the huge range of contributions that women can make to society should be recognized. Neither should women who have no problems reproducing be expected to produce children in quick succession just to prove a man's virility. The whole process should be a co-operative effort which takes into consideration the well-being of the mother as well as that of the children.

Christians must also recognize that the migration of people from rural to urban situations puts severe strains on the capacity of cities to provide. Attention should be paid to tackling the factors that force people to leave rural areas. Attention should also be given to the development of cities into places that encourage human flourishing.

iii) *Justice.* Christians must be realistic about the effects of the Fall on God's world. Two effects stand out in relation to population. The Fall introduced problems into humanity's relationship with the earth on which it depends for its life. Production became more difficult with the possibility of scarcity.[49]

The Fall also led to abusive relationships between humans. Much of the poverty in the contemporary world results from a selfish failure to redistribute wealth on behalf of the rich. Instead they continue to get richer while the poor get poorer.[50] Furthermore, the patterns of consumption in richer nations threaten the environment on which people in poorer nations depend. Christians must strive in the prophetic tradition for the fair

---

[49] Gen. 3:18.

[50] For example the *UN Human Development Report 1996* (Oxford, OUP 1996) records three particularly telling statistics: 1) In 1960 the richest 20 per cent of the world's population were 30 times better off than the poorest 20 per cent. Now they are 61 times richer. 2) In 70 countries average incomes are less than they were in 1980, and in 43 less than in 1970. 3) In 1990–93 average incomes fell by a fifth or more in 21 countries, mostly in E. Europe and the Commonwealth of Independent States (CIS).

distribution of resources. This striving must accompany any family planning provision.[51]

An awareness of the perversity of human nature should also undermine the confidence of some that the free market, in conjunction with improvements in technology, will lead to universal improvements in living conditions. Both the free market and technological innovation can be used to exploit others. They may be neutral tools but in the hands of human moral agents they can be a force for evil as well as good.

Resources

Books

McCloughry, Roy, *Population Growth and Christian Ethics* (Cambridge, Grove Books 1995), provides a balanced introduction to the main population issues and the different ways people have responded to them.

Beisner, E. Calvin, *Prospects for Growth* (Westchester, Crossway 1990). Controversial book arguing that worries about population growth are overexaggerated and reflect a lack of confidence in God's providence.

Not specifically Christian

Simon, Julian, *The Ultimate Resource* (Princeton, Princeton University Press 1981). A controversial, well-argued attempt to debunk theories that continued population growth comprises a threat to the world. People produce more than they consume.

Ehrlich, Paul and Anne, *The Population Explosion* (London, Arrow 1990). In conscious opposition to Simon (there is considerable animosity between the two protagonists!), a well-argued prediction of coming doom if population growth continues at current rates.

---

[51] 'A Christian Response to Population Issues – an Oxford Statement' in *Transformation*, vol. 13, no. 2, pp. 5–17.

Articles

Stafford, Tim, 'Are People the Problem?' in *Christianity Today* (3 October 1994), provides a brilliantly concise introduction to the main issues.

Carter, Isobel, 'The population debate' in *Footsteps*, no. 27 (Teddington, Tearfund 1996), pp. 1–3, provides another useful introduction.

Transformation, vol. 13, no. 2 (1996), contains the following articles:

Guillebaud, John, 'Human needs and human numbers'.

Dan, Oriejji Chimere, 'A Christian demographer's response to human needs and human numbers'.

Tomkins, Andrew, 'Population challenges for the two-thirds world: with specific reference to mother and child health'.

Harris, Harriet A., 'Christian feminism and feminist perspectives on population control'.

Mesach, Olly, 'The role of the christian community in the family planning movement in Indonesia'.

TWELVE

Environment, Poverty and the Kingdom

Any type of human life on earth is only possible because of what the earth produces to sustain it. This is true for everyone: for poor and rich, rural and urban dweller alike. Even to sustain the simplest type of human life with dignity demands that we extract considerable resources from the earth around us: we need food to eat, clothes to wear and a home in which to live. By using the creative gifts given us by God we have developed an incredible variety of means to use natural resources to meet our basic needs and also our desire for comfort and pleasure. In doing so we have not only improved the natural environment but created our own urban environment in which we find ourselves removed almost entirely from the natural environment which continues to sustain us.

The history of human creativity in shaping natural resources to fit a whole range of different purposes is an epic story. Sadly it is also a tragedy. The profound sinfulness of human beings has meant that our most glorious cultural feats have been achieved at a terrible cost in human suffering. The mortar of the wonderful architectural constructions of the ages is full of the blood of the poor and oppressed. Today some have come to the conclusion that we may be witnessing the final chapter of our history as the greed and pride of the minority threatens to destroy the very earth which sustains our life.

Environmentalists are famous for proclaiming woe and destruction on humankind. Since the 1960s they have been predicting that many natural resources such as oil would soon come to an end. A great many of their predictions have already been proved false so that, by at least one biblical test, they must be assigned to the category of false prophets. On the other hand it is possible that they have recognized a very real wolf and that though, so far, the wolf has not come when they have cried wolf, that which threatens our life on earth may very well be on its way to maul us. It is probably true to say that rich people, particularly in the West, are beginning to take the wolf of environmental destruction a little more seriously – but only a little!

Environmental concern: a leisure interest of the rich?

In the prosperous West the need for humans to take care of their environment is increasingly taken for granted. Little may be done, but people see measures such as energy conservation, pollution control, protection of endangered habitats, and reductions in deforestation, as desirable goals. Many have a rudimentary grasp of the dangers of global warming, acid rain and the depletion of the ozone layer. Others deplore their loss of countryside to new roads and cities. Their concern for the environment is, in one sense a luxury of post-industrial prosperity, originating among wealthy people who have achieved the prosperity to purchase the leisure time to observe that industrial development is degrading their environment.[1] Having achieved and sustained material prosperity through industrialization with all its environmental costs, people are now beginning to wonder, not only whether their days off in the country will be threatened, but whether the prosperity of their children might be reduced as well.

---

[1] Houghton, J., *Global Warming: The Complete Briefing* (Oxford, Lion 1994), p. 152. *The New Internationalist*, no. 278 (1996), p. 19.

Pollution, acid rain and global warming clearly have their origins in the industrialization of the West on which the prosperous countries depend for their livelihood. The industrialized Western nations remain the heaviest users of fuel.

So, rich Western eyes have turned with anxiety to the increasing industrialization of the Third World. If Western opulence was won at a heavy cost to the environment what would be the cost if the majority world was to achieve the same standard of living? Total destruction? The point is not made in so many words but the implication is clear. The Third World must not be allowed to achieve the same comforts as the West enjoys because that would threaten the Western lifestyle.

It is not surprising therefore, that some in the Third World have viewed the Western concern for the environment as the hypocritical panic of a rich class worried about luxury issues. It is easy, for example, to campaign about the preservation of rain-forests from the comfort of middle-class Britain. The issue looks very different from the perspective of a landless farmer in Brazil whose family faces starvation if he or she does not occupy a part of the rainforest. Similarly, it is easy to mutter about the production of carbon dioxide by Indian coal-burning electricity plants from the comfort of Britain or the USA where electricity is taken for granted. Most serious is the gross hypocrisy involved, given the vastly higher rates of consumption in the West compared to the Third World.

This is not to say that the poor are disinterested in the environment, but that their concerns are often different from those of the prosperous. For example, in the rural context the environmental agenda of the poor might address the following problems which have a direct effect on daily subsistence: loss of productive land through soil erosion for various reasons such as drought, deforestation or a lack of adequate land holdings to allow for crop rotation; loss of firewood through rapid deforestation; shortage of available water through reduction in underground reserves and difficulties in accessing reserves; commercial interests buying up large tracts of rainforest or prime agricultural land for cash crops or livestock, thereby depriving indigenous people of access. The environmental concerns of the poor grow out of an experience of poverty. They know that the environment must be protected if they are to survive in the long term but short-term necessity sometimes forces them into environmental abuse.

The environmental agenda of the rich may well overlap with this agenda of the poor, but with very different motivations. For example, the concern for the loss of the rainforest is expressed in terms of its effect on global warming and ecological diversity rather than the subsistence needs of indigenous people. A rich agenda also differs in the type of issues raised. The main concerns are the destruction of natural environments and their wildlife; the increase in the production of greenhouse gases which threatens the ecology of the whole planet and the destructive effects of acid rain and ozone depletion. The rich agenda tends to focus on global issues and trends. Its major concern is for the future citizens of the globe. It grows out of the experience of economic security and is concerned to protect that security for future generations. Admittedly, this description of the different agendas is a caricature, but it expresses the different thrusts of the rich and poor when approaching environmental issues.

The perspectives may be different but in the last analysis the agendas of rich and poor are interdependent. It is in everyone's interest to preserve ecological diversity. Valuable sources of medicine and new crops could be protected, which may one day enrich the lives of rich and poor. Our lives are inextricably linked together. But this is a book about God's heart for the poor, so, before looking at the underlying assumptions of the environmental movement and biblical teaching we need to look in more detail at the environment which the poor, in particular, experience.

Environmental problems and their causes

The city

The cities of the Third World are growing very rapidly.[2] This results from rapid rates of population growth among urban populations, migration from rural areas into cities and the

---

[2] Katherine Hagen, Deputy Director of the UN International Labour organization, predicts that 'by 2000 one half of humanity will be living and working in cities, with developing countries accounting for the major share of the world's new urban population.' *The Independent*, 30 May 1996. The UNFPA (United Nations Population Fund) identified 45 per cent of the world's population as living in cities, in their 1995 report.

sprawl of many cities over outlying towns and villages. It results in an increasing number of cities with large populations but infrastructures built for much smaller populations.[3] Cairo, for example, has an expanding population currently estimated at 15 million in a city with an adequate infrastructure for 1 million people. It is not surprising that rapidly expanding cities contain many environmental threats.

Housing is often woefully inadequate. Some 600 million people, it is estimated, live in sub-standard homes.[4] Many basic public services are beyond governments' capacity to provide.[5] The disposal of waste is a major problem – it is often left in the hands of certain poor sections of the community who eke out a living from recycling rubbish. The management of waste, however, always threatens to overtake the ability of cities to cope.

Another threat, which is more in line with accepted environmental thinking, arises because of the density of people living in cities. There is a growing consensus among environmentalists that global warming could threaten the survival of many communities through the world. The production of carbon monoxide by cars is a major contributory factor to this process.[6] Cities have the potential to reduce significantly the quantities of carbon monoxide entering the atmosphere because the density of population means that public transport systems are economically viable. However, all over the world the car is setting the agenda. The West, which is most profligate in its use of the car

---

[3] 'In 1950 the world had 83 cities with populations of 1,000,000 or more. Today there are 280. By 2015 there will be more than 500.' *The Independent*, 30 May 1996. Significantly the rate of urban growth according to the UNFPA '95 report is highest in the 'least developed countries' of the world: 5.2 per cent. This is compared to 0.7 per cent in the 'more developed regions' and 3.3 per cent in the 'less developed regions'.

[4] Editorial, 'Future Cities and Habitat II', *Environment and Urbanisation*, vol. 8, no. 1 (1996), p. 9.

[5] In Third World countries with a crippling debt to pay to the West 'Structural Adjustment Programmes' (SAPs) often draw government money out of the provision of these basic services. For more detail, see subsection 'The Debt Crisis' in ch. 7, 'Economics, Poverty and the Kingdom'.

[6] Carbon monoxide is not the only damaging pollutant to come from cars. Many also are concerned about the social price of our dependence on cars. See, for example, Newman, P., 'Reducing automobile dependence', *Environment and Urbanisation*, vol. 8, no. 1 (1996), pp. 67ff.

is quickly choking its cities while in the Third World massive increases in the use of cars and lorries, with little control of the emission of pollutants, is creating an extremely unhealthy atmosphere for citizens.[7] This is true even though car ownership per head is far lower in Third World cities than in the West. As Third World cities become more prosperous, commercial interest will see to it that car ownership increases with the attendant rise in local pollution and also in the emission of greenhouse gases which could have a global impact.

The rural situation

When looking at environmental problems from the perspective of the world's rural poor it becomes clear that many live in a vicious cycle of environmental degradation leading to poverty, which in turn leads to degrading use of the land in order to survive. The poor and the environment also suffer as a result of the ruthless profit-making activities of commercial interests. They have to contend with vast inequalities of land distribution, with the few owning the bulk of the available land. Many also have to cope with the devastating effects of war upon their environment. Still others suffer as a result of inappropriate development projects instigated by 'well-meaning' overseas governments and international bodies like the World Bank.

The web of cause and effect in which the rural poor live is very complex. We shall examine this web through a focus on one environmental problem that particularly affects the rural poor: soil erosion. Soil erosion is simply the removal of fertile soil by wind or water, leading to the loss of productive topsoil.[8] Some soil erosion is inevitable, but the scale of loss of good soil occurs because of human interaction with the environment. The best antidote to rapid soil erosion is adequate cover of the soil by plants and trees. Trees and plants act as a sponge preventing rapid run-off of water – they soak up heavy rainfall and release it more gradually during drier parts of the year. In the long run they even help to regulate rainfall.

---

[7] Ibid. p. 67.
[8] For details of the processes of soil erosion, its effects and steps that can be taken to prevent it, see *Footsteps*, no. 15 (Teddington, Tearfund 1993).

In many parts of the world there has been widespread destruction of trees for use in cooking, heating, construction and commercial ventures. Obviously the use of wood for these purposes has been occurring for thousands of years with few environmental dangers. However, the scale of demand is unprecedented. Yet to blame shortages simply on population growth is naïve. Land distribution is a major factor. Small landholdings that were once separated from each other by vegetation and trees have been subsumed into large landholdings to be farmed using mechanized techniques. Often these landholdings are commercially owned with local people either leasing their land or simply having it removed from them. Governments often encourage such large-scale farming because the crops grown can be exported to earn foreign currency to meet debt repayments. Soil erosion is a common result of this type of farming. Furthermore, the rural poor are forced to grow their crops on decreasing areas of land. Because they have to use the land more intensively it is much more likely to be degraded.[9] It is, therefore, now becoming clear that commercial exploitation on the one hand and poverty on the other both lead to significant loss of precious topsoil which is needed if the world's growing population are to be fed.

An increase in the number of people does not on its own lead to soil erosion. A report on what was then called the Machakos Reserve in Kenya in 1937 states that due to population growth and a particular method of farming the inhabitants 'are rapidly drifting to a state of hopeless and miserable poverty and their land to a parching desert of rocks, stones and sand'. By 1989 the population was six times larger than it had been in 1932 but soil erosion was 'sharply reduced; . . . agricultural output had risen more than threefold per capita and more than fivefold per

---

[9] This pattern of the poor being forced to over-exploit limited land is repeated in many rural areas in which Tearfund works. For example, Tearfund partner, Society of International Ministries (SIM) has started a reforestation project in the Ethiopian district of Damot Woyde. The average landholding is 0.4 hectares per family with an average of 8–10 persons per family. Ninety-five per cent of the population live off subsistence farming. A member of SIM comments, 'The high density of population, the primitive farming practices, as well as the severe erosion of the area have caused the area to have a history of malnutrition.'

square kilometre'. The reasons given for the dramatic change were 'infrastructural investment, capital inflows from earnings outside, the proximity of the Nairobi market, and marketed crops'. Interestingly, a 'rapidly rising population and labour force' was also seen as a significant factor in the turnaround. Those who researched the area entitled their book *More People, Less Erosion: Environmental Recovery in Kenya*.[10] It is poverty, not people, that destroys the earth on which we all depend.

The global situation

Environmentalists often speak in global terms. They see everyone causing problems for the environment and suffering from the consequences. But it is very likely that everyone will not suffer from any global problem in the same way. It will be the poor who will suffer most because they live in more immediate dependence upon the natural environment and they have the least power to compensate for the losses that result from environmental change. For example, the increase in greenhouse gases produced primarily by Western consumption and the consequent global warming, may well have a catastrophic effect on the capacity of some poorer countries to grow sufficient food.

It also needs to be emphasized that some areas of the world contribute much more to environmental degradation than others. In the case of global warming, for example, the industrialized countries produce the bulk of greenhouse gases. The industrialized world is also responsible for much of the destruction of tropical forests because of its demand for timber and its pressure on Third World governments to repay debts. The logging industry that exports significant quantities of tropical woods to the Western markets often pays little attention to replanting. The beef industry also clears huge tracts of rainforest to rear cattle most famously for beefburgers to be sold to the West. As a Brazilian Workers' Party leader put it, 'If the Amazon is the lungs of the world then debt is its pneumonia.'[11] Similarly, the attempt to provide land for the landless by encouraging

---

[10] Chambers, R., *Whose Reality Counts? Putting the First Last* (London, Intermediate Technology 1997), pp. 25–6.

[11] Jackson, B., *Poverty and the Planet* (Harmondsworth, Penguin 1994), p. 90.

unsustainable colonization of forest areas is related to the chronically unfair distribution of land. Many countries in the Third World are full of those 'who add house to house and join field to field till no space is left and you live alone in the land'.[12]

Underlying assumptions

Much modern thinking on the environment simply multiplies example upon example of ecological danger, hoping to scare people into action. Scientific descriptions of ecological processes dominate alongside predictions of doom for the planet. But underlying these descriptions are various unexpressed world-views. These world-views are crucial since they really drive the debate. It is how we think about the earth that determines what we do with it in the same way that what we think about other humans determines our response to them.

There are at least two world-views that often remain hidden beneath the statistics and predictions of environmentalists. The first defines the value of the earth and all its resources in terms of its usefulness to humans, whilst the second seeks to assign absolute value to the natural world:

1) The natural world exists to be used for the benefit of human-kind. At present this utilitarian attitude to nature finds its primary embodiment in modern business practice. Economics is just beginning to take the environmental cost into consideration in making its calculations, but in the real world of commerce profitability is still the dominant motivation. It is still assumed that the environment will adjust free of charge to whatever humanity demands of it in its commercial ventures. The capital reserves of nature such as its fossil fuels and mineral supplies are treated as if they were limitless.

International commercial relations also put tremendous pressure on Third World countries to satisfy the needs of the present

---

[12]   Isa. 5:7. In the developed world the expansionist ambitions of people express themselves in the ever-increasing monopolization of the world's businesses by a few powerful multinationals. Where people used to build land estates they now build business empires ruthlessly squeezing out the smaller commercial interests. Multinationals also monopolize vast tracts of land.

without regard for the future. The former Brazilian Minister of the Environment provides a good example:

> Today in my country, Brazil, we are flooding thousands of square kilometres of pristine rainforest to make electricity for three mills that export aluminium. In our national account the foreign earnings from exporting the aluminium are added to the GNP, but nowhere do we deduct for the permanent loss of the ore or the demolition of the mountains.[13]

The environmentalist movement is beginning to inject into this view at least a consciousness that the natural world may not have a limitless availability. Some businesses are either voluntarily taking or being forced to take, the idea of sustainability more seriously so that their development 'meets the needs of the present without compromising the ability of future generations to meet their own needs' to quote the Bruntland Commission.[14] The problem comes in defining the needs of the present, particularly since we cannot know for certain what the needs of the future will be. How far into the future should we look? How far into the future can we look, given the technical advances that will be made? In practice the needs of the present dominate attitudes, lifestyle and policymaking.

2) The natural world should be treated with respect because of its own intrinsic value, not because of its usefulness for humanity. Animals, plants, rocks and humans all have absolute value. Humans must learn to take their place as an integral part of a bigger organism that is struggling to survive.[15] It is the earth organism as a whole which has absolute value. This view is very reminiscent of a more ancient pantheism, which identifies the totality of the universe with God, clothed by some environmentalists in the garb of contemporary scientific language.

---

[13] Lutzenberger, J., 'Rethinking progress' in *The New Internationalist*, no. 278 (1996), p. 20.

[14] World Commission on Environment and Development, *Our Common Future* (Oxford, OUP 1987), p. 43.

[15] The Gaia hypothesis is an example of this type of view. See Wilkinson, L., 'Gaia spirituality: a Christian critique' in *Themelios*, vol. 18, no. 3 (1993), pp. 4–8.

Others are happy to recommend a return to a world-view that is close to animism because it encourages belief in a spiritualization of nature. It is a good thing to view the natural world as a habitation of spirits instead of merely as a resource for humans to exploit. Animist cultures are marked by a belief that individual spirits, often of dead ancestors, occupy certain parts of nature like trees or springs. Since this leads to their veneration it also ensures their preservation and anything that leads to the preservation of nature must be good.[16]

A Christian world-view

Some have argued that the Christian approach to the non-human creation is utilitarian. Indeed some have argued that Christian views of nature lie behind all exploitative attitudes to the non-human world. Lynn White, for example, in a seminal article in 1967, claimed that, according to Christian teaching, 'Man shares, in great measure, God's transcendence of nature. Christianity . . . not only established a dualism of man and nature, but also insisted that it is God's will that man exploit nature for his proper ends.'[17] White and others make two allegations against Christianity. First, Christianity removes the spiritual dimension from the non-human creation. Whereas in pre-Christian thinking the natural world was imbued with all sorts of spiritual significance it now becomes an inanimate backdrop to the only possessors of spiritual significance: humans. Nature is a mere machine set up by God. Only humanity bears the image of God and the ability to relate to him. Second, Christianity teaches humanity to exploit creation for its own ends. Creation has no rights in and of itself. Rather it only has rights as the servant of humanity. Its value is relative to the divine image bearers.

---

[16] See the section on animism in ch. 6, 'Religion, Poverty and the Kingdom', pp. 146–8.

[17] White, L., 'The historical roots of our ecologic crisis' in Schaeffer, F., *Pollution and the Death of Man: The Christian View of Ecology* (London, Hodder & Stoughton 1970), p. 79. A more recent edition is published by Crossway 1992, Wheaton, Illinois.

Sadly, White's analysis of the effect of some missionary activity and Christian teaching has some truth in it.[18] Christians are sometimes guilty of absorbing and Christianizing ways of thinking and behaving that are not consistent with biblical teaching. White's mistake is to claim that an aberration is the essence of Christian teaching or practice in this area. A brief survey of biblical teaching, including the key stages in biblical history, will make this very clear.

Creation

The standard Christian doctrine of creation is that God brought the universe into being out of nothing[19] and continually sustains it. Without his sustaining influence it would collapse into nothingness.[20] God has not set up the universe with sufficient power to run in accordance with certain laws of nature. Rather, each moment of natural existence is sustained by him. The so-called laws of nature, therefore, are descriptions of the way that God chooses to uphold the natural world. Such regularity is not absolute, as numerous miracles testified to in the Bible illustrate.

Since God is continually creating the world, he must be its ultimate owner.[21] But he continually offers the world to humanity.[22] Humanity, therefore, has no absolute rights over the creation of which we are a part. Rather, we are commissioned to govern on God's behalf. If we fail to govern in the way that God desires then we abuse our delegated authority. This is at least part of the meaning of being made in the image of God. Humans are meant to image the rule of God over the earth. God's relation to nature throughout the Bible is one of attentive care.[23] Consistent with this, Adam is instructed to 'work . . .

---

[18] See, for example, Enno, S., 'Nature Worship: a paradigm for doing ecumenical theology' in *Asia Journal of Theology*, vol. 8, no. 1 (1994).

[19] Heb. 11:3.

[20] Acts 17:28; Eph. 4:6; Col. 1:17; Heb. 1:3; Matt. 6:30; Ps. 104:24–30; Isa. 40:28; 42:5; 44:2; Job 38:25–41. For a detailed examination of this issue see Helm, P., *The Providence of God* (Leicester, IVP 1993).

[21] E.g. Ps. 24:1–2.

[22] E.g. 115:16.

[23] E.g. Ps. 50:10–11; Ps. 4; Job 38–42; Prov. 3:19; Mt. 6:26–30; Lk. 9:58; 12:6.

and take care'[24] of the garden of Eden. Adam and Eve were to
'subdue' the earth and 'rule over' its creatures.[25] This was a
right to carry on God's creative work of bringing order out of
chaos and not to destroy the earth and its creatures for selfish
ends.

As tenants, governing nature on God's behalf, Adam and Eve's
concern for the Garden of Eden were to be in tune with the overall
purposes of God for his creation. The repeated assertion of Genesis 1 is that all parts of creation are good in themselves. They are
not good only because they fulfil human needs. Creation in its life
and order brings glory to God,[26] testifying to his power and
nature.[27] Therefore, humans in their dominion must 'help' it to
praise God: in their actions they must 'enhance creation's witness
to the glory and nurture of God'.[28] There is no place in Christian
thinking for a utilitarian view of the non-human creation which
defines its value simply in relation to human needs.

Human beings, on the one hand, have a unique place in
creation because they are created in God's image to be co-
workers with him in caring for each other and the rest of the
natural world.[29] This separates human beings from the rest of
creation. On the other hand, human beings are a part of creation
just like everything else.[30] Francis Schaeffer highlights the effect
an awareness of human continuity and discontinuity with the
rest of creation should have on us:

---

[24] Gen. 2:15.

[25] Gen. 1:28. There is much debate over the etymology and meaning of these
two words. Some see them has having exploitative, harsh connotations. The
comment of J. Stott must be remembered at this point: 'It is an elementary
principle of biblical interpretation that one must not establish the meaning of
words by their etymology alone, but also and especially by the way they are
used in their context.' Stott, J., *Issues facing Christians Today* (London, Marshall
Pickering 1990), p. 124.

[26] E.g. Ps. 19:1.

[27] E.g. Jer. 10:12; Rom. 1:20. In Job 38–42 it is the wonder of creation that
produces humility in Job.

[28] Badke, W., *Project Earth* (Oregon, Multnomah 1991), p. 46.

[29] Gen. 1:26.

[30] The account of creation in Gen. 1–2 goes to significant lengths to assert the
continuity of humanity with the rest of nature, particularly through the paral-
lelism of terms used to describe the creation of both.

> As a Christian I say, who am I? Am I only the hydrogen
> atom, the energy particle extended? No. I am made in the
> image of God. I know who I am. Yet on the other hand
> when I turn around and face nature, I face something that
> is like myself. I too am created; just as the animal and the
> plant and the hydrogen atom are created.[31]

An awareness of continuity with the rest of creation should
engender at least two responses. First a respect for and appreciation of creation. The creator who poured all his energies into
the creation of humans also puts all his energies into other parts
of creation.[32] Second, a sense of human interdependence with
nature. We are fundamentally made of the same material and
subject to the same physical conditions. If we damage non-
human creation we damage ourselves. Human beings cannot
live without the earth from which they were made, however
much, in prosperous areas, our technology and lifestyle obscure
this dependence.

The Fall

The primary result of Adam and Eve's sin was the breakdown
in their relationship with God. Inevitably this led to dysfunction
in their relation with each other. It also led to breakdown in their
relationship with the rest of the created order. God states that
the ground is cursed by God because of humanity's sin.[33] The
rest of nature will now obstruct human productive enterprise.[34]
Creation is no longer an untarnished witness to God's providential concern and his glory. Rather, it bears the marks of God's
curse because of human sin. Therefore, the earth may not always
provide for humanity's need; precariousness replaces absolute
security. Similarly, it does not bear witness to God's nature and

---

[31] Schaeffer, F., *Pollution and the Death of Man: The Christian View of Ecology*
(Wheaton, Illinois, Crossway 1992), p. 50.

[32] Mt. 6:28–30.

[33] Gen. 3:17.

[34] Gen. 3:17.

glory in the same way.[35] Creation in its human and non-human form now bears simultaneously the marks of God's creation and his curse. The theme of God cursing the ground is developed through the rest of the biblical story. The experience of Israel in particular illustrates the relationship of blessing and curse.

The history of Israel

Israel was meant to be a pattern for the nations of how the earth should be handled in order to bring glory to God and blessing to the people living off it. God states clearly to Israel that they had no absolute title to the land which he gave them.[36] The earth from which we draw our life can never belong to us absolutely as human beings. Whatever human lawyers may have devised to secure people's title to land, in the last analysis, the earth belongs to God and we can only hold it as his stewards.

Canaan was divided up between the Israelites in such a way as to ensure that everyone had an adequate provision. As Chris Wright puts it in writing of God's endowment to humanity at creation, 'The right of all to use is prior to the right of any to own.'[37] God's law ensures that human patterns of ownership never result in some people not having sufficient to live on.[38] God is also wise to the tendency of some human beings to amass vast estates for themselves thereby leaving insufficient for other people. Various laws were revealed through Moses to ensure the

---

[35] The precise way in which this is true remains a subject of much debate. Paul in Romans 8 writes of creation subjected to 'frustration' and in 'bondage to decay' (Rom. 8:20–21). Perhaps he is pointing to the perpetual cycle of pain and death within nature. From a scientific perspective this cycle has patterns and logic: one species' death means the survival of another species in long food-chains. However from inside these chains and cycles animals experience pain and death. Nature, as Albert Schweitzer put it, is 'the will to live divided against the will to live'. Significantly, the word Paul uses for 'frustration' is the word used in the Septuagint version of Ecclesiastes for 'meaninglessness' (Eccles. 1:2). This may help in understanding what Paul means when he said that the creation is subject to 'frustration'.

[36] Lev. 25:23.

[37] Wright, C., *Living as the People of God* (Leicester, IVP 1983), p. 69.

[38] Ibid. p. 77.

balanced distribution of land.[39] This theme of balanced distribution is also emphasized in the Wisdom Literature.[40]

Not only was God concerned about the distribution of land for people's benefit but also about the land itself and its flora and fauna. So there are laws that ensure the proper treatment of the land and its creatures.[41]

There is always an urgent need to rediscover the biblical principle that the right of all to use the earth's resources is more fundamental than any claim to ownership of them. This proper understanding of ownership can only take place in the context of an understanding that God is the ultimate owner. The earth is not the bountiful product of time plus chance to be exploited mercilessly for selfish ends. It is the creation of a God who loves all equally and commands humankind to administer it for his glory and the well-being of all.

The promised land of Canaan had the potential to overflow with milk and honey.[42] However, this abundance was by no means guaranteed. Unlike Egypt it was a land dependent on the regular provision of rain[43] so that God's constant upholding care could be clearly seen.[44] Dependence on factors beyond Israel's control was a strong incentive to trust and obey God. And laws such as the Sabbath rest of the land heightened such dependence.[45]

It is an aspect of human rebellion against God that we try to create absolute physical security for ourselves in this world. But we deceive ourselves if we think that we can ensure security without reference to God or to other people who may suffer as

---

[39] E.g. Lev. 25. C. Wright comments on Leviticus 25, 'The combined effect of these regulations was to take the land itself right off the market as a commodity. Speculation in land or amassing huge private estates by permanent land purchase was technically impossible in Israel.' Wright, *People of God*, p. 82. See also Deut. 19:14 in conjunction with Hos. 5:10; Job 24:2; Prov. 23:10.

[40] Distribution of land: Prov. 15:25; 22:28; 23:10. Distribution of produce: Prov. 13:23.

[41] E.g. Lev. 19:23–6; 25:1–7; Deut. 22:4,6–7; 25:4; Ex. 20:10; 23:12. See also Prov. 12:10.

[42] E.g. Deut. 8:7.

[43] Deut. 11:11.

[44] Deut. 11:12.

[45] E.g. Lev. 25:20–22.

a result.[46] The pattern established before the Fall is developed in the experience of Israel. If Israel trust and obey, God promises richly to provide for all their needs. However, if they disobey, God promises to bring destruction on the environment's ability to provide.[47]

God's destruction of the natural environment, which is his own creation, points to the centrality of his relationship with human beings. God's first intention is to draw people to himself as they respond to his abundant provision. However, if this response is not forthcoming he will use scarcity and destruction. Nature is a mirror of humanity's spiritual state. As humanity moves away from God nature reflects this by becoming a place of dysfunction, decay and death. As Paul says, 'the creation waits in eager expectation for the sons of God to be revealed'.[48] In writing this Paul is taking his place in the prophetic tradition which saw an inevitable link between the spiritual renewal of Israel and the transformation of nature into what it should be.[49] In the experience of Israel there is an indissoluble tie between the spiritual health of the nation and the health of the natural environment.

This indissoluble tie needs to be rediscovered. Pantheistic environmentalists proclaim that a spiritual understanding of the earth is necessary for its preservation. But their position is closer to Old Testament Baal worship than the worship of the one true God. Baal worship was essentially manipulative. The gods were served so that the fertility of the earth, including humans, was secured. Pantheism says that if we worship the earth it will look after us. Baal worship, like pantheism fails to see that the relationship between God and human beings is the key to the history of the earth. If the earth and its creatures are longing for the full revelation of God's family, as Paul says, then we are proclaiming something of vital importance for the environment when we proclaim the gospel of Jesus Christ.

[46] Mt. 6:34,45.
[47] E.g. Deut. 28; 1 Kgs. 16:29ff.; Hag. 1:10–11; Jer. 4:22–31.
[48] Rom. 8:19.
[49] E.g. Jer. 31:1–12.

Jesus and the early Church

That God became incarnate in Jesus makes a wonderful statement about the goodness of the physical world and the centrality of human beings in creation. In Jesus God came to save us and with us the earth, our environment, also. Because he rose from the dead our hope as Christians is not some disembodied existence but a new heaven and a new earth where righteousness dwells.[50] Those who have this hope are freed from the desire, born of rebellion against God, to look for security in this world.

This is seen very clearly in the behaviour of the first Christians who saw their possessions and resources as a gift from God to be used for the blessing of others, and in particular for the support of their fellow believers.[51] It is wrong to paint too idyllic a picture of the early church as portrayed in Acts because they soon experienced difficulties which are honestly recorded in chapters 5 and 6. What is striking is the way that people full of the Spirit and of love for Jesus shared their possessions. This is possible only for those who see the earth as providing needs and blessings and not security and ultimate meaning. The promise stands to such people that the earth will yield abundantly so that they can continue to honour God and bless their fellow human beings.[52]

It would be an anachronism to say that Jesus developed a 'green' lifestyle during his time on earth. However the seeds for such a lifestyle are contained within his ministry. For example, his criticism of unrestrained greed and his principle of simple, humble dependence upon God for all human needs. Furthermore his teaching reveals a deep interest in the non-human world and a belief in the love of God for all non-human creatures.[53] Perhaps most importantly, if the Fall disrupted human relationship with God, each other and the non-human creation,

---

[50] See, for example, Isa. 65:17–25; Rev. 21:1. C. Wright comments: 'The transformation of nature in passages such as Isa. 2:2; 11:6–9; Jer. 31:1–14 and Hos. 2:18–23 is clearly not intended literally. Yet neither should it be utterly spiritualized or taken as merely metaphorical.' Wright, *People of God*, p. 91.

[51] E.g. Acts 2:42–7; 4:32–7.

[52] 2 Cor. 9:6–11.

[53] E.g. Mt. 6:26–30; Lk. 9:58; 12:6. Many of Jesus' parables are also drawn from nature.

then the complete salvation won by Jesus must bring the beginnings of a restoration of all things.

The last things

There seem to be two different visions of the future in the New Testament. One sees the ultimate renewal of everything through the work of Christ.[54] Paul describes this renewal most poignantly when he says that 'the creation itself will be liberated from its bondage to decay and brought into the glorious freedom of the children of God'.[55] For Paul the liberation of nature is a part of God's plan of salvation. As such, he is in the prophetic tradition which also looked forward to a time when creation would be renewed. In this vision the 'new heaven' and the 'new earth'[56] have significant continuity with the heaven and earth which exist now. They are the renewal of the sin-affected heaven and earth.

However, there is another vision of the future which predicts the destruction of the current natural order. In this the 'new heaven' and 'new earth' are utterly different from those which exist now.[57] This vision seems to indicate discontinuity between the current creation and the new creation. The 'new heaven' and 'new earth' indicate the absolute destruction of the old.

This apparent anomaly disappears when we remember that the Bible can use the language of discontinuity to express the scale of change that happens to a person or thing. A good example would be the language used to describe a person's salvation. Christians are a new creation. However, this does not mean that there is no significant continuity in the physical appearance, character, temperament and abilities of a person before and after their conversion. The present created order will be liberated into such a changed quality of life that it is necessary to use the language of newness to illustrate it. The new heaven and new earth will come together, thus fulfilling God's will 'to

---

[54] E.g. Col. 1:19–20; Eph. 1:9–10.
[55] Rom. 8:21.
[56] Rev. 21:1.
[57] 2 Pet. 3:7–11; Heb. 1:11.

bring all things in heaven and on earth together under one head even Christ'.[58]

The implications of the future for the contemporary church simply re-emphasize the implications of the past and present. The earth is the loving provision of a Creator who poured his creative energy into producing a very good creation. This creation in a sense 'deserves more' than to be consigned to destruction, so God will renew it when Christ returns. Since God has no intention to throw his creation away but to perfect it, we should treat it with great respect now as the scene of our probation as his stewards.

From theory to practice

The Bible makes it very clear that the environment is first and foremost the environment for human beings. It is the resource that God has handed into our care to use for his glory and for the blessing of the whole human race. Because of our sin we tend to exploit this wonderful resource for selfish ends. Two results follow. On the one hand, many are denied access to its blessings, and on the other hand, it is exploited to destruction. Therefore, as Christians, we should be passionately committed to enabling the poor to experience the blessings of the earth and to opposing its destructive exploitation. It is not surprising to find many Christians already active in these two areas.

One such group of Christians working in Honduras have called themselves MOPAWI. MOPAWI is an abbreviation of the Miskito Indian words for the 'development of the Mosquitia'. Mosquitia is a region of Honduras with a distinctive geographical, and diverse ethnic, identity. It covers an area of 20,000 sq. km., about 20 per cent of the territory of Honduras, and contains areas of coastline, swamp, savannah and humid tropical forest in the valleys of the principal rivers. Between 45,000 and 50,000 people live in the area. The majority of the people are indigenous Miskitos who live in sensitive relationship to their environment, having developed agricultural methods that suit their context.

---

[58] Eph. 1:10.

Other Miskitos living near the coast make a living by diving for shellfish.

However, the position of the indigenous people has become increasingly vulnerable in recent years due to the exploitative ambitions of various non-indigenous groups who see the forest areas as a resource to be plundered. Areas of the Mosquitia have been colonized by loggers looking for precious species of timber in the rainforest, cattle ranchers, speculators looking for gold in the rivers and poor agriculturists from other zones of Honduras looking for land upon which to house and provide for their families. These newcomers may benefit in the short term, but any gains are temporary, as the land rapidly becomes degraded through overuse and ignorance of the ecological dynamics of the area. When one area has been exhausted, the colonizers move on to another tract of land as more people follow on behind them. Indigenous people are displaced, often suffering violence. They can do little to resist incoming forces because they rarely have legally recognized land rights. No one had told them that they needed them.

The colonizers operate within a broader context of political and economic interests. The Honduran government is keen to let logging companies and cattle ranchers into the region since the resultant timber exports boost foreign currency coming into an impoverished, debt-plagued country. Equally, in a country where 4 per cent of the population own 60 per cent of the usable land, the government is pleased to have a region where it can encourage landless poor to go to find livelihoods, even if most ultimately fail to make an adequate living in the area. This pattern echoes what happened to the Amazonian rainforest during the 1960s. Faced with mounting economic and social pressures, military governments offered the rainforest as the answer to the people's problems. Here was a theoretically 'uninhabited' wilderness area that could provide for people. People were allowed in with no idea as to how best to use the fragile ecosystem of the rain forest. Consequently the indigenous populations, the incoming landless poor and the environment all suffered.

Indigenous people making a living in Mosquitia coastline areas from shellfish sales are also suffering as the marine environment on which they depend is overexploited. Growing numbers of divers are competing for a diminishing resource base. Young shellfish are caught illegally before they reach the end of their reproductive lives thus further cutting back the fish resources. Ultimately, the shellfish industry may die unless resources are managed effectively.

Faced with these different manifestations of environmental destruction and consequent suffering among the poor, MOPAWI has developed a number of responses. At the heart of MOPAWI's response is a long-term initiative to secure officially recognized land rights for the indigenous population. Given the greater sensitivity of the indigenous to their environment, secure landownership would protect both the indigenous people and the environment on which they depend. MOPAWI has undertaken significant research, therefore, into the past and present land use and ownership patterns of the Mosquitia region. Armed with this information they have brought issues of ecology and land rights to the attention of Honduran society and international audiences. They have also encouraged the indigenous themselves to grasp the importance of land rights to their livelihoods. The government has been pressured into steps to protect indigenous populations, although there is much progress still to be made.

While MOPAWI recognizes that the indigenous people are the best managers of the environment they have lived in for centuries, they also work to foster some new initiatives in the management of the different resource bases in Mosquitia. In particular they have encouraged the use of new crops that are suitable for their environment, as for example, the growth of cocoa in forest areas which both provides the indigenous with a potential source of nutrition and some income, and protects the soil against erosion. Similarly, MOPAWI has educated many divers concerning the sustainable use of the marine resources, although until all divers embrace more sensible fishing, little progress will be made. MOPAWI has also set up vocational training in order to create new sources of income, thus reducing dependence on the fragile resource base.

This case study has not done justice to the range of responses MOPAWI make to the problems of the indigenous people and the environment on which they depend. Other responses do not seem directly related to environmental concerns, but they do in the long-term have an impact – for example, MOPAWI's work on bilingual education, which encourages indigenous people to learn the national language, Spanish, through their indigenous language. Previously indigenous people had been banned from using their own language in schools, a move which threatened their identity and reduced their chances of effectively learning Spanish. A new generation is now emerging who both respect their own culture and are confident in the official state language. They are in a much stronger position to stand up for the rights of their people and their environment.

This sample of MOPAWI's work highlights just one example of Christians who, motivated by a Christian attitude to the whole of creation, are seeking to enable the poor to experience the blessings of the earth and to stop its destructive exploitation.

Resources

Books

Roberts, W. Dayton, *Patching God's Garment: Environment and Mission in the 21st Century* (Monrovia, MARC 1994). A mix of biblical teaching and case studies outlining how Christians should react to ecological problems.

Schaeffer, Francis, *Pollution and the Death of Man: The Christian View of Ecology* (London, Hodder & Stoughton 1970/Wheaton, Crossway 1992). A prophetic book which is yet to be surpassed in terms of the contrast it draws between Christian worldviews and non-Christian world-views in relation to nature. It also contains useful articles on common non-Christian perceptions of the Christian attitude to nature, such as, White, L., 'The Historical roots of our ecologic crisis' and Means, R.L., 'Why worry about Nature?'

Cooper, Tim, *Green Christianity* (London, Spire 1990). Detailed, scientifically credible evangelical framework for engagement with ecological issues, including useful biblical engagement with other worldviews.

Badke, William B., *Project Earth* (Oregon, Multnomah 1991). Stimulating, surprising and plausible treatment of biblical material on nature.

Elsdon, Ron, *Greenhouse Theology* (Tunbridge Wells, Monarch 1992). Written by a scientist with a good grasp of theology and the Bible.

Not specifically Christian

World Watch Institute, *State of The World*, published annually (London, Earthscan). The authoritative, annually published 'Bible' of many who are concerned with ecological issues.

Jackson, Ben, *Poverty and the Planet* (Harmondsworth, Penguin 1994). Brilliant introduction to environmental issues in relation to poverty.

Kirby, John, O'Keefe, Phil, and Timberlake, Lloyd (eds.), *Sustainable Development* (London, Earthscan 1995). Detailed and authoritative for those already introduced to issues of environmentally sustainable development.

Articles

Transformation, vol. 10, no. 2 (1993). Contains the following articles:

Wilkinson, Loren and Mary Ruth, 'The depth of the danger'.

Drane, John, 'Biblical theology of the creation and the New Age'.

De Witt, Cal, 'A scientist's theological reflection on creation'.

Robbins, A.M.J., 'Deforestation in Nepal'.

Sheldon, J.K., 'Select bibliography on Christians and the environment'.

Seaton, Chris, 'The environment and youth'.

Alpine, Thomas, 'Case study in wholistic mission: A Catholic parish in Mexico'.

Footsteps, for articles on the following:

General Environmental issues including a focus on MOPAWI, see no. 20 (1994).

Soil Erosion and Water Conservation, see no. 5 (1990), no. 7 (1991), no. 13 (1992), no. 15 (1993), no. 25 (1995).

Energy-/Fuel-efficient cooking methods, see no. 5 (1990), no. 16 (1993), no. 21 (1994), no. 22 (1995).

The New Internationalist, no. 278 (New Internationalist Publications 1996). Introductory articles on environmental problems and a proper response to them.

Conclusion

A Prayer

Lord, as I think of the path that has been trod through this volume my heart is full of gratitude for your grace to me. At the same time I am more conscious than ever that I live in a world where an awful lot of people do not know you or experience life as a blessing. Thank you for the many Christians who are devoting their lives to make you known in word and deed. Thank you, too, for those who though they do not know you yet care enough to devote themselves to improving the lot of the poor. I thank you, also, that I belong to the evangelical tradition in your church which has done, and is doing, so much for the poor.

As I expose myself to the pain of the poor, the weight of their suffering threatens to crush me. I know that I can neither carry such a weight of pain, nor do anything to lighten the burden in my own strength. I am so grateful that you are a king who has already taken all this pain to the cross and carried it away for me. Not that you are indifferent to it now. You still feel it. As the incarnate Son of God you still look out on the multitudes of this world who are harassed and helpless, like sheep without a shepherd. In your compassion you reach out to them in mercy and you use the hands and feet of people like me, who have experienced your mercy, to do it. Lord, may I always be available to do your work with you.

I sometimes wish that your kingdom was the same as the kingdoms of this world. Then I could justify going in there with all guns blazing to sort out the wicked who are oppressing the poor. But I know deep in my heart that your way is best.

Transition that comes through the message and practice of the gospel in the power of the Holy Spirit is the only way really to bless the poor.

Thank you, Lord, that your purpose of establishing an ever-lasting kingdom ruled over by your son Jesus is not some new idea. Right through history you have been working to this end. At the dawn of history you focused that purpose on the family of Adam and Eve's son Seth. You made it quite clear, from Seth's descendant Abraham onwards, that your special interest in him and his family was for the benefit of all the nations. So, your kingdom was never meant to be for just one nation. It has always been something for everyone. That is why your Son commands his followers to go and make disciples for him from all nations.

Not only does your kingdom stretch back to the beginning of history and extend to all nations, but it also goes very deep into our human nature. Because sin has corrupted every aspect of my being, Lord, your kingdom needs to be established over every corner of my personality. I know that this is a task that can take a lifetime but I long to make progress. I also know that it is to the extent that I make progress here that I can become an instrument in your hand. Blessing the poor is one of the many things I will be able to do if I am thoroughly submitted to you. O Lord fire me with this glorious vision of the revelation of your kingdom through history, all over the world and in every aspect of my being.

Lord, you know that the culture to which I belong is very individualistic. It encourages me continually to be self-centred. This is not how you want us to be. Living for self is a complete contradiction of your intention. You want us to live for you and for each other. That is really the thrust of the law that you revealed through Moses so long ago and endorsed so strongly through your Son. Forgive me, Lord, that I have not taken your law as seriously as I ought. Even if we as your church today took serious note of what your law says about how we are to use our resources to encourage the poor, a huge dent would be made in the problem of poverty. Help us to do it, Lord.

It must break your heart to see us, who claim to be your church, making such a mess of things so often. But thank you that, despite the mess, the real church does still exist all over the world. You do have a people in many localities who love you and each other – communities of reconciliation who honour you and do good to each other and to the needy in their localities and beyond. Lord, I long to see a rapid multiplication of this type of community all over the world.

Thank you, Lord, that in your providence you continue to bless humankind with abundant provision for all our needs. Forgive us that some of us demand so much of your provision for ourselves that others have to go without. This is so true of us in the West and also of those who have managed to jump on the bandwagon of a Western lifestyle in the Third World. We find it so difficult to be responsible with the riches that you give us and get sucked into the awful spiral of wanting more and more security in this world, that we end up being thoroughly worldly. Lord, help us to break free from this delusion and begin to see that the abundant resources that you give us are to be used, not to put down roots in this world, but to furnish and decorate our home in the next. Help us to be heavenly minded so that we can use our resources to extend your kingdom. When this happens justice will be done to the poor.

The fact that it is so difficult to be obedient to you, Lord, is proof that there is very stiff opposition to face. The struggle with my own individual sin is bad enough, but that sin is fed by powerful worldly structures which are, in turn, driven by very real powers of evil in the spiritual realm. Thank you, Lord, that the empty tomb is certain proof that this whole plethora of evil that we have to contend with, has been vanquished once and for all on the cross. However, the battle is real enough and I lose the battle all too often. I cannot be triumphalistic, Lord, because I know my own weakness. Yet, I must press on in the certain knowledge that truth and justice will prevail and that you have provided all the armoury that I need to win the day.

It is amazing how deeply deluded we can become as human beings. The evidence of your being and glory, Lord, is so clear in your creation, that falling down to worship you should be as natural as breathing. Instead, we suppress the truth and set up all sorts of idols to take your place. In the West we commonly worship ourselves, but increasingly we are also returning, like people in many other parts of the world, to worship a whole range of gods and spirits. We do this despite the fact that the worship of false gods does so much harm to so many people. Idolatry and injustice are very close allies. Lord free me from idolatry, particularly from the worship of Mammon/money, the favourite god of the West. May the light of the gospel break the power of false gods and spirits which keep people in bondage to injustice.

In painting a very black picture of the state of things on earth, help me to remember, Lord, that you are still the sovereign creator and sustainer of this world. You are not a king who has been dethroned. Your power and authority is vigorously challenged but you have not been thrown out of this world altogether. Just as the earth itself, though marred by sin, still witnesses to your glory the same is true of fallen human beings. All our rebellion and all the efforts of Satan cannot wipe out your indelible stamp on us. We make a terrible mess of the way in which we handle the resources of the earth but we still display wonderful creativity in doing so, which witnesses to our origin. We have learnt to produce so many things from the raw materials that you have given us and to create a wonderful system for distributing and marketing them. Help those of us who belong to you, Lord, to use this gift to make sure that the poor have access to the means of production so that there will be a more equitable distribution of this earth's goods.

I also want to thank you, Lord, for the institutions of government. Your Son, my saviour, is a king so the kingdom of heaven is not without its government. When I think of the way the kingdoms of this world operates, your government is so different. In your kingdom the king bows down to wash his disciple's feet! He is the supreme servant. Lord, how wonderful it would be if the governments of the world existed to serve their people rather than to satisfy ambition and lust for power. Yet, Lord, there are those in politics who take service seriously. Many such politicians, at all levels, belong to you. Strengthen them. Add to their number. Keep them from the temptations that power brings. Help them to prove their faithfulness to you by being particularly concerned for the weak and marginalized in their communities.

It is staggering to realize, Lord, that there are some 27 million refugees in the world. Ethnic conflict is so often the cause of their sadness. Yet, Lord, that does not mean that my ethnic identity is an evil thing. You know how strongly I feel my Welshness and how keen I am that people I meet understand that I am Welsh – and not English. I really believe, Lord, that it is in your goodness that I am what I am. This ethnic identity that you have given me is a precious gift which it is my duty to foster and preserve for your glory. At the same time the moment I begin to think that my ethnic identity is superior to someone else's I am bringing to birth an evil which has had terrible consequences all over the world. It almost wiped away my identity when the English adopted it and everyone knows of its terrible fruit in former Yugoslavia and Rwanda. Help me as a Christian to affirm people's identity, to strive for justice for all and to rejoice in ethnic diversity.

There is another diversity, Lord, where one of the parties often suffers terrible injustice, and that is the diversity of the sexes. I will never forget those women in an Indian slum who asked me whether I beat my wife. All over the world women work terribly hard, bear many children and care for them with little help from men, who often ill-treat and even abandon them. I know, Lord, that there are many happy families, where the wife and mother is valued, but it is now estimated that a quarter of the world's families are headed by a woman on her own. Forgive me if I have devalued women at all. Help us in the church to value them as you do and to make sure that they get a just reward from all their labour.

Talking about value, Lord, I am afraid that as the world's population grows, and the voices of the prophets of doom become more shrill, that the value of any human being will fall. Many millions of human beings are already considered a nuisance even before they are born, and are aborted, so the climate is ripe for considering human beings a nuisance, even after they have been born. I thank you, Lord, that you put such a value on us as to be prepared to die for us. Help us as your people to defend the dignity of our human existence as strongly as we can. Yet, I thank you that in your providence it is now possible to have children well spaced and that many of us can choose how many children to have. Thank you for the five children that my wife and I have, and for being able to give them what children need to grow up strong and healthy. Help me, Lord, to work towards making sure that all the children born into this world have the same advantages.

As I sit here in my study, on a beautiful May evening, with the sun setting behind the wooded hillside on the other side of the valley, I marvel again, Lord, at the beauty of your creation. The voices of those who warn us that we are destroying, not only the beauty, but the capacity of the earth to sustain us, is getting more shrill every day. There is evidence, Lord, that the warnings are not groundless. We are not surprised, because the Bible teaches clearly that selfishness is destructive. You gave us the earth to care for and not to exploit mercilessly to destruction. Help me, Lord, to be careful of your earth and to use its resources responsibly so that many more people in my generation can enjoy them, and that the earth will be left in better shape for coming generations.

Lord, I thank you for the privilege of being called to teach your word. Thank you for the gift of many individuals that has been used over the years to teach me so many different aspects of the truth of your word. Forgive me that the word has not always borne fruit in my life as it should. You saved me, Lord, to do good works. I thank you for those who have taught me that 'good works' means doing a very wide range of different things. Help me to be a better teacher of your word, and a better example of what it means to live by it, so that when you come or call I will be found about your business.

> Who then is the faithful and wise manager, whom the master puts in charge of his servants to give them their food allowance at the proper time? It will be good for that servant whom the master finds doing so when he returns. I tell you the truth, he will put him in charge of all his possessions . . . From everyone who has been given much, much will be demanded; and from the one who has been entrusted with much, much more will be asked.[1]

---

[1]   Lk. 12:42–4,48b.

Index of Bible Passages

General Index

Leadership Images from the New Testament
A Practical Guide
David Bennett

ISBN 1 85078 309 8

In an age where the church is increasingly embracing the methods and style of business management and leadership, this book brings the question of leadership back to the Bible. Bennett proposes that biblical leadership has more to do with learning to follow than with learning to command, supervise of manage. In a readable, alphabetized reference format, he examines the various images or metaphors used in the New Testament for leaders and draws out the important implications for today's spiritual leaders.

This book is essential for any church leader, or aspiring leader.

" 'Images are powerful,' says Bennett. So is this book! Scholarly, yet practical, it moves beyond leadership skills and managerial techniques to a serious consideration of the relationships, dispositions and attitudes which are indispensable both to leadership and discipleship."
Kenneth Mulholland, Professor at Columbia Biblical Seminary, South Carolina, USA.

David Bennett is Senior Pastor of Mountain Park Church in Lake Oswego, Oregon. Over the past twenty years he has led numerous short-term missions and has experience in church organization in Asia, Africa, Latin America and Europe.

Carey, Christ and Cultural Transformation
The Life and Influence of William Carey
Ruth and Vishal Mangalwadi

ISBN 1 85078 258 X

Here, for the first time since Carey set foot in India two hundred years ago, Indians, themselves evaluate the contribution of the 'father of the modern missionary movement' to the modernization of India.

Their unique insights into the life and work of William Carey highlight the many facets of his efforts on behalf of the oppressed. He was not merely a social reformer but a missionary with firm theological assumptions undergirding his social reforms. His work is discussed against the background of the moral, social, intellectual and spiritual bankruptcy of nineteenth century India.

Whilst illustrating the positive effects of Carey's reforms, the authors reveal many of the causes of oppression in India today and establish the importance of the Christian faith as a basis for social renewal. Their vauable insights make this important reading for all those currently involved in missionary activities.

"a welcome addition to the existing literature about the missionary reformer of India . . . Carey has a lot to say about the strategic response needed in today's mission context."
Tetsuanao Yamamori, President of Food for the Hungry International.

Vishal Mangalwadi is well-known in India and the West as a political campaigner and champion of social reform. He lectures and broadcasts widely in the US and Britain, particularly on the New Age. His previous books include *Truth and Reform*, *The World of Gurus* and *In Search of Self*.
Ruth Mangalwadi teaches at Woodstock International School.